INTERNATIONAL DEVELOPMENT IN FOCUS

Markets and People

Romania Country Economic
Memorandum

Contents

Acknowledgments   *vii*
Executive Summary   *ix*
Abbreviations   *xiii*

Overview   1
Drivers of growth   5
Competition: Allocating resources more efficiently   10
Human capital: Forming present and future workers   15
Notes   20
References   21

CHAPTER 1   **Productivity   23**
Estimating productivity   24
Leaders and laggards   27
Productivity drivers: Within-firm improvements and
    reallocation effects   32
A policy agenda   35
Annex 1A: Measures of productivity   37
Annex 1B: List of 2-digit sectors   38
Notes   39
References   39

CHAPTER 2   **Romania's Product Market Regulations   41**
Benchmarking product market regulations   42
Regulations with economywide effects   44
Sector-specific regulations   49
Boosting growth with procompetition reforms   55
Notes   56
References   58

CHAPTER 3   **State Ownership and Competitive Neutrality   59**
The SOE sector in Romania   60
Romanian SOEs hold significant market positions   61
Regulations and policies protect SOEs from competition   66
Romania lacks an economic test for government intervention
    through SOEs   72
Reducing anticompetitive market outcomes   73
Notes   75
References   77

CHAPTER 4 **Romania's Human Capital Deficit** **79**

Measuring Romania's human capital   81

Estimating the subnational HCI for Romania   82

Lagging the rest of the EU   83

Regional disparities are driven by education, more human capital
    for girls, and a wide urban-rural divide   84

Annex 4A: Human Capital Index for Romania: Data and
    methodology   92

Notes   95

References   96

CHAPTER 5 **Closing Learning Gaps in Primary and Secondary
Education   97**

Learners: Performance is characterized by systemic gaps and
    disparities   99

Teachers: Challenges in recruitment, deployment,
    and motivation   101

School management: Driving toward greater professionalization   103

School inputs: Skewed funding mechanisms
    and allocations   104

Improving school performance in Romania: Suggested policy
    actions   105

Notes   110

References   110

CHAPTER 6 **Romania's Skills Challenge   113**

Multiple causes for skills mismatches   114

Quantity of general education   114

Levels of skills   115

Quality of education   116

Skills specialization   117

Economic activity and labor demand   118

The changing nature of work   119

Asymmetry of information   120

Sociocultural influences   121

Responding to skills mismatches with work-based training   122

Workplace training practices: Case study evidence   123

Identifying opportunities to respond to the challenges   124

Concrete steps to overhaul Romania's skills-development system   126

Notes   129

References   130

CHAPTER 7 **Policy Recommendations   133**

Market competition   133

Human capital   138

APPENDIX   **145**

Boxes

O.1   The firm as a central actor of economic growth   7

1.1   Management capabilities and firm productivity   36

2.1   Product market regulation methodology: Economywide score   43

2.2   Tackling entry restrictions in professional services in Romania   53

2.3   Tackling price regulation and estimating benefits to the service users   54

3.1   The Sovereign Fund for Development and Investments   68

3.2   Corporate governance of Romania's SOEs   69

3.3   State aid in Romania   71

5.1   Conceptual framework from the *World Development Report 2018*   98

6.1   Taking training to the workplace in Romania   125

Figures

O.1 Romania's GDP growth, 1990–2018 2
O.2 Growth drivers (demand side) in Romania, 2013–17 2
O.3 Growth drivers (supply side) in Romania, 2013–17 3
O.4 Structural change in the composition of gross value added, Romania, 1995–2018 3
O.5 Changes in employment and productivity shares by industry, Romania, 2018 versus 2009 4
O.6 Industry distribution of exports, 1996–2018 4
O.7 Labor productivity in Romania relative to the EU-15, 2000–17 5
O.8 Shares of growth attributable to TFP, labor, capital, and other factors during four periods, 1990–2018 6
BO.1.1 A model economy 7
O.9 GDP per capita (2011 PPP adjusted) versus economywide PMR indicator 12
O.10 GDP per capita (2011 PPP adjusted) versus PMR subcomponents 12
1.1 Average annual growth rate of median productivity values, 2011–17 (manufacturing versus services) 26
1.2 Average annual growth rate of productivity dispersion values, 2011–17 (manufacturing versus services) 27
1.3 Average differences in firm characteristics, 2017 28
1.4 Labor productivity growth: Frontier versus laggards, 2011–17 29
1.5 TFPR productivity growth: Frontier versus laggards, 2011–17 30
1.6 Churning at the frontier 32
1.7 Average employment growth across the firm TFPR markup-adjusted distribution; all firms: Deviation from the 2011–17 average 32
1.8 Average employment growth across the firm TFPR markup-adjusted distribution: Manufacturing versus services, deviation from the 2011–17 average 33
1.9 Olley and Pakes decomposition of TFPR adjusted, 2011–17, accumulated percentage change 33
1.10 Olley and Pakes decomposition of TFPR adjusted, 2011–17, annual percent change 34
1.11 The national productivity system 35
B2.1.1 Economywide PMR methodology 43
2.1 Product market regulation in Romania and comparator countries 45
2.2 Restrictiveness of state control regulation in Romania and comparator countries 45
2.3 Romania: State control indicator composition 46
2.4 Regulatory barriers to entry and rivalry in Romania and comparator countries 47
2.5 Romania: Regulatory barriers to entry and rivalry indicator composition 47
2.6 Regulatory barriers to trade and investment in Romania and comparator countries 48
2.7 Regulations in network sectors (energy, telecom, and transport): Overall score in Romania and comparator countries 49
2.8 Restrictive regulations in network sectors 50
2.9 Are there any special regulations prohibiting or restricting sales below costs beyond a prohibition of predatory pricing? 51
2.10 Are sales promotions restricted to appear within a particular period of the year? 52
3.1 Probability of an SOE operating in a sector or subsector 62
3.2 Factors related to market position and regulations that may increase the risk of negative effects of SOEs in the market 63
3.3 Competitive neutrality gap analysis for Romania 67
3.4 Degrees of business separation 70
4.1 Romania's workforce is both shrinking and aging 80
4.2 The HCI is based on three components 81
4.3 Romania's HCI score is the lowest among EU countries, 2017 83
4.4 Subcomponents, in particular education, are also low compared with other EU countries, 2017 84

4.5   Marked disparities in human capital exist across counties
      within Romania, 2017   85
4.6   There is a high negative correlation between HCI and poverty rates
      between counties   86
4.7   Education explains low performance at the county level   87
4.8   Expected years of schooling decrease in all the counties when adjusted for
      quality of learning, and there is high variability in the reduction   88
4.9   The gap with respect to full health and education is driven mainly
      by test scores   88
4.10 On average, more than two years of additional schooling is required to close the
      gap with Bucharest-Ilfov   89
4.11 Adult survival rates explain most of the gender gap   89
4.12 The Human Capital Index is positively correlated with the level of urbanization
      of counties   90
4.13 Harmonized tests scores are higher in urban areas   91
B5.1.1 WDR determinants of learning   98
5.1   Early school leaving in lower middle school in Romania, 2017   100
5.2   Annual gross salaries for full-time teachers in lower secondary education   102
5.3   Public expenditure on education by education level as percentage of
      GDP in the EU, 2015   104
5.4   Policy actions and interventions in education: Goals and outcomes   105
6.1   Romania's working-age population is relatively less educated than
      international peers; Bucharest-Ilfov is the most educated region in the
      country   115
6.2   Vertical skill mismatching by all occupations, 2017   116
6.3   High proportion of employees with a tertiary education level in some
      fields are either vertically or horizontally mismatched   117
6.4   Contributions to total vacancy rates by region, 2017   118
6.5   Jobs in Romania have become intensive in cognitive skills, 1998–2014   119
6.6   Romania labor demand is shifting toward high-skilled workers   120

Tables

O.1   Romania's *Doing Business* scores, by indicator, 2010–18   9
1.1   Main economic sectors   26
2.1   Policy options to remove economywide and sector-specific barriers to
      firm entry and rivalry   55
2.2   Potential effect on GDP of reforms across service sectors   56
3.1   SOE market shares and private sector participation in sectors/subsectors
      with SOEs   64
3.2   Market failures   72
3.3   Examples of competition constraints in markets where SOEs breached the
      competition law   74
3.4   Policy options to ensure competitive neutrality of SOEs   74
4A.1 Data sources   93
4A.2 Comparative data   93
4A.3 HCI breakdown by administrative components   94
5.1   Examples of education policy actions to address determinants of
      learning   106
5.2   Policy options to close learning gaps in primary and secondary
      education   109
6.1   Policy options to overhaul Romania's skills-development system   128
7.1   Boosting market competition   134
7.2   Building human capital   139
A.1   Basic indicators   145
A.2   Investment   146
A.3   Labor   147
A.4   Human capital   149
A.5   Business environment   151

Acknowledgments

This report was written by a team co-led by Donato De Rosa (Lead Economist) and Alexandria Valerio (Lead Education Specialist), and including Reena Badiani-Magnusson (Senior Economist), Vincent Belinga (Economist), Neil Butcher (Consultant), Ioana Ciucanu (Consultant), Elia De la Cruz Toledo (Consultant), Andrei Silviu Dospinescu (Consultant), Georgeta Gavriloiu (Consultant), Arti Grover (Senior Economist), Zohar Ianovici (Consultant), Mariana Iootty (Senior Economist), Sonja Loots (Consultant), Leonardo Lucchetti (Senior Economist), Mariana Moarcas (Senior Education Specialist), Mohamed Mukhtar Qamar (Consultant), Myra Murad Kahn (Consultant), Constantino Navarro (Consultant), Tilsa Guillermina Ore Monago (Consultant), Catalin Pauna (Senior Economist), Jorge Pena (Consultant), Georgiana Pop (Senior Economist), Alina Sava (Education Specialist), Geomina Turlea (Consultant), and Michal Tulwin (Research Analyst). Helpful support in the production of the report was provided by Anastasia Gadja, Leah Laboy, Maria-Magdalena Manea, Cindy A. Fisher, and Stefanie Heim. Box 1.1 was contributed by Arti Grover.

The team received guidance from Arup Banerji (Country Director), Tatiana Proskuryakova (Country Manager), Gallina Vincelette (Practice Manager), and Harry Patrinos (Practice Manager). The team is grateful for the many helpful comments received from peer reviewers Paulo Correa (Lead Economist), Ivailo Izvorski (Lead Economist), Elizabeth Ninan (Senior Education Specialist), Shwetlena Sabarwal (Senior Economist), and from several colleagues at the World Bank. The report benefited immensely from the comments of Romanian authorities, as well as from discussions with representatives of the Romanian private sector and academia.

Executive Summary

Romania's income per capita increased from 26 percent of the EU-28 average in 2000 to 64 percent in 2018. The economy has opened to trade and investment and has gone through a structural transformation from heavy industry to services, while agriculture still contributes 4.8 percent of total gross value added and 23 percent of total employment.

Romania's economic success rests on the wobbly foundations of unfavorable demographics, weak human capital, and ineffective institutions. These shortcomings are taking a toll on the pace of convergence with wealthier European Union (EU) partners, with average annual labor productivity growth dropping from 9.0 percent in 2000–08 to 3.1 percent in 2009–17.

Between 2000 and 2018, Romania's population fell from 22.5 million to 19.5 million, with emigration accounting for more than 75 percent of the decline. Meanwhile, labor force participation in 2018 stood at 67.8 percent, one of the lowest rates in the EU, and only 58.3 percent for women. However, it has increased steadily over the past decade for both men (by 6 percent) and women (by 3.4 percent).

Weak human capital aggravates the plight of labor supply. Forty percent of 15-year-old Romanian students do not achieve minimum literacy proficiency, and only 15 percent of the working-age population has completed tertiary education.

The generally low quality of institutions adds to the structural weaknesses of the economy. Reforms that would help enhance the economy's growth potential are often held back by poor coordination among different parts of government, ineffective policy implementation and monitoring, and politicization of decision making.

Based on consultations with stakeholders, competition and human capital were chosen as the focus of the *Romania Country Economic Memorandum 2019*. These two pillars were recognized as critical to increasing the economy's growth potential and as areas that can stimulate a constructive policy debate.

COMPETITION: ENABLING MORE PRODUCTIVE FIRMS TO GROW

Romania has a dual enterprise sector with a strong and widening gap between productivity leaders and laggards. From 2011 to 2017, leaders appeared to be older, larger, and more capital intensive, and they paid higher wages. Leading firms also charge higher markups over cost, especially in manufacturing, because of their ability to wield market power or to produce higher-quality goods and services that command higher prices than others. Higher markups, however, are not accompanied by increased technical efficiency—the ability to combine inputs in more cost-effective ways.

The reallocation of market shares to more efficient players has been the main driver of productivity growth in manufacturing but not in services. Since the 1990s, Romanian manufacturing firms have been exposed to domestic and international competition, ensuring the flow of resources and market shares to more efficient players. This has not been the case for services, either because they are intrinsically nontradable or because regulations restrict firm rivalry and entry of new firms, resulting in significant misallocation of resources. At the same time, productivity improvements within individual firms have contributed little or negatively to aggregate productivity growth, suggesting that there is scope to improve firm capabilities, particularly in services.

Impediments to competition are associated with state control of the economy and barriers to entry and rivalry, especially in services, as revealed by the Organisation for Economic Co-operation and Development product market regulation indicator. Removal of these restrictions would have a significant positive impact on gross domestic product growth. Helpful measures would include (i) streamlining burdensome administrative procedures to facilitate market entry for businesses; (ii) eliminating unnecessary entry requirements for road freight services; (iii) removing unnecessary entry requirements for professional services (for example, unnecessary membership requirements in professional associations or double licensing from public and professional bodies to lawyers and engineers); and (iv) reassessing the application of minimum and maximum prices for lawyers and of recommended price guidelines for engineers and architects.

Romanian state-owned enterprises (SOEs) do not compete on an equal footing with private sector firms, distorting market outcomes and hampering the efficient allocation of resources. Competitively neutral policies are needed to ensure that all enterprises—public or private, domestic or foreign—face the same set of rules. Achieving competitive neutrality for SOEs would require (i) removal of exemptions from the law on corporate governance; (ii) separation of commercial and noncommercial functions; (iii) imposition of positive rates of return on investments; (iv) less fragmented oversight; (v) improved reporting; (vi) clear compensation rules for public service obligations; and (vii) transparent state aid allocation.

HUMAN CAPITAL: ADAPTING SKILLS TO CHANGING NEEDS

The World Bank's Human Capital Index (HCI) at the subnational level highlights weaknesses in Romania's human capital endowment. Romania's human capital accumulation—proxied by the HCI—is the lowest in the EU and varies widely across counties. A child born in Romania today is expected to reach only 60 percent of his or her productive potential as an adult, compared to 100 percent if the individual were to receive the full benefit of high-quality education and health available in some other EU countries. There is also a marked association between the HCI and county-level poverty rates, with children born in poorer counties comparatively less productive than they would be if they received full health and education as available in some other counties. For every county, productivity gaps are unambiguously associated with a lack of education quality.

Disparities in education outcomes remain relevant across and within regions of Romania. Changes are taking place, but learning gaps in primary and secondary education persist. These can be seen clearly between urban and rural areas, across regions, and across social groups. Changes need to happen both at the system level and at the learning-center level. Useful reform measures would include (i) using evidence to hold the system and stakeholders accountable for achieving student learning; (ii) tracking progress of program interventions through systematic measurement of impacts; (iii) designing and implementing a more flexible approach to teacher development and appraisal; (iv) upgrading the teaching profession by using innovative teacher recruitment, motivation, and development practices that recognize teachers as valued professionals; (v) providing schools with the ability to plan school-level improvements tailored to their needs; and (vi) offering systematic support to school leaders and teachers to prepare school staff on methodologies that can engage students meaningfully.

A deficient skills supply system is preventing Romania from responding to changing global circumstances. Automation of production processes has started driving a demand for higher levels of cognitive skills, while the number of jobs involving routine application of procedural knowledge is shrinking. A paradigm shift would require reforms in primary and secondary schooling to ensure adequate literacy, numeracy, socioemotional skills, and other core foundational competences. In addition, more targeted actions to establish an effective skills-development system would include (i) ongoing review, rationalization, and streamlining of vocational programs and qualifications; (ii) policy and financing incentives to implement public-private partnerships; (iii) recognition of prior learning to underpin the development of a precision training framework to ensure workers can access training when, where, and how they need it; and (iv) effective coordination of efforts among key players in the skills development ecosystem.

Abbreviations

ALMP	active labor market policies
ASR	adult survival rate
CAGR	compound average growth rate
CEE	Central and Eastern Europe
CN	competitive neutrality
CVT	continued vocational training
EC	European Commission
ESL	early school-leaving
EU	European Union
EYS	expected years of schooling
GDP	gross domestic product
HCI	Human Capital Index
HP filter	Hodrick-Prescott filter
HTS	harmonized test scores
ICT	information and communication technology
IT	information technology
LP	labor productivity
MSMEs	micro-, small, and medium-size enterprises
NACE	Nomenclature des Activités Économiques dans la Communauté Européenne
NUTS	Nomenclature of Territorial Statistics
OECD	Organisation for Economic Co-operation and Development
PISA	Program for International Student Assessment
PMR	product market regulation
PPP	purchasing power parity
RCC	Romanian Competition Council
ROE	return on equity
RPL	recognition of prior learning
SFDI	Sovereign Fund for Development and Investments
SIIIR	Integrated Education Information System in Romania
SMEs	small and medium enterprises
SOE	state-owned enterprise
TESDA	Technical Education and Skills Development Authority (the Philippines)

TFP	total factor productivity
TFPR	revenue total factor productivity
TIMSS	Trends in International Mathematics and Science Study
TNER	total net enrollment rates
TVET	technical and vocational education and training
U-5 SR	under-5 survival rate
WDR	World Development Report

Overview

Romania's income per capita increased from 26 percent of the EU-28 average in 2000 to 64 percent in 2018. Economic growth, however, has been uneven and rests on the foundations of ineffective institutions, unfavorable demographics, and weak human capital. In this context, the Romania Country Economic Memorandum 2019 *focuses on competitive markets and educated and skilled workers as drivers of future growth. Productivity dynamics at the firm level suggest that product market policies can be made more competition friendly, while direct intervention of the state in the economy should be informed by competitive neutrality. At the same time, raising the quality of human capital requires renewed attention to education policies and a country system able to provide the right skills for the changing needs of the Romanian economy.*[1]

Romania's growth performance has been impressive but uneven and characterized by macroeconomic imbalances. In the early stages of the transition, prices were liberalized and the legal framework for private property and a market-based economy was established. The opening of the economy led to a large initial contraction in output after 1990. After the initial collapse, the early 2000s were a period of unsustainable growth, driven by procyclical fiscal policies that boosted domestic consumption. Public wages more than doubled between 1999 and 2008, public employment increased by 13.4 percent in only four years (between 2005 and 2008), and between 2003 and 2008 household credit increased more than sevenfold. A 7.1 percent contraction in output in 2009 led to a painful adjustment, with a 14.2 percent reduction in the number of public employees between 2008 and 2011 and an increase in the ratio of nonperforming loans from 7.9 percent in December 2009 to 21.9 percent in December 2013. In 2013, the growth cycle resumed, boosted again by procyclical fiscal policies, which now risk creating new macroeconomic imbalances (figure O.1).

In recent years, growth has had a narrow base and has been driven by domestic consumption, although the country's real growth rate was among the highest in the European Union (EU). Investments (gross fixed capital formation) have tended to be procyclical and volatile. The public sector has contributed to the volatility of total investment, because cuts in public investment, rather than in current expenditure, have been the safety valve through which the government has often met the fiscal deficit targets imposed by the EU's Stability and Growth Pact. The contribution of net exports to gross domestic product (GDP) growth has been, on average, small and highly procyclical. Particularly striking is the large role of consumption and the small role of net exports in Romania's growth recovery since 2013, as compared with both high-income EU and Organisation for Economic Co-operation and Development

Romania's GDP growth, 1990–2018 (HP filter)

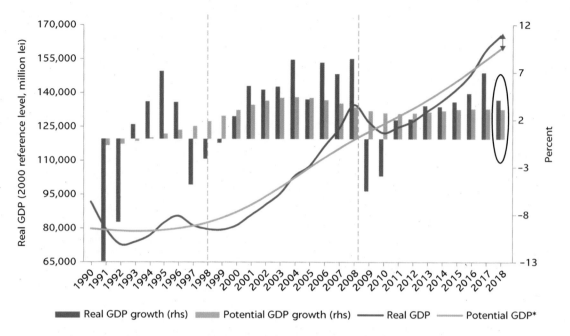

Real GDP growth (rhs) ▪ Potential GDP growth (rhs) ▪ Real GDP — Potential GDP*

Sources: Original estimations based on data from Eurostat 2019 (database), European Commission, Brussels, https://ec.europa.eu /eurostat/data/database; National Institute of Statistics 2019, TEMPO (online database), Bucharest, http://statistici.insse.ro:8077/tempo -online/#/pages/tables/insse-table; AMECO (macro-economic database), European Commission Economic and Financial Affairs, Brussels, https://ec.europa.eu/economy_finance/ameco/user/serie/SelectSerie.cfm.
Note: GDP = gross domestic product; HP filter = Hodrick-Prescott filter; rhs = right-hand side.
* Based on the HP filter.

Growth drivers (demand side) in Romania, 2013–17

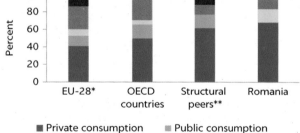

▪ Private consumption ▪ Public consumption
▪ Changes in inventories ▪ Gross fixed capital formation
▪ Net exports

Sources: UNSD 2018; World Bank 2018d.
Note: The contributions to growth for Romania's peers are expressed as shares of real gross domestic product (GDP) growth and are based on 2013–17 data. EU-28 = for list of countries see Note 3 on page 20; OECD = Organisation for Economic Co-operation and Development; OECD countries = for list of countries see Note 2 on page 20.
* EU-28 countries exclude Luxembourg and Malta, for which data are not available.
** Structural peer countries are selected based on population and GDP per capita and include Bulgaria, Chile, Colombia, Dominican Republic, Ecuador, Malaysia, Peru, and Poland.

(OECD) countries[2] and even with peer countries at a similar level of development (figure O.2).

Structural transformation has been visible on the supply side, with services becoming a major growth driver, while agriculture still plays an important role. Since 1990, Romania's economy has gone through a significant structural transformation from heavy industry to services. Industrial sectors like the chemical industry and textile manufacturing were especially hard hit by the early transition, registering a permanent loss of output capacity. Services, mainly wholesale and retail trade, have been driving growth in recent years, reflecting robust domestic demand. It is noteworthy that the information and communication technology (ICT) sector is one of the main contributors to growth and, as of 2017, was the seventh largest as a share of GDP (5.2 percent) in the EU. The contribution of agriculture to GDP growth is still higher than the average for OECD and EU countries, and also higher compared to structural peers of similar size and income per capita (figure O.3).

The composition of gross value added since the mid-1990s has changed dramatically. The shares of services and ICT have been increasing, while agriculture, albeit down from almost 20 percent in the mid-1990s, still contributes a significant 4.8 percent to total gross value added. As with most other economies, the share of construction tends to be procyclical and volatile (figure O.4).

In terms of employment, the share of agriculture is still high, but new sectors are emerging. In 2018, agriculture continued to make up 23 percent of total employment

FIGURE O.3

Growth drivers (supply side) in Romania, 2013–17

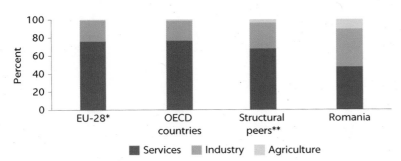

Sources: UNSD 2018; World Bank 2018d.
Note: The contributions to growth for Romania's peers are expressed as share of real gross
domestic product (GDP) growth and are based on 2013–17 data. EU-28 = for list of countries see
Note 3 on page 20; OECD = Organisation for Economic Co-operation and Development; OECD
countries = for list of countries see Note 2 on page 20.
* EU-28 countries exclude Luxembourg and Malta, for which data are not available.
** Structural peer countries are selected based on population and GDP per capita and include
Bulgaria, Chile, Colombia, Dominican Republic, Ecuador, Malaysia, Peru, and Poland.

FIGURE O.4

**Structural change in the composition of gross value added,
Romania, 1995–2018**

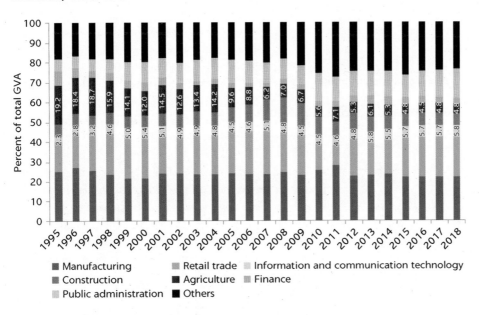

Source: National Institute of Statistics, http://www.insse.ro/cms/en.
Note: Current prices. GVA = gross value added.

in Romania, largely consisting of unskilled workers; this compares with 5.2 percent, on average, among its regional peers (Czech Republic, Hungary, Poland, and Slovak Republic) and 4.3 percent in the EU as a whole. Overall, however, the labor force has steadily been moving to higher-productivity sectors such as ICT (figure O.5).

The changing structure of the economy and of its comparative advantage is reflected in the composition of Romania's exports. The trade-to-GDP ratio increased from 60.8 percent in 1996 to 86.5 percent in 2018. Romania successfully diversified its export basket by switching from labor-intensive low-tech sectors (garments and footwear) to more advanced sectors (automotive, machinery, and electronics). Notably, "medium-tech" exports increased from 23 percent in 1996 to 46 percent in 2016, while high-tech exports are consistently below 10 percent of total exports. This structural transformation of the export basket seems to have slowed somewhat since the 2008–09 financial crisis (figure O.6) (World Bank 2018c).

FIGURE O.5

Changes in employment and productivity shares by industry, Romania, 2018 versus 2009

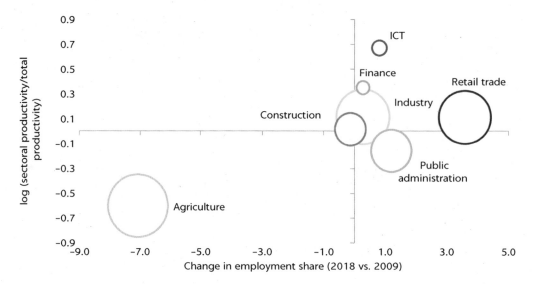

Source: Original estimates for Romania based on data from Eurostat (database), European Commission, Brussels, https://ec.europa.eu/eurostat/data/database.
Note: The size of the bubble indicates the number of employees. The vertical axis captures the relative sectoral increase in productivity. The horizontal axis captures the average relative increase in sectoral employment. ICT = information and communication technology.

FIGURE O.6

Industry distribution of exports, 1996–2018

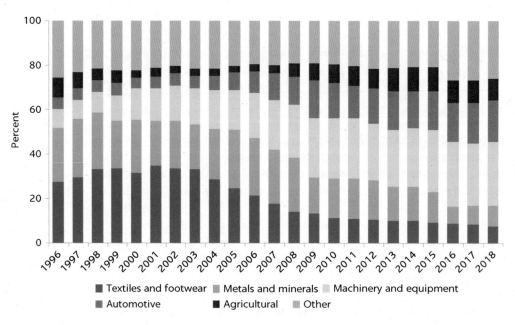

Source: UN Comtrade (United Nations Commodity Trade) 2018 (statistics database), United Nations, New York, https://comtrade.un.org.

DRIVERS OF GROWTH

Romania's success has been driven by the convergence of its labor productivity with the levels of richer EU member states. But the pace of convergence has slowed since 2009. Romania's income per capita rose from 26 percent of EU-28[3] average in 2000 to 64 percent in 2018. As of 2017, the level of labor productivity in Romania was 65.3 percent of the (unweighted) average of the older member states (EU-15[4]), up from 28.3 percent in 2000. The pace of convergence, however, slowed dramatically in the postcrisis period, with the compound average growth rate (CAGR) of labor productivity plummeting to 3.1 percent in 2009–17 from 9 percent in the 2000–08 period (figure O.7).[5]

The global financial crisis appears to have changed the pattern of labor productivity growth in Romania, with a decreasing contribution of productive efficiency and an increasing contribution of capital intensity. Both capital accumulation (the capital-labor ratio) and total factor productivity (TFP)[6] have been driving labor productivity improvements in Romania. The CAGR of capital intensity over the 2000–17 period was 4.2 percent, slightly faster than the 4 percent CAGR for TFP. Prior to the crisis (from 2000 to 2008), the CAGR of TFP was 5.9 percent, somewhat faster than the pace of growth of the capital-labor ratio (5.4 percent). After the crisis (2009–17), the trend reversed, with capital intensity experiencing a CAGR of 5.5 percent and TFP growth slowing to 4.5 percent. Sustaining the country's convergence to a high-income level will depend not only on more and better investment in (physical and human) capital but also on efficiency improvements.

Growth accounting confirms that growth has been driven by physical capital accumulation and efficiency gains (TFP), while the role of labor has been negative. TFP has been an important driver of Romania's economic growth, reflecting the efficiency gains from the gradual correction of resource misallocation during the transition to a market economy. But the role of TFP as a growth driver is diminishing. At the same time, the role of physical capital accumulation appears to have increased in the postcrisis period, while the contribution of labor, although negative throughout the entire period, appears to have become less negative after 2009 (figure O.8).

Capital accumulation and productive efficiency, in Romania and elsewhere, are influenced by many factors: some are exogenous while others are determined by policy choices. Some forces are broadly outside the control of an individual country's policy makers, at least in the short run. These include international trade and capital flows, demographic trends, technological progress, and the like. Other influences on economic growth are the result of policy choices. The latter policies, and the institutions that underpin them, can be defined in many ways. They comprise the monetary and fiscal frameworks needed to reduce macroeconomic volatility and encourage investment in physical and human capital, a sound legal system to enforce contracts to lend credibility to all types of economic interactions, and, crucially, a public administration with the capacity to design and enforce these policies. In all these aspects, Romania's policies and institutions have often not been up to the challenge (World Bank 2018a).

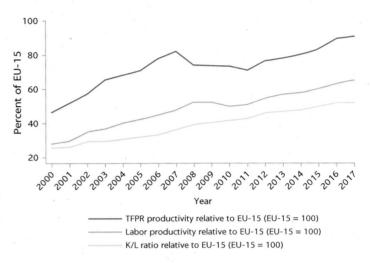

FIGURE O.7

Labor productivity in Romania relative to the EU-15, 2000–17

- TFPR productivity relative to EU-15 (EU-15 = 100)
- Labor productivity relative to EU-15 (EU-15 = 100)
- K/L ratio relative to EU-15 (EU-15 = 100)

Source: Penn Table 9.0 (database), Groningen Growth and Development Centre, University of Groningen, https://www.rug.nl/ggdc/productivity/pwt/.
Note: Labor productivity is output-side real GDP at current purchasing power parities (PPPs, in millions of 2011 US$), divided by the number of persons engaged (in millions). The capital-labor ratio is defined as capital stock at current PPPs (in millions of 2011 US$) divided by the number of persons engaged (in millions). Country-level TFPR is reported as the TFP level at current PPPs (EU-15). All values are converted as a proportion of EU-15 (unweighted) average. EU-15 = for list of countries see Note 4 on page 20; GDP = gross domestic product; K = capital; L = labor; TFP = total factor productivity; TFPR = revenue total factor productivity.

Shares of growth attributable to TFP, labor, capital, and other factors during four periods, 1990–2018

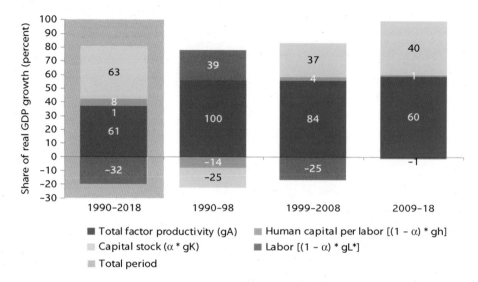

Source: Original calculations based on a human capital adjusted Solow (1957) model.
Note: The depreciation rate of capital is set at 5 percent, the value used in the literature for Romania. A = total factor productivity; α = income share of capital; g = growth; GDP = gross domestic product; h = estimated level of human capital per unit of labor input; K = capital stock; L = labor force (population 15+); TFP = total factor productivity.

Romania's economic success is fragile and rests on the foundations of ineffective institutions, unfavorable demographics, and weak human capital. An overview of the dynamics of labor, human capital, and physical capital accumulation, as well as of various possible determinants of total factor productivity, can help shed light on the drivers of Romania's economic growth. Box O.1 illustrates how these forces see the firm as the actor at center stage.

Availability of labor

Romania's total and working-age populations declined by about 3.7 and 2.4 million, respectively, between 1990 and 2018, and are expected to continue falling. Romania's fertility rate declined from 1.8 in 1990 to the current 1.7, while the age structure has shifted, with the share of the population age 65 and over increasing from 10.3 to 18.2 percent.

Between 3 million and 5 million Romanians currently live and work abroad, mostly in OECD and European countries. Between 2000 and 2018, Romania's population fell from 22.5 to 19.5 million, with emigration accounting for more than 75 percent of this decline (World Bank 2018a). This has had important consequences for the labor market and for the contribution of labor to the potential growth of the Romanian economy. However, policies have been implemented to try to reduce this "brain drain," including income tax breaks for workers in the IT and construction sectors and substantial increases of funding in the health and education sectors.

In 2000, Romania's labor force participation rate for persons ages 15 to 64 was 68.4 percent, below the EU-15 average of 69.2 percent. By 2018, it had dropped to 67.8 percent, one of the lowest rates in the EU. While about 76.9 percent of men

BOX O.1

The firm as a central actor of economic growth

The growth in GDP (Y) per capita may be decomposed into the product of labor productivity growth and labor participation growth (the ratio between labor force, L, and total population, N). Labor productivity is, in turn, affected by aggregate TFP, as well as by the aggregate accumulation of inputs, the capital/labor ratio. Dynamic issues aside, each of these components has its own determinants at the level of the individual firms that form the productive base of an economy. The productive efficiency of the economy as a whole (TFP) is the result of aggregating firm-level TFPs (efficiency levels). Likewise, the accumulation of inputs depends on firms' decisions regarding investment in physical capital, demand for labor, and demand for skilled labor. Also, labor participation increases when, for a given population, the demand for labor at the firm level increases. This model economy is illustrated in figure BO.1.1, which shows the transmission mechanism from individual firms to the whole economy.

FIGURE BO.1.1

A model economy

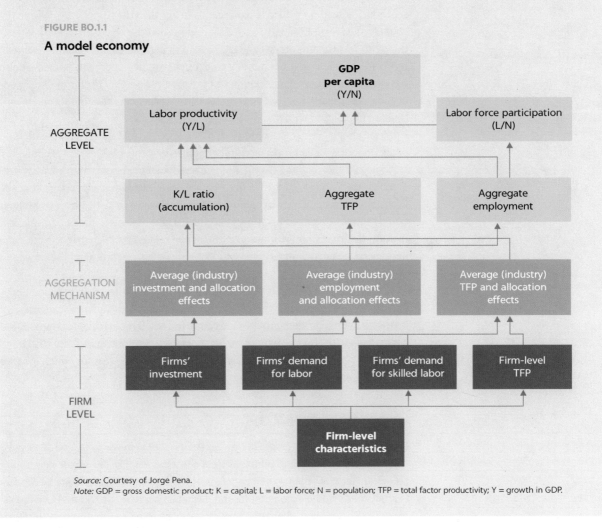

Source: Courtesy of Jorge Pena.
Note: GDP = gross domestic product; K = capital; L = labor force; N = population; TFP = total factor productivity; Y = growth in GDP.

were active in the labor market in 2018, only 58.3 percent of women were. The participation rate for people with tertiary education was 88.4 percent, compared with 68.6 percent for people with upper-secondary education and only 42.6 percent for people with less than an upper-secondary education.

Quality of human capital

The quality of Romania's human capital is low. Forty percent of 15-year-old Romanian students do not have minimum literacy proficiency; and the proportion of those who leave school early—at 18.5 percent—is one of the highest in the EU (World Bank 2018a). About 40 percent of 15-year-old students have low reading and numeracy proficiency according to the 2015 OECD Program for International Student Assessment (PISA).[7] This rate is almost double the EU average (23 percent). Romanian students lag those in other EU countries by about 1.5 years, and the achievement gap in Romania between the top and bottom quintile's PISA scores is among the highest in the EU. In 2017, only 15 percent of Romania's working-age population had completed tertiary education, and of concern is the comparatively low proportion of graduates per population ages 20–29 in STEM (science, technology, engineering, and mathematics) disciplines. Meanwhile, overall 27 percent of the working-age population had completed less than upper-secondary education, which is significantly lower than the EU average. Within the country, the North East and South East regions had the highest shares of population with less than upper-secondary education completed, at 36 and 33 percent, respectively, with, on the other extreme, Bucharest at 14 percent. Bucharest also has the highest share of working-age population (33 percent) holding tertiary education. After Bucharest, the West and South-West regions have the second lowest share of population with the lowest level of education.

Skills shortages are documented in key sectors, including ICT, health, and education, as well as for science and engineering professionals and technicians. Institutional shortcomings in the Romanian education system, coupled with emigration patterns, have led to insufficient numbers of highly skilled workers available to sustain the pace of growth.[8] Skills shortages also exist in skilled manual occupational groups, including machinery mechanics and repairers; cooks; car, van, and motorcycle drivers; and workers in garment and related trades, partly reflecting the low development and quality of vocational training and technical school education (World Bank 2018a).

The emigration of highly skilled workers aggravates the plight of human capital. In the first decade of the 2000s, Romania recorded the largest increase of high-skilled immigration into the G20 countries, reaching a stock of about 492,000 persons in 2010–11. The share of highly educated emigrants out of the total of all emigrants was also high, at 23 percent as of 2010, the latest year for which data are available (World Bank 2018a).

Investment in physical capital

Romania invested, on average, 25.1 percent of its GDP between 2000 and 2018, most of it in manufacturing and nonresidential construction. Private-sector investment accounted for more than 80 percent of total investment, and equipment and nonresidential construction accounted for more than 85 percent of private-sector investment. Despite the high share of private investment, a shallow financial sector limits the availability of long-term finance. The banking sector is the main financial intermediary, but bank loans to private enterprises amounted to a meager 11.7 percent of GDP in 2018. Foreign direct investment inflows—a conduit for the transfer of capital, access to modern technologies, competition, and better managerial skills—remain below precrisis levels.[9]

Public investment has not played a supportive role because of institutional weaknesses. Romania ranks 113th out of 140 countries in the quality of its transport infrastructure, according to the World Economic Forum's *Global Competitiveness Report 2018* (Schwab 2018). High levels of public investment, bolstered by the large influx of EU funds since EU accession in 2007, have not yielded the expected results in terms of quality and quantity of transport infrastructure. Insufficient institutional coordination, ineffective policy implementation and monitoring, politicization of decision making, poor human resource policies in public administration, and delays in implementing results-based budgeting have contributed to weak public investment performance (World Bank 2018a).

Some determinants of total factor productivity

The unpredictability of the business environment—a direct consequence of institutional failures—is a significant challenge for the private sector. In recent years, for instance, businesses were faced with many fiscal measures that were first introduced and then reversed, which severely impacted businesses' ability to plan operations (World Bank 2018a). Because of their size and scarce resources, micro-, small, and medium-size enterprises (MSMEs) tend to be more affected by the regulatory burden. Although Romania has made progress on the World Bank's Doing Business indicators—in 2018 it scored 72.9 out of 100 in the "ease of doing business" score (table O.1)—getting electricity, dealing with construction permits, resolving insolvency, protecting minority investors, and enforcing contracts are key areas that remain a burden on businesses.

Restrictive regulation of services constrains aggregate productivity. The service sector in Romania employs more than 50 percent of the workforce and accounts for more than 60 percent of GDP. Although competition in services is in a relatively nascent phase in the EU as a whole, Romania stands out for particularly restrictive regulation of professional, transport, and airline services. Reducing barriers in service sectors can increase productivity across the EU by an average of 5 percent, provide more and better jobs, stimulate investment, and encourage deeper integration among EU countries (World Bank 2016).

TABLE O.1 **Romania's *Doing Business* scores, by indicator, 2010–18**

	STARTING A BUSINESS	DEALING WITH CONSTRUCTION PERMITS	GETTING ELECTRICITY	REGISTERING PROPERTY	GETTING CREDIT	PROTECTING MINORITY INVESTORS	PAYING TAXES	TRADING ACROSS BORDERS	ENFORCING CONTRACTS	RESOLVING INSOLVENCY
DB2018	89.7	58.1	53.3	74.7	80.0	60.0	80.9	100.0	72.3	59.8
DB2017	89.5	58.1	53.2	73.8	80.0	60.0	80.9	100.0	72.3	59.2
DB2016	90.5	57.4	53.1	74.0	80.0	60.0	80.6	100.0	72.3	58.2
DB2015	90.5	62.2	53.0	80.8	80.0	60.0	80.0	77.2	66.1	57.1
DB2014	90.4	54.0	35.4	80.7	87.5	56.7	64.0	76.9	66.1	32.2
DB2013	88.9	53.9	35.2	80.6	87.5	56.7	62.0	76.3	66.1	31.5
DB2012	87.8	53.8	36.2	80.5	87.5	56.7	49.4	75.9	66.1	30.8
DB2011	90.4	55.3	35.4	80.3	87.5	56.7	48.8	77.4	66.1	27.7
DB2010	90.3	61.0	35.3	80.3	87.5	56.7	49.4	76.9	66.1	30.7

Source: Doing Business (database), World Bank, Washington, DC, https://www.doingbusiness.org/.
Note: The ease of doing business score captures the gap of each economy from the best regulatory performance observed on each of the indicators across all economies in the *Doing Business* sample since 2005. An economy's ease of doing business score is reflected on a scale from 0 to 100, where 0 represents the lowest and 100 represents the best performance. DB = Doing Business.

Poor corporate governance of state-owned enterprises (SOEs) and their presence in markets that are, or could be, open to the private sector are further sources of inefficiency. It drags down aggregate productivity both directly, in the sectors where SOEs are active, and indirectly, through the inefficient provision of inputs to other sectors of the economy. State aid is directed to declining industries, worsening the misallocation of resources. Consistently over time, the poorly performing railway sector has absorbed a sizeable portion of overall state aid: 37.5 percent on average per year between 2010 and 2015. Conversely, the state aid allocation for research and development or risk capital for MSMEs—areas that have the potential to spark growth— has been limited (World Bank 2018b).

Among several concurrent determinants of economic growth, the *Romania Country Economic Memorandum 2019* focuses on the role of competition and human capital. The common purpose of the six independent essays in this report is to identify policy actions that will help drive Romania's future economic growth and continued convergence toward the income levels of wealthier EU partners. Competition and human capital were chosen, based on consultations with various public and private sector stakeholders, as policy areas that are apt to stimulate a constructive dialogue on impactful reforms for the short and medium term.

COMPETITION: ALLOCATING RESOURCES MORE EFFICIENTLY

Since the global financial crisis, the world economy has experienced a general productivity slowdown, accompanied by a reduction in the pace of convergence of less productive economies, including Romania. Since 2010, annual labor productivity growth in OECD countries has slowed to 0.9 percent, half the rate recorded in the precrisis period. Furthermore, the slowdown has been more pronounced in countries with relatively low labor productivity levels, slowing the pace of convergence in countries like Romania (see figure O.7). In many economies, the employment growth seen since the crisis has been in activities with relatively low labor productivity, compressing aggregate productivity (OECD 2019). In Romania, the 2009–18 period saw employment losses in agriculture (by 28 percent, from 2.8 million to less than 2 million) and in manufacturing (by 8 percent, from 1.7 million to 1.6 million), compensated by increased employment in wholesale and retail trade, transport, and accommodation (by 5 percent, from 1.7 million to just under 2 million), and even in more sophisticated services, such as information and communication technology, where employment increased by 28 percent, from 122,000 to 185,000. These trends show that in Romania the structural transformation away from agriculture is ongoing and remains a key driver of the patterns of employment growth.

The postcrisis period witnessed a widening productivity gulf between leading and lagging firms, both within and across countries, and Romania is no exception to this trend. OECD (2015) suggests a distinction among three types of firms: the globally most productive, the most productive domestic firms, and laggard firms. The *global frontier* comprises large and skills-intensive firms, often multinationals, that account for a substantial portion of global patents and trademarks and undertake innovation that pushes out the global productivity frontier. *Domestic frontier* firms are the most productive in the domestic economy within their industries, are open to international engagement, are relatively young, and are more likely to innovate.

Laggard firms are more focused on local markets and relatively less productive in their industry within the domestic economy. Andrews, Criscuolo, and Gal (2016) find that, even as aggregate productivity growth began to slow down, frontier firms continued to reap larger productivity gains than laggards. The increasing productivity gap suggests that lagging firms have become less effective at learning from the global frontier, especially in services.

More intense competition enables more productive firms to command a larger share of resources—labor, skills, and capital—thus allowing them to grow, boosting aggregate productivity.[10] Competition can also favor the diffusion of existing technologies to laggards, allowing productivity improvements within firms and facilitating their catching up with the national productivity frontier. A welcome consequence of allowing the best domestic firms to emerge and grow is that the economy would benefit from lower- cost and higher-quality goods and services, which in turn would facilitate participation in global value chains.

The intensity of competition is affected by product market regulation, which tends to be less restrictive in countries with higher incomes per capita. A simple correlation analysis using OECD product market regulation (PMR) cross-sectional data available for 70 countries, including Romania, suggests that GDP per capita is higher for countries with lower incidence of regulatory barriers that inhibit competition (figure O.9). This result is robust to different levels of PMR measurement, whether it captures state involvement in business sectors ("state control"), the ease of creating firms and expanding them ("barriers to entry and rivalry"), or the ease of entry of foreign products and firms ("barriers to trade and investment") (figure O.10).

Against this background, chapters 1, 2, and 3 in this report provide an assessment of productivity and competition in Romania. Chapter 1 presents an analysis of firm-level productivity, trying to identify the domestic leaders and laggards and to understand the extent to which productivity growth, or the lack thereof, has come from more efficient operation of individual firms or from the reallocation of resources from less efficient to more efficient players. Chapter 2 benchmarks product market regulation in Romania to that of EU and OECD countries, trying to establish which of its aspects hamper market competition. Finally, chapter 3 looks at the degree to which the state's presence in the economy through SOEs is (or is not) informed by principles of competitive neutrality, allowing SOEs and private players to operate on equal terms.

Productivity leaders and laggards

Anecdotal evidence suggests that a vibrant enterprise sector has been the engine of Romania's growth over the past two decades. At the same time, regulated services sectors and those with a large state presence are perceived as inefficient and a drag on growth (World Bank 2018b). The firm-level analysis in chapter 1 confirms this impression.

Firm-level data suggest that companies at the domestic productivity frontier are older, larger, pay higher salaries, charge higher markups, and have higher capital intensity. Data also suggest that the labor productivity of laggard firms has been increasing faster than that of frontier ones, especially after 2013, and this catching-up process has been driven mostly by capital deepening rather than gains in (revenue-based) total factor productivity (TFPR). When one analyzes the gap between frontier and laggard companies in terms of growth of TFPR, one finds a widening gap for manufacturing, and this appears to be driven mostly by frontier companies

FIGURE O.9

GDP per capita (2011 PPP adjusted) versus economywide PMR indicator

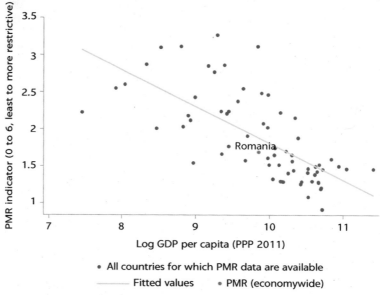

PMR indicator (0 to 6, least to more restrictive)
3.5
3
2.5
2
1.5
1
7
8
9
10
11
Log GDP per capita (PPP 2011)
Romania
All countries for which PMR data are available
Fitted values
PMR (economywide)

Source: Original analysis.
Note: GDP = gross domestic product; PMR = product market regulation; PPP = purchasing power parity.

FIGURE O.10

GDP per capita (2011 PPP adjusted) versus PMR subcomponents

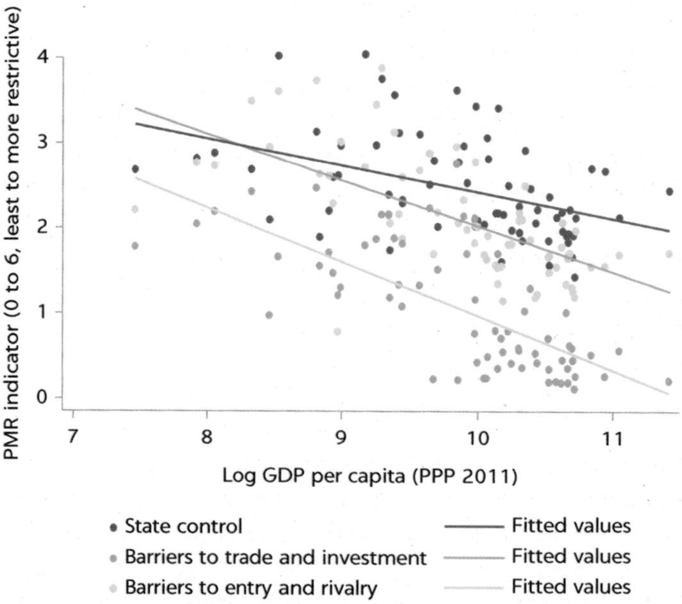

PMR indicator (0 to 6, least to more restrictive)
4
3
2
1
0
7
8
9
10
11
Log GDP per capita (PPP 2011)
State control
Barriers to trade and investment
Barriers to entry and rivalry
Fitted values
Fitted values
Fitted values

Source: Original analysis.
Note: GDP = gross domestic product; PMR = product market regulation; PPP = purchasing power parity.

charging increasingly higher markups (relative to nonfrontier firms) rather than by actual gains in technical efficiency (proxied by TFPR markup-adjusted). This would suggest that the higher markup performance of manufacturing productivity leaders might come either from higher market power or differences in the quality of and demand for their products, rather than from their ability to successfully invest in and combine new technology to succeed in the market. For services, the average gap in TFPR growth between frontier and laggard companies is almost nonexistent, and again this result is driven by markup performance of leader companies, which tend to increase their markups faster than laggards.

Reallocation of market shares to more efficient players has played an important role only in manufacturing and not in services. An Olley and Pakes (1996) decomposition shows that the "between" margin was relatively more important than the "within" margin to explain productivity growth from 2011 to 2017, but it was positive only for manufacturing.[11] For services—which typically are more sheltered from competitive pressure, with lower exposure to foreign competition and more stringent product market regulations—the reallocation margin is negative on average, suggesting that the most productive firms are not capturing larger market shares. When the analysis is broken down by year, the results show a small and mostly positive "within" component for manufacturing, while the same component for services displays an unsteady performance, alternating signs throughout the period. This suggests that individual firms are becoming less productive, with space to improve firm capabilities (management quality, technological learning, and so forth), particularly in services.

Pervasive state control and remaining barriers to entry and rivalry

The restrictiveness of product market regulation is a key driver of the efficient allocation of resources across firms. To identify and benchmark regulatory restrictiveness in Romania, the analysis in chapter 2 relies on the OECD PMR indicator for Romania. The indicator includes three pillars: (i) state control, (ii) barriers to entry and rivalry (also known as barriers to entrepreneurship), and (iii) barriers to trade and investment. PMR indicators assess the extent to which public policies promote or inhibit market forces. Each of the areas addressed within the PMR methodology sheds light on specific restrictions of the regulatory framework, both economywide and in key sectors of the economy, such as electricity, gas, telecom, postal service, transport, water, retail distribution, professional services, and other sectors, as well as administrative requirements for business start-ups, treatment of foreign parties, and such other policies as governance of public-controlled enterprises or antitrust exclusions and exemptions. The economywide PMR methodology is a useful instrument for pinpointing rules that are likely to restrict competition.

Overall, the regulatory framework in Romania is more restrictive of competition than the average for OECD and EU-15 countries. Considering its projected PMR score based on 2017 information, Romania's overall PMR score would have marginally improved between 2013 and 2017, which implies that unless other countries have worsened their performance over those four years, Romania's regulatory restrictiveness would not only be higher than the OECD and EU averages but also higher than in some of its neighbors, such as the Czech Republic, Hungary, or the Slovak Republic.

Impediments to competition are mainly associated with state control of the economy and several remaining barriers to entry and rivalry. This indicates persistent state intervention in the economy through SOEs in markets where private sector participation and competition are typically viable (such as energy generation and transport). In relative terms, Romania's regulations appear to be more restrictive than the total sample average in the case of state control regulations. Regarding barriers to entry and rivalry, Romania exhibits a less restrictive regulatory framework than the total sample average, but it is still more restrictive when compared to the EU-15 and OECD averages.

A number of policy actions could be taken to reduce the restrictiveness of Romania's product market policies. The most transformational among these would include the following:

- Streamlining burdensome administrative procedures for businesses to facilitate market entry;

- Limiting interventions by the trade association in the entry decision in road freight services;

- Removing unnecessary entry requirements for road freight services (for example, the requirement to notify the government or regulatory agency and wait for approval before road freight businesses can start operation);

- Removing unnecessary entry requirements for professional services (for example, unnecessary membership requirements in professional associations and double licensing from public and professional bodies to lawyers and engineers);

- Reassessing the application of minimum and maximum price for lawyers and of recommended price guidelines for engineers and architects.

Ensuring competitive neutrality for state-owned enterprises

The government's direct involvement in markets is not in itself problematic, but in Romania there is still a significant SOE footprint. Romania has more than 1,500 SOEs and has at least one SOE in 23 out of the 30 PMR sectors, as compared to the Slovak Republic (12 sectors); the EU-15 average (15 sectors), the Czech Republic (17 sectors), and Hungary (18 sectors). SOE presence goes beyond typical network industries, for example, in sectors where state presence is not justified by a clear economic or strategic rationale. Furthermore, the government is kept liable for losses in the railway sector. In the energy sector, it recently reintroduced price regulation and reversed reforms toward full liberalization, to the detriment of the quality of the service (notably, shortages in electricity provision).

SOEs compete on uneven (nonneutral) terms with the private sector because of gaps in the current regulatory framework and in its implementation. In terms of the regulatory framework itself, lack of competitive neutrality emerges from restrictive SOE governance rules, exemptions of newly set-up SOEs from the law on corporate governance, lack of rules mandating the separation of commercial and noncommercial functions despite legal separation (for example, in the railway and energy sectors), and the lack of specific provisions that require SOE investments to show positive rates of returns. Important competitive neutrality gaps associated with the implementation of the regulatory framework emerge from the protracted application of corporate governance rules, fragmentation of SOE oversight across institutions with frequent overlaps, inconsistent reporting of SOE performance that prevent full monitoring and comparability with the private sector in comparable situations, little clarity in terms of compensation for public service obligations, and lack of transparency in state aid allocation.

Reassessing the SOE presence under a clear economic rationale and abiding by the principle of subsidiarity can help systematize the roles of the state in the economy—as an operator through SOEs and as a regulator—and avoid conflicts of interests and market distortions. State aid in Romania targets sectors with an SOE presence, such as railways and energy, providing another avenue for direct state intervention in the economy. Despite being subject to the EU rules, state aid amounting to at least 0.45 percent of Romanian GDP was found to be illegal in 2017 (the total legal state aid accounted for 0.63 percent of the GDP in Romania in the same year). The state's presence has also been creeping up in the past five years with the creation of several new SOEs: Bucharest city government alone created around 22 companies in such diverse areas as travel arrangements, advertising spaces, and even taxi services. In some cases, such as that of the airline TAROM, costs seem to outweigh the benefits. These instances dictate that direct intervention of the state in the economy must be subject to a clear economic rationale.

Measures should be taken to ensure that SOEs and privately owned firms compete on an equal footing. The most important among these would include the following:

- Restricting publicly controlled firms to markets where the presence of the state is needed as last resort and ensuring competitive neutrality where private and public firms coexist,

- Requiring that SOEs must achieve a rate of commercial return and show positive net present value,

- Ensuring that government interventions in markets follow the principle of the subsidiarity role of the state in the economy, with a clear economic rationale.

HUMAN CAPITAL: FORMING PRESENT AND FUTURE WORKERS

Human capital is fundamental for economic growth. Human capital consists of the knowledge, skills, and health that people accumulate over their lives, enabling them to realize their potential as productive members of society (World Bank 2019b, 50). Human capital is a key determinant of economic growth through its influence on labor productivity.[12] In neoclassical models, a one-off increase in the stock of human capital leads to a one-off increase in productivity growth. Endogenous growth models place even greater emphasis on human capital, suggesting that the same one-off increase can lead to a permanent increase in productivity growth. This implies increasing returns on investments in human capital and emphasizes the importance of education and innovation as engines of long-run growth. Empirical evidence has substantiated the theory, and human capital inputs—captured through a quantity or quality dimension, either in terms of years of schooling or the quality of education—have been found to increase productivity and, therefore, economic growth.[13] Finally, higher levels of human capital are also associated with positive externalities—a cleaner environment, higher levels of public health, and greater social cohesion—that indirectly contribute to economic growth.

As the fourth industrial revolution unfolds, investing in the right workforce skills and training models is essential to keep pace with rapid changes in technology and markets. Countries at the economic frontier are forward-looking, have robust economies, are open to investment and technology, and have competitive, well-matched workforces. But the frontier is an ever-moving target and keeping up with it requires ongoing strategic investments in human capital. Moreover, rapid technological change implies that all types of jobs, including low-skill ones, require adaptability and more advanced cognitive skills. Education and training models need to allow individuals, firms' employees, and countries' workforces to update their skills frequently and efficiently to meet changing needs.

Advanced cognitive skills such as complex problem-solving skills, sociobehavioral skills such as teamwork, and skill combinations that facilitate adaptability, such as reasoning and self-efficacy, are increasingly important (World Bank 2019b). Building these skills requires strong human capital foundations and lifelong learning opportunities. Since jobs that rely on interpersonal interaction will not easily be replaced by machines and job tasks across occupations are increasingly requiring higher-order cognitive skills, it is essential that the education and training system be geared toward developing integrated skills sets—sociobehavioral, higher-order cognitive, and problem-solving skills—in addition to developing foundational skills. Preparing students to learn throughout life equips individuals with the flexibility and resilience needed to partake in new job opportunities and safeguard against economic downturns.

Romania's human capital foundations and skills development systems are not up to the challenges ahead. In 2015, the country's public spending on nontertiary education accounted for less than 2 percent of GDP, less than half the EU-28 average. Low public spending contributes to poor student performance, exacerbating long-standing income and regional disparities in educational outcomes. Results from the 2015 PISA show high levels of inequality in student performance between socioeconomic groups and a large share of students underperforming in literacy, numeracy, and problem-solving skills. Differences in performance between students in the top and bottom socioeconomic quintiles is equivalent to three years of schooling. This performance gap is one of the highest in Europe. Students from rural and poor households consistently perform below standards and have substantially higher rates of leaving school early. In fact, the early-school-leaving rate is six times greater in rural areas compared to urban areas—25.4 percent and 4.2 percent, respectively (Eurostat 2019, indicator edat_lfse_30).

Against this background, chapters 4, 5, and 6 in this report provide an assessment of human capital, education, and skills in Romania. Chapter 4 computes the World Bank's Human Capital Index (HCI) at the subnational level, finding stark differences in human capital endowments across Romanian regions and socioeconomic groups. Chapter 5 examines the gaps in the pretertiary education system that hamper the quality of learning. Finally, chapter 6 assesses skills mismatches and proposes solutions that will enable Romania to successfully participate in the so-called fourth industrial revolution.

Wide disparities across regions and social groups in the Human Capital Index

Romania's human capital accumulation—proxied by the HCI—is the lowest in the EU and varies widely across counties. Assuming a status quo in education and health conditions, a child born today in Romania is expected to reach only 60 percent of his or her productive potential as an adult, compared to 100 percent if the individual were to receive the full benefit of high-quality education and health interventions. As expected, there is a marked association between the HCI and county-level poverty rates (World Bank 2016b); children born in poorer counties are comparatively less productive than they would be if they received full health and education. Low education quality is associated with low student performance and accumulated skills deficits. The HCI for Romania shows that the years of schooling a child born today can expect to achieve by the age of 18, given the current enrollment rates in the county where the child resides, decrease significantly—across all counties—when adjusted by the quality of education. The analysis finds large inequities between rural counties and better-off and more densely populated urban ones.

The HCI is highest in Bucharest-Ilfov and Cluj counties and lowest in Giurgiu county. A child born today in Bucharest-Ilfov and Cluj counties, is expected to reach 69 percent and 66 percent potential, respectively, as productive adults, compared to 53 percent for a child born in Satu Mare and 49 percent in Giurgiu. Looking at the relative contribution of each of the HCI components (child survival, health, and education), the analysis reveals that productivity gaps are unambiguously associated with a lack of education quality in every county. On average, the productivity loss associated with low education quality is about 22 percent nationally and ranges from 18 percent in Braila to about 29 percent in Harghita.

A simulation exercise suggests that significant investment in education is needed—an average of 2.2 quality-adjusted years of schooling—for most counties to reach the HCI levels of Bucharest-Ilfov. On average, more than two quality-adjusted expected years of schooling are needed. These results vary from county to county. For instance, Giurgiu would require almost four years of additional learning-adjusted years of education to catch up with Bucharest-Ilfov. On the other hand, Cluj would require less than a year of quality-adjusted years of education to close that gap.

Closing learning gaps in education

Although the Romanian government has made some progress in improving education outcomes, school segregation, student performance gaps, and leaving school early characterize the learning environment in the country. Policy priorities and programs have focused on strengthening education institutions, encouraging better teaching practices, changing school curricula, and improving students' evaluations (Kitchen et al. 2017). However, implementation challenges and relatively limited funding have slowed or halted progress, leaving several gaps. First, school social segregation and marginalization drive students to attend schools with children and young people of the same socioeconomic status, lowering potentially positive peer effects and biasing teachers' expectations of students. Second, wide performance gaps in several key foundational competencies and subject areas (math, reading, and science) have shown little narrowing over the years, placing Romania behind other comparable countries. Third, high rates of leaving school early are closely related to poverty, with differences evident both between urban and rural areas and by socio-economic status.

Difficulty in recruitment of teachers and poorly designed school funding mechanisms exacerbate social and geographical inequalities in access to education. Only 3.8 percent of university graduates complete programs in education. Moreover, recruitment of teachers in rural areas is not effective, as the current merit-based allowance system rewards teachers whose students achieve exceptional results in assessments and competitions, making it difficult for disadvantaged and hard-to-staff schools to attract and maintain high-quality teachers. The problem is exacerbated by the current school funding formula. Resources are allocated on a per capita basis, leading many schools in urban areas to overcrowd their classrooms, while rural schools struggle to assemble enough students to break even. These funding inequities are exacerbated by stark differences in the revenue base available in local municipalities, which are responsible for financing a significant portion of the per capita formula. Of equal concern is the lack of incentive mechanisms attached to the formula to incentivize better education outcomes or increased student learning. Finally, the relatively low teacher compensation level makes it difficult to entice young and talented candidates to pursue teaching as a professional career.

To tackle challenges in the education system, interventions and policies have centered on broadening access and improving learning. Most interventions to improve education can be categorized under two types: *incentives-based* interventions, aiming to reduce barriers to access, and *instructional* interventions, aiming to improve learning and enhance education curriculum delivery. In Romania, given the prevalence of regional gaps and lagging subnational regions, it is relevant to review interventions that focus on increasing access to education to understand how to reduce initial disparities, that is, leveling the playing field to improve conditions that are conducive for learning for all students. In urban areas, where schools tend to have more qualified teachers, better school infrastructure, and a higher proportion of top-performing schools, relevant suggested interventions should focus on improving student achievement. In rural areas, basic needs should also be covered, and interventions that address leaving school early, enrollment, and attendance can be stepping-stones to reducing education gaps more effectively.

Transformational policy actions to close gaps in primary and secondary education would include the following:

- Using evidence, including international and national student assessments, to hold the system and stakeholders accountable for achieving student learning;

- Tracking progress of program interventions through systematic measurement of impacts;

- Designing and implementing a more flexible approach to teacher development and appraisal that focuses on improving teaching performance and the student's learning experience;

- Upgrading the teacher profession using innovative teacher recruitment, motivation, and development practices that recognize teachers as valued professionals;

- Providing schools with the ability to plan school-level improvements tailored to the teaching force and diverse needs of the student populations they serve; and

- Offering systematic support to school leaders and teachers to prepare school staff on methodologies that can engage students meaningfully.

Creating a skilled workforce

Automation of production processes has started driving demand for higher levels of cognitive skills, while jobs involving routine application of procedural knowledge are shrinking. This suggests that the Romanian economy is particularly vulnerable, as it currently has a disproportionate share of routine type of jobs in the manufacturing, ICT, and agriculture sectors, and most of Romania's labor force (55 percent) is in blue-collar occupations. Between 2012 and 2017, the job vacancy rate at the national level doubled from 0.6 percent to 1.3 percent. The vacancy rate increased in all of Romania's eight regions, with the West region experiencing the largest increase of 1.1 percentage points, where the vacancy rate passed from 0.6 percent to 1.7 percent. Across all regions, high-skilled white-collar and low-skilled, blue-collar occupations are the most difficult occupations to fill, except in Bucharest-Ilfov, where high-skilled (managers, professionals, and technicians and associate professionals) and low-skilled (clerical support workers, and service and sales workers) white-collar occupations contributed to almost 80 percent of the total vacancy rate in 2017. Some of the faster-growing sectors—transport and storage, ICT, manufacturing, administrative support services, and professional, scientific, and technical services—also face a significant challenge in filling open positions.

Skills mismatches are exacerbated by limited provision of continued vocational training (CVT). Many enterprises in Romania do not provide CVT, which is the traditional way by which employers respond to skills mismatches. Results from a recent employer survey show that the main reasons CVT is not offered regularly in enterprises is that companies believe that the existing qualifications, skills, and competencies are aligned with the current needs of enterprises (84 percent) and employers are recruiting people with the right skills needed for the job (78 percent). The number of Romanian enterprises providing CVT declined significantly between 2005 and 2010 but increased slightly between 2010 and 2015. By comparison, most other EU-28 countries show a progressive increase in providers over the same periods. However, more people, and more highly skilled people, are taking part in CVT in Romania. In 2010, around 18 percent of employees in Romania took part in CVT courses, increasing to 21 percent in 2015 (National Institute of Statistics 2017). The likelihood of participation in education and training is related to levels of educational achievement, making people with a tertiary-level education more likely to participate in work-based training (66 percent for the EU-28 and 16 percent for Romania), while those having completed at most upper-secondary or postsecondary levels are second-most likely (41 percent for the EU-28 and 6 percent for Romania), and those with at most lower secondary education least likely (24 percent for the EU-28 and only 1 percent for Romania) (Eurostat 2018, adult learning statistics).

There are significant opportunities for Romania to develop new models of skills development that will position it to benefit from the possibilities of the fourth industrial revolution. A disconnect between employers, workers, and education and training providers results in a model of skills development in which the various actors act in isolation and achieve suboptimal levels of training. According to the National Strategy for Lifelong Learning 2015–2020 (Ministry of Education and Scientific Research 2015), expanding lifelong learning in Romania will require addressing accumulated skills deficits in the stock of the workforce, improving information asymmetries, introducing incentive schemes to entice more people to participate in education and training, and ensuring there is adequate capacity and resources for relevant training to take place. A paradigm shift will require strong determination to introduce new models and approaches, as it is clear that business as usual will not move Romania in the direction it wishes to head. From this perspective, the so-called precision training framework provides a strong conceptual model for introducing suitable new approaches.

Several measures would ensure progress toward creating a workforce with adequate skills to meet the challenges facing the Romanian economy. A high impact would be obtained from the following:

- Implementing appropriate reforms in primary and secondary schooling to ensure adequate literacy, numeracy, socioemotional skills, and other core foundational competences;

- Undertaking ongoing review, rationalization, and streamlining of all vocational programs and qualifications to ensure that formal skills development programs in both technical and vocational education and training (TVET) schools and universities are relevant, up-to-date, and sufficiently flexible to allow for reskilling;

- Introducing policy and financing incentive mechanisms to implement public-private partnerships, combined with clear guidelines for participation, as a specific strategy to share the cost, risk, and reward in skills areas where vacancies are highest and skills are not readily available in the labor market;

- Designing recognition of prior learning (RPL) processes within the framework of existing Government Orders to enable more flexible completion of skills development programs, accumulation of credits, portability of credentials, and flexible entry into programs;

- Implementing an accompanying RPL system, also within the framework of existing Government Orders, to underpin the development of a precision training framework to ensure workers can access training when, where, and how they need it;

- Establishing structured mechanisms to enable effective coordination of efforts among all the key players in Romania on whom a skills development ecosystem for the country will depend;

- Ensuring the sustainability of the effective coordination with a combination of legislation, funding, and well-publicized strategic leadership from the government and industry.

NOTES

1. This overview is authored by Donato De Rosa and Alexandria Valerio. It builds on the background papers for this report and on "Romania's Growth Challenges: Country Scan for the Country Economic Memorandum 2.0" authored by Donato De Rosa, Andrei Dospinescu, and Catalin Pauna.

2. OECD countries include: Australia, Austria, Belgium, Canada, Chile, the Czech Republic, Denmark, Estonia, Finland, France, Germany, Greece, Hungary, Iceland, Ireland, Israel, Italy, Japan, Korea, Latvia, Lithuania, Luxembourg, Mexico, the Netherlands, New Zealand, Norway, Poland, Portugal, the Slovak Republic, Slovenia, Spain, Sweden, Switzerland, Turkey, the United Kingdom, the United States.

3. The EU-28 includes the following countries: Austria, Belgium, Bulgaria, Croatia, Cyprus, the Czech Republic, Denmark, Estonia, Finland, France, Germany, Greece, Hungary, Ireland, Italy, Latvia, Lithuania, Luxembourg, Malta, the Netherlands, Poland, Portugal, Romania, the Slovak Republic, Slovenia, Spain, Sweden, and the United Kingdom.

4. The EU-15 includes the following countries: Austria, Belgium, Denmark, Finland, France, Germany, Greece, Ireland, Italy, Luxembourg, the Netherlands, Portugal, Spain, Sweden, and the United Kingdom.

5. In the postcrisis period, the CGAR of Romania's labor productivity slightly accelerated from 1.21 percent in 2009–12 to 4.53 percent in 2013–17.

6. Productive efficiency is proxied by TFP, an imperfect measure of technical efficiency since it includes prices and should properly be termed "revenue total factor productivity," or TFPR. In this chapter, for simplicity of notation, we refer to TFP and TFPR interchangeably. See chapter 1 for a discussion of the various definitions of productivity at the firm level.

7. Measured through PISA test scores, 38.5 percent of 15-year-old students are below basic proficiency in science, 38.7 percent are below proficiency in reading, and 39.9 percent are below proficiency in mathematics.

8. See the background paper on skills for a comprehensive description of the education and training system in Romania (World Bank 2019a).

9. The large inflows of foreign direct investment (FDI) recorded before the 2009 economic crisis were mainly due to the acquisition of large state-owned enterprises (SOEs) in industry and banking.

10. Competition can help reduce slack (Vickers 1995), increase efficiency in resource reallocation (Restuccia and Rogerson 2007), and encourage technology adoption and innovation (Aghion and Griffith 2005). Several microlevel studies provide empirical evidence of the positive impact

of procompetitive regulation on productivity growth. See, for instance, Nicoletti and Scarpetta (2003), Conway et al. (2006), and Alesina et al. (2005).

11. TFP growth can be achieved by efficiency improvements within firms ("within" margin) or reallocation of resources and market shares from less to more efficient players ("between" margin).

12. For a neoclassical view, see, for instance, Mankiw, Romer, and Weil (1992) as an extension of Solow (1957). Seminal endogenous growth models are proposed in Romer (1986), Lucas (1988), and Aghion and Howitt (1998).

13. Sianesi and Van Reenen (2003) conclude that an overall 1 percent increase in school enrollment rates raises GDP per capita growth by a range of 1 to 3 percent. An additional year of secondary education, which increases the stock of human capital, is associated with a more than 1 percent increase in economic growth each year. Hanushek and Woessmann (2008) reach the conclusion that only an increase in the quality of schooling—measured by international test scores—rather the quantity of schooling explains cross-country differences in income per capita. Breton (2011) finds that both a nation's average test scores and average schooling attainment explain income differences across countries, therefore economic growth. Using a different input for education, Sylwester (2000) finds that current educational expenditure leads to future economic growth, implying a significant time lag in the causal relationship.

REFERENCES

Aghion, P., and R. Griffith. 2005. *Competition and Growth: Reconciling Theory and Evidence.* Cambridge, MA: MIT Press.

Aghion, P., and P. W. Howitt. 1998. *Endogenous Growth Theory.* Cambridge, MA: MIT Press.

Alesina, A., G. Ardagna, G. Nicoletti, and F. Schiantarelli. 2005. "Regulation and Investment." *Journal of the European Economic Association* 3 (4): 791–825.

Andrews, D., C. Criscuolo, and P. Gal. 2016. "The Best versus the Rest: The Global Productivity Slowdown, Divergence across Firms and the Role of Public Policy." *OECD Productivity Working Papers* 5, OECD Publishing, Paris.

Breton, T. R. 2011. "The Quality vs. the Quantity of Schooling: What Drives Economic Growth?" *Economics of Education Review* 30 (4): 765–73.

Conway, P., D. De Rosa, G. Nicoletti, and F. Steiner. 2006. "Regulation, Competition and Productivity Convergence." OECD Economics Department Working Paper 509, OECD Publishing, Paris.

Eurostat. 2018. "Adult Learning Statistics." Eurostat (database), European Commission, Brussels, https://ec.europa.eu/eurostat/statistics-explained/index .php/Adult_ learning_ statistics.

———. 2019. Eurostat (database), European Commission, Brussels, https://ec.europa.eu/eurostat /data/database.

Hanushek, E. A., and L. Woessmann. 2008. "The Role of Cognitive Skills in Economic Development." *Journal of Economic Literature* 46 (3): 607–68.

Kitchen, H., E. Fordham, K. Henderson, A. Looney, and S. Maghnouj. 2017. *Romania 2017.* OECD Reviews of Evaluation and Assessment in Education. Paris: OECD Publishing. https://doi.org/10 .1787/9789264274051-en.

Lucas, R. E. 1988. "On the Mechanics of Economic Development." *Journal of Monetary Economics* 22 (1): 3–42.

Mankiw, N. G., D. Romer, and D. N. Weil. 1992. "A Contribution to the Empirics of Economic Growth." *Quarterly Journal of Economics* 107 (2): 407–37.

Ministry of Education and Scientific Research. 2015. *The National Strategy for Lifelong Learning 2015–2020.* Retrieved from http://pubdocs.worldbank.org/en/944481496304564701/The -National-Strategy-for-Lifelong-Learning-mare.pdf.

National Institute of Statistics (Romania). 2017. TEMPO (online database), Bucharest, http://www .insse.ro/cms/en.

Nicoletti, G., and S. Scarpetta. 2003. "Regulation, Productivity and Growth: OECD Evidence." *Economic Policy* 18 (36): 9–72.

OECD (Organisation for Economic Co-operation and Development). 2015. *The Future of Productivity*. Paris: OECD Publishing.

———. 2019. *OECD Compendium of Productivity Indicators 2019*. Paris: OECD Publishing.

Olley, G., and A. Pakes. 1996. "The Dynamics of Productivity in the Telecommunications Equipment Industry." *Econometrica* 64 (6): 1263–97.

Restuccia, D., and R. Rogerson. 2007. "Policy Distortions and Aggregate Productivity with Heterogeneous Plants." NBER Working Paper 13018, National Bureau of Economic Research, Cambridge, MA.

Romer, P. M. 1986. "Increasing Returns and Long-Run Growth." *Journal of Political Economy* 94 (5): 1002–37.

Schwab, K., ed. 2018. *The Global Competitiveness Report 2018*. Cologny/Geneva: World Economic Forum.

Sianesi, B., and J. Van Reenen. 2003. "The Returns to Education: Macroeconomics." *Journal of Economic Surveys* 17 (2): 157–200.

Solow, R. 1957. "Technical Change and the Aggregate Production Function." *Review of Economics and Statistics* 39 (3): 312–20.

Sylwester, K. 2000. "Income Inequality, Education Expenditures, and Growth." *Journal of Development Economics* 63 (2): 379–98.

UNSD (United Nations Statistics Division). 2018. (National Accounts database), UNSD, New York, http://data.un.org/Explorer.aspx.

Vickers, J. 1995. "Concepts of Competition." *Oxford Economic Papers* 47 (1): 1–23.

World Bank. 2016a. *EU Regular Economic Report 3—Growth, Jobs and Integration: Services to the Rescue*. Washington, DC: World Bank. http://pubdocs.worldbank.org/en/930531475587494592/EU-RER-3-Services-to-the-Rescue.pdf.

———. 2016b. "Pinpointing Poverty in Romania." Poverty in Europe Country Policy Brief, World Bank, Washington, DC. https://openknowledge.worldbank.org/handle/10986/23910.

———. 2018a. *From Uneven Growth to Inclusive Development: Romania's Path to Shared Prosperity*. Systematic Country Diagnostics. Washington, DC: World Bank.

———. 2018b. "Productivity." Background Paper, *From Uneven Growth to Inclusive Development: Romania's Path to Shared Prosperity*, World Bank, Washington, DC.

———. 2018c. "Trade." Background Paper, *From Uneven Growth to Inclusive Development: Romania's Path to Shared Prosperity*, World Bank, Washington, DC.

———. 2018d. World Development Indicators (database), World Bank, Washington, DC, https://datacatalog.worldbank.org/dataset/world-development-indicators.

World Bank. 2019a. "Precision Training for Workforce Romania. Romania's Skills Challenge: Ending Mismatches with Training-Ready Workers. Preparing Current and Future Workers to Thrive in a Changing Labor Market in Romania." World Bank, Washington, DC.

———. 2019b. *World Development Report 2019: The Changing Nature of Work*. Washington, DC: World Bank.

1 Productivity

Productivity analysis allows us to identify the drivers of economic growth in Romania in 2011–17. Companies at the productivity frontier are older, larger, have higher capital intensity, and pay higher wages than others. Market leaders also charge higher markups, especially in manufacturing—but they are not becoming more efficient. Reallocation of market shares to more efficient players has been the main driver of productivity growth in manufacturing but not in services, which are typically more sheltered from competition. Individual firms are becoming less productive, suggesting that there is scope to improve firm capabilities, particularly in services. These findings suggest a policy agenda for Romania centered on removing distortions to competition and boosting human capital.[1]

Productivity, the technical efficiency with which firms transform inputs into production, is the ultimate driver of economic growth. As Paul Krugman noted in 1994, "Productivity isn't everything, but, in the long run, it is almost everything. A country's ability to improve its standard of living over time depends almost entirely on its ability to raise its output per worker" (Krugman 1994). Differences in output per worker (labor productivity) are driven by capital deepening and efficiency gains obtained through technological change, resulting in total factor productivity (TFP) growth. Empirical evidence suggests that almost half of the difference in per capita income across countries is explained by differences in TFP (Easterly and Levine 2001; Caselli 2005; Hsieh and Klenow 2010). Therefore, it is key to boost TFP to ensure continued growth, expand potential, and achieve convergence to higher income levels.

TFP growth can be achieved by efficiency improvements within firms or reallocation of resources and market shares from less to more efficient players. Incumbent firms can become more productive—that is, they can increase the amount of output they produce with a given amount of inputs (the *within* component)—by upgrading their internal capabilities through innovation, adoption of new technologies, and use of better managerial practices. Improved *resource allocation*—and therefore, economic activity and market shares—across firms and industries can be explained by more productive existing firms gaining market shares (*between* firms), new and more productive firms entering the market (*entry*), and less productive firms exiting the market (*exit*).

To understand the drivers of Romania's economic growth, it is important to investigate productivity patterns at the firm level. Since 2000, Romania's income per capita

23

has been converging to the level of richer European Union (EU) members, driven by labor productivity growth, whose level jumped from 28.3 percent of the EU-15 average in 2000,[2] to 65.3 percent in 2017. It is important to discern how much of this increased output per worker has been determined by greater availability of complementary factors of production per worker—more capital, for example, in the form of machinery and equipment—and how much has derived from TFP improvements. Information at the level of individual firms allows us to disentangle the drivers of labor productivity in Romania. Firm-level analysis can also help identify productivity leaders and laggards, determine whether productivity growth is the result of within-firm improvements or reallocation effects, and indicate policies that can help boost productivity.

Firm-level analysis suggests that there are significant differences between leading and laggard firms, that reallocation toward more efficient firms plays a role only in manufacturing, and that within-firm productivity gains are weak across the board. In the period 2011–17, companies at the productivity frontier are older, larger, have higher capital intensity, and pay higher salaries than others. Leaders are not becoming more efficient but are charging increasingly higher markups, suggesting market power deriving from rents or differences in quality and demand for their products compared to the laggards, rather than an ability to successfully invest in new technology. Reallocation is relatively more important than within-firm improvements to explain productivity growth. However, this reallocation process is productivity enhancing only for manufacturing. In services, typically with lower exposure to foreign competition and more stringent product market regulations, more productive firms are not capturing larger market shares. Overall, within-firm productivity improvements contribute little to productivity growth, suggesting that there is room to improve firm capabilities (management quality, technological learning, and so forth). These findings can help to outline the contours of a productivity policy for Romania, centered on removing distortions in the regulatory environment and boosting human capital.

ESTIMATING PRODUCTIVITY

When estimating productivity, it is important to go beyond the aggregate data and to the firm level. Aggregate TFP numbers carry measurement problems, especially related to the emergence of information and communication technologies (ICT) that are difficult to capture in output statistics (Brynjolfsson, Rock, and Syverson 2019). Furthermore, aggregate TFP is estimated as the residual of an aggregate production function for the whole economy, which ignores technological differences across sectors within countries. Finally, aggregate TFP masks heterogeneity among individual firms. Firms have different intrinsic characteristics and differ in terms of performance, even within very narrowly defined industries (Syverson 2004). These differences persist either because of supply factors, such as management skills, research and development, or investment patterns (Bartelsman and Doms 2000), or due to demand factors related to product differentiation, customer-producer relationship, or geographical segmentation.

It is also crucial to distinguish technical efficiency from other supply and demand factors that may affect a firm's revenues. Not doing so may lead to misguided interpretations of the evidence offered by the data. When output and input prices at the firm level are not observed, the productivity measure conflates both demand and supply factors, and therefore the productivity residual is a measure of firm performance rather than efficiency. What appears to be technical efficiency in transforming factor inputs (land, labor, and capital) into products or services, could, in fact, reflect the market structure in which firms operate, distortions induced by policy—for example, when price competition is restricted by regulation—or higher-quality products and services that command a higher price because of their characteristics (Cusolito and Maloney 2018).

To differentiate among various possible influences on productivity, three productivity measures are computed (see annex 1A):

- *Labor productivity (LP)*: defined as value added per full-time employee.

- *Revenue total factor productivity (TFPR)*: defined as the portion of firm-level revenue or sales that cannot be explained by the contribution of capital, labor, energy, and other inputs. To account for differences in production technologies across sectors, the TFPR estimation allows for heterogeneous sector-specific production functions (statistique des activités économiques dans la Communauté européenne, or NACE, 2-digit). Being a revenue-based measure, TFPR is not free of price effects; this means this proxy of efficiency might capture not only technical efficiency but also market power deriving differences in quality and other factors affecting demand for the product.

- *Revenue total factor productivity adjusted for markups (TFPR adjusted)*: correcting TFPR firm-year varying markups to mitigate the price effects described in the previous bullet.

The analysis draws on balance sheet data collected by the Romanian National Agency for Fiscal Administration (Agenția Națională de Administrare Fiscală). The dataset covers the 2011–17 period and contains key information to compute productivity—such as value added, number of employees, costs of labor and of different material inputs, and fixed tangible and intangible assets, among others. The variables included in the dataset are presented in annex 1A. Given the focus of the study, firms outside the business economy were excluded. The business economy, defined following the Eurostat definition, covers all industry, construction, and market services sectors (sectors NACE rev. 2 B to N, plus sector S95). The final list of 2-digit sectors included in the analysis is presented in annex 1B. For firms that move across sectors, the industry mode (most common industry) along the period is used. Since *exit* is overrepresented (as firms might stop reporting balance sheets while still being in operation) and a firm's year of incorporation does not always coincide with the year a firm starts reporting balance sheets, the analysis is restricted to a balanced panel of 183,856 surviving firms (24,433 in manufacturing and 159,423 in services). All nominal variables are expressed in Romanian lei 2010 prices (using Eurostat gross domestic product implicit price deflator). Table 1.1 shows that the value-added composition of these surviving companies is highly skewed toward services, which account for 80 percent of total value added in 2017 (excluding mining and agriculture).

Apart from a common growth pattern in terms of labor productivity, manufacturing and services seem to have experienced distinct trends. In manufacturing, median TFPR experienced positive growth, which could suggest increasing efficiency. However, this trend does not seem to be sustained when the markup effect is discounted. This implies that technical efficiency has, in fact, decreased in the 2011–17 period. For services, the median values of both TFPR and TFPR adjusted experienced negative growth over time (figure 1.1).

Firms are converging in labor productivity and diverging in TFP, in both manufacturing and services. There is decreasing dispersion of the labor productivity distribution, suggesting that the gap in labor productivity is diminishing both for manufacturing and services, whereas dispersion of firm efficiency measured through TFP—adjusted and nonadjusted TFPR—has been increasing over time (figure 1.2).

TABLE 1.1 Main economic sectors (percent of total value added in the sample)

	PERCENT OVER TOTAL VALUE ADDED
MANUFACTURING TOTAL	**19.60**
Top 10 (manufacturing)	**14.55**
Manufacturing of motor vehicles	4.12
Manufacturing of food	2.31
Manufacturing of rubber and plastic	1.40
Manufacturing of fabricated metal products	1.30
Manufacturing of basic metals	1.02
Manufacturing of other nonmetallic mineral products	0.95
Manufacturing of machinery and equipment	0.91
Manufacturing of wearing apparel	0.85
Manufacturing of beverages	0.85
Manufacturing of electrical equipment	0.83
SERVICES TOTAL	**80.40**
Top 10 (services)	**68.60**
Wholesale trade	27.83
Retail trade	19.60
Wholesale and retail trade of motor vehicles	5.29
Land transport	4.20
Electricity, gas, steam, and air conditioning	2.40
Telecommunications	2.24
Construction of buildings	2.19
Warehousing and support activities for transportation	1.86
Computer programming	1.56
Specialized construction activities	1.38

FIGURE 1.1.

Average annual growth rate of median productivity values, 2011–17 (manufacturing versus services)

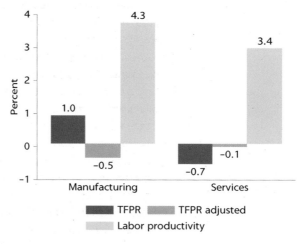

Note: TFPR = revenue total factor productivity.

The reasons behind this increasing dispersion in terms of TFPR (adjusted and nonadjusted) can be multiple, and not necessarily related to policy distortions. As highlighted by Cusolito and Maloney (2018), several factors can explain this, including not only policy distortions but also differences in technology, quality,

FIGURE 1.2

Average annual growth rate of productivity dispersion values, 2011–17 (manufacturing versus services)

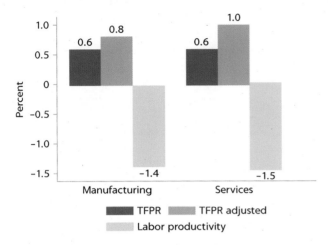

Note: TFPR = revenue total factor productivity.

markups, adjustment costs to capital coupled with volatility in sales, or even different levels of experimentation. On the other hand, irrespective of the underlying drivers, the data show unequivocal evidence that firms are becoming increasingly heterogenous in terms of TFP, which then reinforces the need to go beyond the average firm and explore firm heterogeneity to inform the design of policies for specific segments of the productivity distribution in Romania.

LEADERS AND LAGGARDS

To shed light on firm heterogeneity and further explore the differentiated performance of firms, frontier and laggard companies are identified following the approach presented in Andrews, Criscuolo, and Gal (2016). Frontier companies are defined as the top 5 percent—in terms of TFPR, LP, or TFPR adjusted—in each year and 2-digit sector. Hence, neither the number of companies nor the set of frontier firms is fixed over time, which allows us to capture turbulence at the frontier, as laggard companies in a given year can enter the frontier the following year. By the same token, the group of laggard companies is also allowed to change over time, reflecting the churning process at the frontier, which would push some former leaders into the laggard group.

Frontier firms are larger, older, pay higher wages, are more capital intensive, and charge higher markups than others. Figure 1.3 shows cross-sectional differences in average characteristics for frontier and laggard firms—with the frontier measured in terms of TFPR—along key dimensions (age, size, capital intensity, and markup) for 2017, the latest year of observation. All reported differences in averages—frontier relative to laggards—are statistically significant. A t-test comparing average variables across laggards and frontier groups (for both manufacturing and services) rejects equality at least at 5 percent. On average, firms that are on the TFPR frontier are significantly larger (in terms of employment size) than laggards, both in manufacturing and services. Frontier firms also pay higher wages—ranging between 26,880,000 and 32,300,000 (in 2010 Romanian lei)—and are more capital intensive, irrespective of the industry. Finally, firms at the frontier charge higher markups (3.4 to 4.0 times higher, depending on the industry) than laggard companies.

FIGURE 1.3

Average differences in firm characteristics, 2017

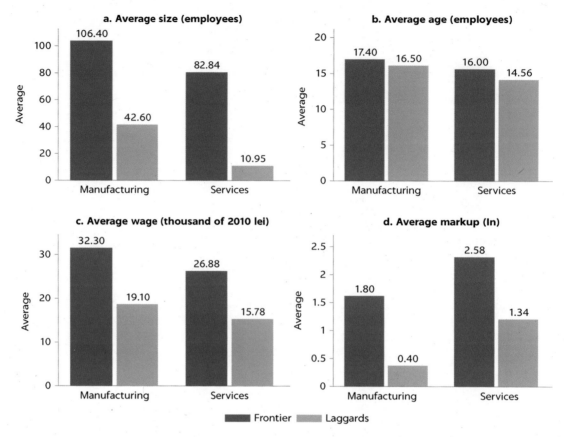

Note: Frontier firms are identified as the top 5 percent in terms of revenue total factor productivity (TFPR) level, within each 2-digit sector and year. ln = natural logarithm.

Labor productivity of laggard firms has been catching up since 2013, driven more by capital deepening than technical efficiency gains. To assess divergence of productivity behavior between these two groups of firms, figure 1.4 shows the evolution of the (unweighted) average of log labor productivity across frontier and laggard companies, for all firms under analysis, as well as distinguishing between manufacturing and services. In this case, the frontier is defined as the top 5 percent performers in terms of labor productivity (within each 2-digit sector and year). Because labor productivity growth can be achieved through either higher capital intensity or revenue-based TFP, the figures plot not only the labor productivity growth evolution itself but also these two components. Overall, data suggest that labor productivity of laggard firms has been increasing faster than that of frontier ones, especially after 2013, and this catching up process has been driven mostly by capital deepening rather than gains in (revenue-based) TFP. This applies to both manufacturing and services industries.

Focusing on TFPR allows us to disentangle the productivity differences between leaders and laggards due to higher markups from those due to technical efficiency. Since the TFPR measure is based on revenue data, the differential growth performance between laggards and frontier firms might in fact reflect disparities between these groups in terms of ability to charge higher markups, instead of differences in technical efficiency. Figure 1.5 shows the evolution of (unweighted) average log TFPR across frontier and laggard companies, as well as the evolution TFPR adjusted (a proxy of technical efficiency) and markup performance for all firms together, and

FIGURE 1.4

Labor productivity growth: Frontier versus laggards, 2011–17

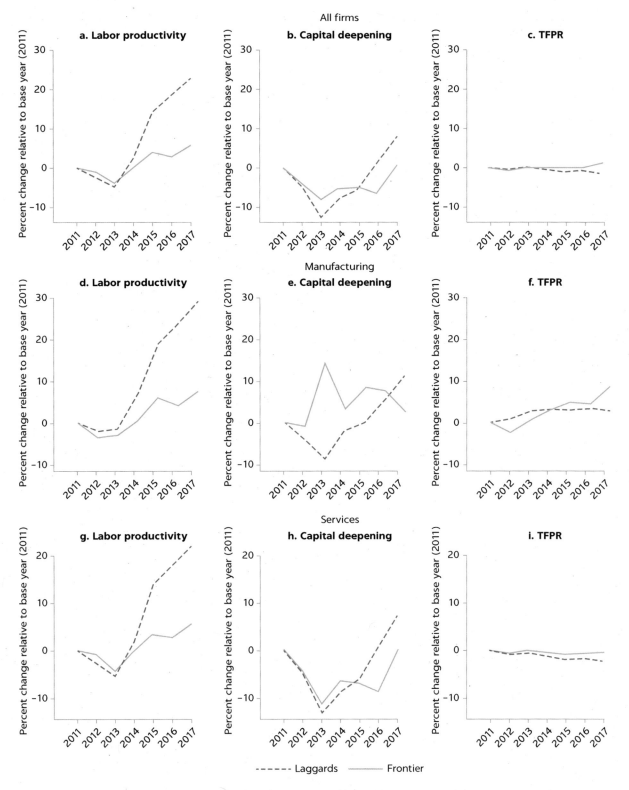

Note: Frontier firms are identified as the top 5 percent performers in terms of labor productivity, within each 2-digit sector (in manufacturing or services industry) and year. The frontier line captures the average of log labor productivity for the top 5 percent companies (by 2-digit sector, within manufacturing or services, and year). The laggards line captures the average log productivity of all other firms. The vertical axes represent log-differences from the starting year. TFPR = revenue total factor productivity.

FIGURE 1.5

TFPR productivity growth: Frontier versus laggards, 2011–17

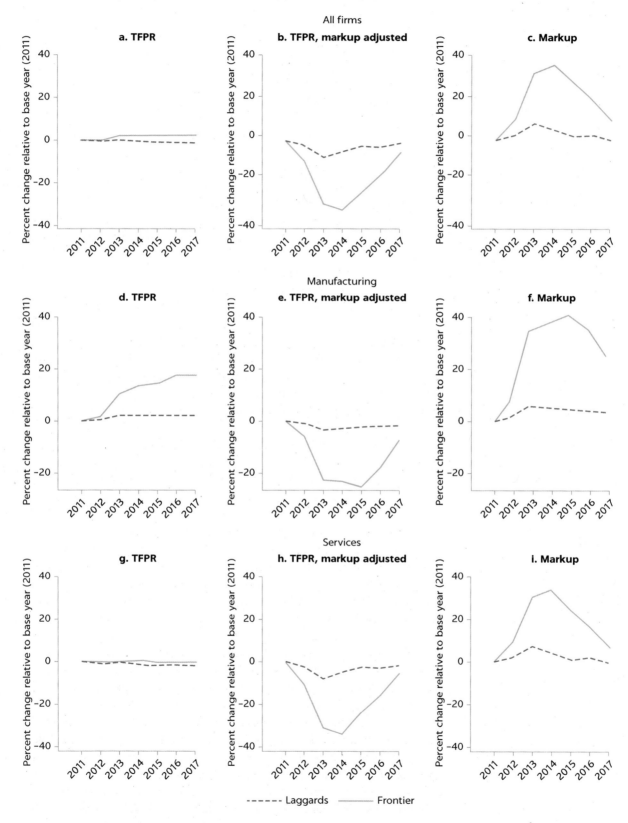

Note: Frontier firms are identified as the top 5 percent performers in terms of TFPR productivity, within each 2-digit sector (in manufacturing or services industry) and year. The frontier line captures the average of log TFPR productivity for the top 5 percent companies (by 2-digit sector, within manufacturing or services, and year). The laggards line captures the average log TFPR productivity of all other firms. The vertical axes represent log-differences from the starting year. TFPR = revenue total factor productivity.

manufacturing and service firms separately. In this case, the frontier is defined as the top 5 percent performers in terms of TFPR (within each 2-digit sector and year).

In manufacturing, there is an increasing divergence in TFPR growth between frontier and laggard companies, with leaders charging increasingly higher markups. This widening gap in productivity growth is not driven by gains in technical efficiency, proxied by TFPR markup adjusted. Hence, it is not necessarily related to the ability of leading firms to successfully invest in or adopt new technologies to succeed in the market. Rather, it may reflect either their ability to charge higher markups thanks to the market power deriving from rents or differences in quality and demand for their product, factors that are not necessarily related to more efficient production methods.

This overall trend is confirmed in most manufacturing subsectors. However, there are some exceptional cases where markups of productivity leaders tend to grow slower than those of laggard companies. These are manufacturing of textiles, manufacturing of other transport equipment, manufacturing of wood, printing, and manufacturing of rubber and plastic. Among them, the examples of manufacturing of textiles and manufacturing of other transport equipment are particularly striking, as these sectors are more exposed to foreign competition given their integration into global value chains. The fact that markup of productivity leaders is growing more slowly than that of laggard companies might reflect either a decrease in market power or a deterioration of product quality.

In services, there is little difference in TFPR growth between leaders and laggards, although leaders have exercised their market power by imposing high markups without improving their technical efficiency. The (unweighted) average gap in growth of TFPR between frontier and laggard companies is almost inexistent over the period under analysis. This result is driven by markup performance of leader companies who tend to increase their markups faster than laggards. This overall trend, seen across for the whole service industry, is observed for most of NACE 2-digit sectors. This is particularly true for water collection, treatment, and supply; civil engineering; retail trade; land transport; telecommunications; computer programming; legal and accounting activities; activities of head offices; architectural and engineering activities; and rental and leasing activities.

The example of legal and accounting activities is particularly telling. As shown in chapter 2, according to Organisation for Economic Co-operation and Development Product Market Regulation data, regulatory barriers to entry or conduct for legal and accounting services are more stringent in Romania than in other countries in the region. In the case of lawyers and accountants, Romania has very restrictive entry regulations when compared to other countries. For instance, lawyers are subject to burdensome accreditation requirements (specifically in terms of additional licensing by state or other public authorities) and must undergo a mandatory professional examination and a compulsory two-year relevant practice to become full members of the profession. In addition, compulsory chamber membership is applied to accountants and lawyers, while accountants are also required to complete two years of higher education, in addition to a three-year college degree, to enter the profession. In terms of conduct regulations, lawyers are subject to price controls (minimum and maximum set prices), can operate only under a restricted legal form of business (they are not allowed to provide services as public limited companies), and are not allowed to advertise or do marketing for their services. This suggests reduced market contestability in the sector, implying that the observed differential growth performance of markups between leaders and laggards can be reflecting an increase in market power of leading firms.

Data also suggest an increasing persistence of incumbent firms at the frontier. As shown in figure 1.6, the average proportion of firms classified as frontier companies in a

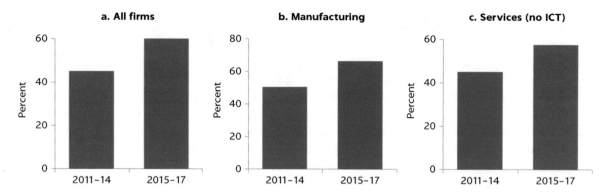

FIGURE 1.6

Churning at the frontier

Note: The figure shows the proportion of firms classified as frontier firms at time t—that is, in the top 5 percent of the industry TFPR distribution—that were already at the frontier one year earlier (t-1). ICT = information and communication technology; TFPR = revenue total factor productivity.

FIGURE 1.7

Average employment growth across the firm TFPR markup-adjusted distribution; all firms: Deviation from the 2011–17 average

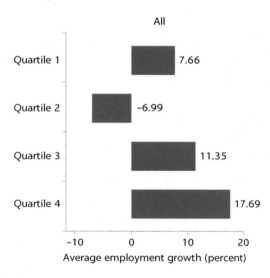

Note: TFPR = revenue total factor productivity.

given year (t) that continue in the frontier in the following year (t+1) increases over time. When considering manufacturing and services together, in 2011–14, on average, 50 percent of frontier firms were already in the frontier the year before. By 2015–17 this figure had risen to 60 percent. The same rising trend is observed for manufacturing and services, separately. This result holds if frontier is measured in terms of TFPR adjusted for markup, which provides a purer measure of technical efficiency. Overall, this result might reflect a decline in contestability of markets, which is either reducing the pressure on frontier firms to adopt better technologies or decreasing the incentives for laggard companies to adopt frontier technologies.

PRODUCTIVITY DRIVERS: WITHIN-FIRM IMPROVEMENTS AND REALLOCATION EFFECTS

Productivity growth can be decomposed into three margins: *within*, *between*, and *selection* (entry/exit). As highlighted in Cusolito and Maloney (2018), the first component reflects the ability of incumbent firms to become more productive and is related to the process of upgrading firms' internal capabilities (by innovating, adopting new technologies, and applying best managerial practices). The *between* component is associated with the reallocation of factors of production and economic activity toward more efficient firms. The third and last component reflects the entry of more productive firms in the market (relative to the industry average) and/or the exit of less productive firms. As the dataset used in this chapter focuses on surviving companies, the analysis can cover only the *within* and *between* components.

The three drivers of productivity are inextricably linked. Impediments to competition imposed by trade barriers, poor regulation, or an overbearing presence of state-owned enterprises (SOEs) can hinder the reallocation of factors of production to the most efficient players, thus negatively impacting the *between* margin. But such distortions can also have negative dynamic consequences on the *within* margin, as they may discourage investment and innovation in sheltered incumbents and potential challengers, as well as on *selection* by preventing the exit of less productive firms and the entry of more productive firms.

A first (and indirect) trial to detect the main drivers of productivity growth reveals that labor reallocation has generally been productivity enhancing, with some signs of misallocation in services. Figure 1.7 shows average employment growth

FIGURE 1.8

Average employment growth across the firm TFPR markup-adjusted distribution: Manufacturing versus services, deviation from the 2011–17 average

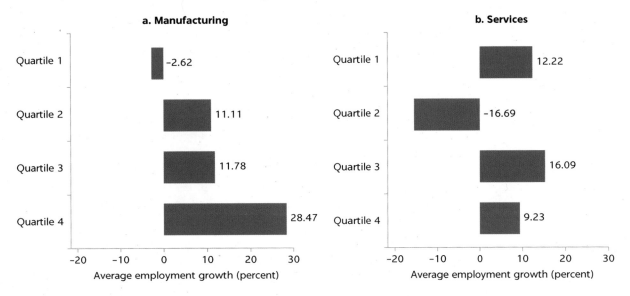

Note: TFPR = revenue total factor productivity.

differentials across the quartiles of the TFPR-adjusted distribution of Romanian firms. As an indirect way to measure misallocation, if labor is efficiently allocated across firms in the same sector, then employment in more productive firms should expand, while employment in less productive firms should contract. Results show that employment has been expanding faster in firms belonging to more productive quartiles (not to firms with more market power, as the analysis uses markup-adjusted TFPR), which suggests that labor reallocation has been productivity enhancing in the country. Some nuances are unveiled when splitting the economy across manufacturing and services (figure 1.8). Services, in fact, show some signs of misallocation, as firms in the first quartile in terms of TFPR-adjusted performance are expanding employment faster than the ones in the most productive quartile. This could provide another clue of the negative effects on productivity of entry and conduct regulations, which are prevalent in services.

When applying a more direct way to disentangle productivity growth margins, results suggest that reallocation of market shares to more efficient firms—the *between* effect—was the main driver in 2011–17. A direct way to measure allocative efficiency is to apply the work of Olley and Pakes (1996). The decomposition goes beyond the reallocation (*between*) component and includes the *within* margin and measures the difference between size—

FIGURE 1.9

Olley and Pakes decomposition of TFPR adjusted, 2011–17, accumulated percent change

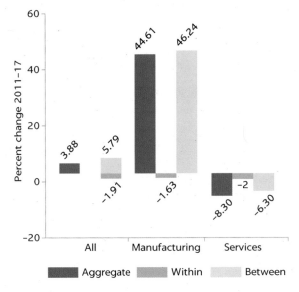

Note: TFPR = revenue total factor productivity.

here measured by firms' market share in the industry/sector in terms of value added—and productivity to estimate the efficiency with which output is allocated across firms, by industry and sector. Results suggest that the reallocation element is indeed the main driver for productivity expansion for the whole economy in the 2011–17 period (figure 1.9). On average, TFPR adjusted grew by 3.88 percent per year in the period, mostly driven by the positive reallocation component.

Meanwhile, productivity improvements within individual firms have been a drag on aggregate productivity growth. This may reflect the potential deterioration of managerial skills, innovation capacity, or, more broadly, internal capabilities. Romanian firms lag in different dimensions of innovation, as shown by the low number of patent application to the European Patent Office or the low research and development expenditures. Romania also shows a poor performance when compared to EU peers in terms of reliance on professional management (World Bank 2018). As discussed in chapter 6, another important drag on the productivity of individual firms are the skills mismatches that characterize the Romanian labor market.

In services, reallocation has resulted in market shares flowing to less efficient players. When breaking this down by industry, the *between* component is positive only for manufacturing. For services—typically more sheltered from competitive pressures, given the lower exposure to foreign competition and more stringent product market regulations—the reallocation margin is negative, suggesting that more productive firms are not earning larger market shares.

When looking at the annual evolution of productivity drivers of 2011–17, reallocation to more efficient players has been a consistent driver of productivity growth only in manufacturing, whereas in services the contribution of within-firm improvements has been consistently small and not always positive over the years. Data show a clear picture for manufacturing, confirming that the reallocation process has been productivity enhancing for all years, except 2012, while the *within* margin was negative only until 2013. For services, the *within* and *between* components alternate in magnitude and sign, an indication of large remaining inefficiencies (figure 1.10).

Some nuances are revealed by examining subsectors within manufacturing and services. Within the manufacturing industry, the only sectors for which aggregate productivity growth and the *between* component are both positive are manufacturing of wood, manufacturing of machinery and equipment, and manufacturing of motor vehicles. Within the services industry, most subsectors experience the same pattern observed for the whole service industry, with negative aggregate productivity growth and negative *within* and *between* components. The exceptions are sewerage, civil engineering, retail trade, water transport, architectural and engineering activities, scientific research and development, and employment activities.

FIGURE 1.10

Olley and Pakes decomposition of TFPR adjusted, 2011–17, annual percentage change

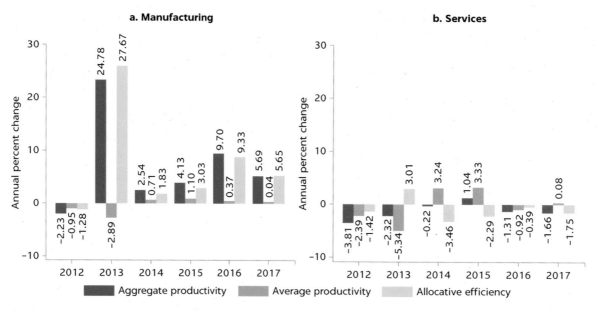

Note: TFPR = revenue total factor productivity.

A POLICY AGENDA

Policies to boost productivity span a wide range and are highly complementary. Figure 1.11 from Cusolito and Maloney (2018) presents the elements of a "national productivity system," the set of policies and institutions necessary to improve the productivity of an economy. The firm is the critical player in the system, and its decisions on accumulating capital, labor, or knowledge are influenced by supply and demand factors.

Macroeconomic policies, the trade and competition regime, internal capabilities, and entrepreneurship together determine a firm's incentives to invest, innovate, and become more productive. Monetary and fiscal policies may affect the volatility of aggregate demand and of firms' sales, thus determining their willingness to take risk, invest, and innovate. Competition and trade may be conduits for learning and may encourage firms to make efforts to profit from market opportunities. Adequate capabilities within firms are also necessary to manage production, as well as to recognize, develop, and adopt new technologies (box 1.1). Finally, grit, risk tolerance, and openness to recognizing new opportunities are essential features of entrepreneurship that influence the willingness to invest and innovate. These factors are interrelated. For instance, participating in international markets increases the benefits of technological upgrading and informs entrepreneurial opportunities, while better capabilities allow firms to take advantage of these markets. Higher macroeconomic volatility leads to less firm entry and upgrading, while low growth may induce governments to experiment with unsustainable policies.

The trade and competition regime guaranteed by membership in the EU has undoubtedly been a positive force for Romania, providing learning opportunities and positively affecting incentives to invest and innovate. On a negative note, a sometimes volatile fiscal policy has been creating uncertainty and has negatively affected the investment decisions of Romanian firms (World Bank 2018). At the

FIGURE 1.11

The national productivity system

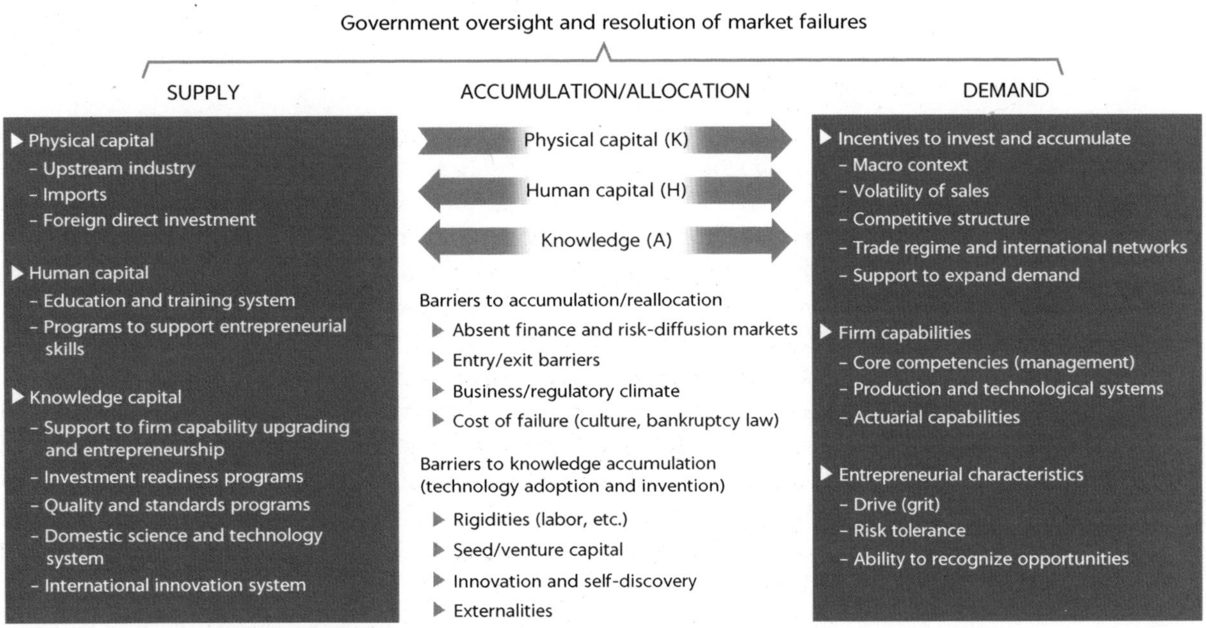

Source: Cusolito and Maloney 2018.

BOX 1.1

Management capabilities and firm productivity

Why focus on management? The persistence in productivity differences between firms within the same industry is striking and puzzling. For example, labor productivity for plants at the 90th percentile, within narrowly defined four-digit U.S. manufacturing industries, is four times as high as that for plants at the 10th percentile. Likewise, the difference in total factor productivity (TFP) is twice as high, when controlling for other factors (Syverson 2011). Although within-industry productivity differentials have historically been attributed to "hard" technological innovations (for example, advanced equipment), recently Bloom and Van Reenen have significantly advanced the empirical foundations for measuring management practices across firms and countries to show a robust association of such practices with firm performance. In fact, differences in managerial quality are critical in explaining cross-country differences in income levels, productivity, innovation, and firm dynamism (Bloom and Van Reenen 2010).

How is management measured? Management is measured based on the U.S. Census Management and Organizational Practices Survey, which uses a multiple choice–based evaluation tool that defines 16 key management practices in three broad areas: (i) performance monitoring—collecting and analyzing information on daily activities of the firm for continuous improvement; (ii) target setting—using and stretching short- and long-run targets; (iii) performance incentives—rewarding high-performing employees and retraining or moving underperformers. For each management practice, the responses are bounded by the choices in the questionnaire, and an unweighted score is computed based on a predefined scoring matrix.

Where have management capabilities surveys been implemented? While several countries such as Canada, China, Japan, the United Kingdom, and the United States have implemented the management survey, the World Bank has been involved in these surveys in Croatia, Mexico, Pakistan, and the Russian Federation.

What is the magnitude of the associated impact on firm performance? A 10 percent increase in management score is associated with a 14.5 percent increase in sales per worker in the United States (Bloom, Brynjofsson, et al. 2019), 18 percent in Russia (Grover and Torre 2019), and 30 percent in Croatia (Grover, Iacovone, and Chakraborty 2019). Other measures of firm productivity are also positively associated with management score. For instance, a 10 percent increase in management score in Russia is associated with 2.6 percent increase in TFP and 6 percent in value added per worker. The associated increase in value added per worker is 9 percent in the United States, 12 percent in Pakistan (Lemos et al. 2016), and 15 percent in Mexico (Bloom, Iacovone, et al. 2019). In Mexico and Croatia, management quality is also associated with innovation (Iacovone and Pereira-López 2017; Grover, Iacovone, and Chakraborty 2019), while in Croatia there is evidence on greater likelihood of adoption of sophisticated technology for procurement and quality management with higher quartiles of management capabilities. Finally, the likelihood of accessing external finance also increases with management capabilities among manufacturing firms in Croatia (Grover, Iacovone, and Chakraborty 2019).

How do these results inform firm-level interventions? A simple answer to this question is that management can be improved with concerted effort. For example, an experiment with textile firms in India provides a proof of concept that intensive individualized consulting can deliver lasting improvements in the practices of badly managed firms, resulting in productivity improvements by 17 percent (Bloom et al. 2013). Since such interventions are costly and likely to be prohibitive for many small and medium enterprises to finance themselves, and for governments seeking to scale up to assist large numbers of firms, Iacovone, Maloney, and McKenzie (2019) piloted two alternative approaches for improving management capabilities among auto parts firms in Colombia. The first uses intensive and expensive one-on-one consulting, while the second draws on agricultural extension approaches to provide consulting to small groups of firms at approximately one-third of the cost of the individual approach. Both approaches led to improvements in management practices of a similar magnitude (8–10 percentage points), so that the new group-based approach dominates on a cost-benefit basis. This points to the possibility of using group-based approaches as a pathway to scaling up management improvements.

same time, available information indicates that Romania lags its EU peers in terms of the internal capabilities of its firms. For instance, the country ranks 106th out of 140 countries for its reliance on professional management (Schwab 2018).

Firms can acquire knowledge through physical capital, human capital, and an effective science, technology, and quality system. Knowledge can be acquired through physical capital, when upstream industries are able to supply inputs, as well as through foreign direct investment and easy access to imported intermediate goods, both of which have been favored by Romania's integration in the EU. An obvious source of knowledge is the pool of available human capital, which is determined by education and training policies and institutions. As discussed in chapters 4, 5, and 6, the availability of human capital is a particularly weak spot for Romania. The science, technology, and quality systems are also important to facilitate technology transfer, adapt existing knowledge, or generate new knowledge. Finally, it is important for firms to have access to the international innovation system, the source of most new knowledge.

A number of barriers can hinder the accumulation of all forms of capital. Difficult access to finance, the absence of risk mitigation markets, entry and exit barriers, poor regulation, and cumbersome bankruptcy regimes that increase the cost of failure can discourage investment in physical assets, human capital, and knowledge.

Governments play a crucial role in overseeing the national productivity system and resolving potential market failures or distortions. In this respect, at least four dimensions shape the quality of government action: rationale and design of policy, efficacy of implementation, coherence of policies across various actors, and policy consistency and predictability over time. In all these areas, Romania has struggled to meet the expectations of its citizens and firms (World Bank 2018).

Whereas many policy variables concur to shape productivity, a feasible agenda for Romania in the short to medium term can focus on competition and human capital. As discussed in chapters 2 and 3, constraints to better resource allocation can be eased by streamlining entry and conduct regulation in service sectors and ensuring competitive neutrality in markets where SOEs are active. Policies to improve human capital are also of crucial importance, as highlighted in chapters 4, 5, and 6. These should aim at forming a healthy and educated workforce that is knowledgeable, responsive to changing demands, capable of embracing new technologies, innovative, and entrepreneurial.

ANNEX 1A: MEASURES OF PRODUCTIVITY

Three productivity measures are computed:

Labor productivity (LP) is defined as value added per full-time employee, where value added is defined as revenues minus cost of raw materials.

Revenue total factor productivity (TFPR) is defined as the portion of firm-level revenue or sales that cannot be explained by the contribution of capital, labor, energy, and other inputs. The functional form used to represent the production technology is a flexible translog, where the measure of output (Y) is net revenue (turnover) and the inputs are the average number of employees per year (L), cost of raw materials (M), and capital stock (K) measured using both tangible and intangible assets. TFPR is estimated using an extended Ackerberg, Caves, and Frazer (2015) algorithm, where the Markov process of TFPR is allowed to be more general, while the log of firm age, measured in terms of number of years defined as current year minus birth year, is used as control variable. To account for differences in production technologies across sectors, the TFPR estimation allows for heterogeneous sector-specific (NACE 2-digit) production functions. Observations with revenue, employment, capital (tangible assets and intangibles), and cost of raw materials with value 0 or lower than 0 is excluded from the TFPR estimation.

Revenue total factor productivity adjusted for markups (TFPR adjusted) is a TFP-adjusted measure partially free of price effects because it might still carry quality and/or demand effects. Also, the "partial" price correction done through the method applied here—via firm-year level markup—does not use price firm-level data, which are not available in the dataset. To mitigate price effects, the TFPR is corrected by firm-year varying markups as follows:

$$TFPR_{it}^{adj} = TFPR_{it} - markup_{it}$$

where TFPR is expressed in logs and markup is estimated using the approach presented by De Loecker and Warzynski (2012). In this case, markup—defined as the ratio of price over marginal cost—is derived from the first order condition of the firm's minimization problem with respect to the flexible input (material). Specifically, it is computed as the estimated output elasticity related to flexible input (material)—as estimated through the Ackerberg, Caves, and Frazer (2015) algorithm—divided by the observed share of cost of flexible input (material) in turnover.

ANNEX 1B: LIST OF 2-DIGIT SECTORS

NACE[3] 2-DIGIT SECTORS

1	Manufacturing of motor vehicles
2	Manufacturing of food
3	Manufacturing of rubber and plastic
4	Manufacturing of fabricated metal products
5	Manufacturing of basic metals
6	Manufacturing of other nonmetallic mineral products
7	Manufacturing of machinery and equipment
8	Manufacturing of wearing apparel
9	Manufacturing of beverages
10	Manufacturing of electrical equipment
11	Manufacturing of wood
12	Manufacturing of chemicals
13	Manufacturing of computers electronic and optical equipment
14	Manufacturing of furniture
15	Manufacturing of leather
16	Manufacturing of textiles
17	Manufacturing of other transport equipment
18	Manufacturing of coke and refined petroleum
19	Repair of machinery and equipment
20	Manufacturing of pharmaceuticals
21	Manufacturing of paper
22	Printing
23	Other manufacturing
24	Wholesale trade
25	Retail trade
26	Wholesale and retail trade of motor vehicles
27	Land transport
28	Electricity, gas, steam, and air conditioning
29	Telecommunications
30	Construction of buildings

31	Warehousing and support activities for transportation
32	Computer programming
33	Specialized construction activities
34	Architectural and engineering activities
35	Real estate activities
36	Civil engineering
37	Advertising and market research
38	Waste collection
39	Food and beverage service activities
40	Activities of head offices
41	Office administration
42	Accommodation
43	Water collection treatment and supply
44	Postal and courier activities
45	Travel agency
46	Rental and leasing activities
47	Security and investigation activities
48	Publishing activities
49	Employment activities
50	Programming and broadcasting activities
51	Legal and accounting activities
52	Services to buildings and landscape activities
53	Information service activities
54	Scientific research and development
55	Air transport
56	Activities auxiliary to financial services
57	Other professional scientific and technical activities
58	Motion picture video and television program production
59	Repair of computers
60	Financial service activities
61	Water transport
62	Veterinary activities
63	Remediation activities
64	Sewerage

NOTES

1. This chapter draws on the background paper "Productivity Growth in Romania: A Firm-Level Analysis," authored by Mariana Iootty, Jorge Pena, and Donato De Rosa (Iootty, Pena, and De Rosa 2019).
2. EU-15 labor productivity is expressed as the unweighted average of the levels of the EU member states prior to 2004: Austria, Belgium, Denmark, Finland, France, Germany, Greece, Ireland, Italy, Luxembourg, the Netherlands, Portugal, Spain, Sweden, and the United Kingdom.
3. NACE = Nomenclature des Activités Économiques dans la Communauté Européenne.

REFERENCES

Ackerberg, D., K. Caves, and G. Frazer. 2015. "Identification Properties of Recent Production Function Estimators." *Econometrica* 83 (6): 2411–51.

Andrews, D., C. Criscuolo, and P. N. Gal. 2016. "The Best versus the Rest: The Global Productivity Slowdown, Divergence across Firms and the Role of Public Policy." OECD Productivity Working Paper 05, OECD Publishing, Paris.

Bartelsman, E. J., and M. Doms. 2000. "Understanding Productivity: Lessons from Longitudinal Microdata." *Journal of Economic Literature* 38 (3): 569–94.

Bloom, N., E. Brynjolfsson, L. Foster, R. Jarmin, M. Patnaik, I. Saporta-Eksten, and J. Van Reenen. 2019. "What Drives Differences in Management Practices?" *American Economic Review* 109 (5): 1648–83.

Bloom, N., B. Eifert, A. Mahajan, D. McKenzie, and J. Roberts. 2013. "Does Management Matter? Evidence from India." *Quarterly Journal of Economics* 128 (1): 1–51.

Bloom, N., L. Iacovone, M. Pereira-López, and J. Van Reenen. 2019. "Spillovers, Market Size, and Misallocation: Management in Mexico." Unpublished report.

Bloom, N., and J. Van Reenen. 2010. "Why Do Management Practices Differ across Firms and Countries?" *Journal of Economic Perspectives* 24 (1): 203–24.

Brynjolfsson, E., D. Rock, and C. Syverson. 2019. "Artificial Intelligence and the Modern Productivity Paradox: A Clash of Expectations and Statistics." In *Economics of Artificial Intelligence*, edited by Ajay Agrawal, Joshua Gans, and Avi Goldfarb, 23–57. Chicago: University of Chicago Press.

Caselli, F. 2005. "Accounting for Cross-Country Income Differences." In *Handbook of Economic Growth*, vol. 1A, edited by Philippe Aghion and Steven N. Durlauf, 679–741. Amsterdam: Elsevier.

Cusolito, A. P., and W. F. Maloney. 2018. *Productivity Revisited: Shifting Paradigms in Analysis and Policy*. Washington, DC: World Bank.

De Loecker, J., and F. Warzynski. 2012. "Markups and Firm-Level Export Status." *American Economic Review* 102 (6): 2437–71.

Easterly, W., and R. Levine. 2001. "What Have We Learned from a Decade of Empirical Research on Growth? It's Not Factor Accumulation: Stylized Facts and Growth Models." *World Bank Economic Review* 15 (2): 177–219.

Grover, A., L. Iacovone, and P. Chakraborty. 2019. "Management in Croatia: Drivers and Consequence for Firm Performance." Unpublished document.

Grover Goswami, A., and I. Torre. 2019. "Management Capabilities and Performance of Firms in the Russian Federation." Policy Research Working Paper 8996, World Bank, Washington, DC.

Hsieh, C.-T., and P. J. Klenow. 2010. "Development Accounting." *American Economic Journal: Macroeconomics* 2 (1): 207–23.

Iacovone, L., M. Maloney, and D. McKenzie. 2019. "Improving Management with Individual and Group-Based Consulting: Results from a Randomized Experiment in Colombia." Policy Research Working Paper 8854, World Bank, Washington, DC.

Iacovone, L., and M. Pereira-López. 2017. "Management Practices as Drivers of Innovation: New Evidence from Mexico." Unpublished report.

Iootty, M., J. Pena, and D. De Rosa. 2019. "Productivity Growth in Romania: A Firm-Level Analysis." Policy Research Working Paper 9043, World Bank, Washington, DC.

Krugman, P. R. 1994. *The Age of Diminished Expectations: U.S. Economic Policy in the 1990s.* Cambridge, MA: MIT Press.

Lemos, R., A. Choudhary, J. Van Reenen, and N. Bloom. 2016. "Management in Pakistan: First Evidence from Punjab." Working Paper, International Growth Centre, London.

Olley, G., and A., Pakes. 1996. "The Dynamics of Productivity in the Telecommunications Equipment Industry." *Econometrica* 64 (6): 1263–97.

Schwab, K., ed. 2018. *The Global Competitiveness Report 2018*. Cologny/Geneva: World Economic Form.

Syverson, C. 2004. "Product Substitutability and Productivity Dispersion." *The Review of Economics and Statistics* 86 (2): 534–50.

———. 2011. "What Determines Productivity?" *Journal of Economic Literature* 49 (2): 326–65.

World Bank. 2018. *From Uneven Growth to Inclusive Development: Romania's Path to Shared Prosperity*. Systematic Country Diagnostics. Washington, DC: World Bank.

2 Romania's Product Market Regulations

The degree to which Romania's product market regulations restrict competition is still higher than the average in the countries of the European Union and Organisation for Economic Co-operation and Development (OECD). Business surveys also indicate a perceived low intensity of competition in the economy. This perception can be related to, among other things, persisting formal regulatory restrictiveness that inhibits competition as well as to implementation gaps for procompetition regulations. The latter are mainly associated with state involvement in the economy through state-owned enterprises (SOEs) and command and control, as opposed to incentive-based regulation, and remaining barriers to entry and rivalry mainly in the services sector. Removal of these formal restrictions in the services sector would have a significant positive impact on gross domestic product (GDP) growth in Romania.[1]

Business surveys indicate that competition is perceived to be less vibrant in Romania than in some of its Central and Eastern European (CEE) neighbors.[2] According to the Global Competitiveness Index, which captures the views of business executives in 140 countries on a scale of 1 to 7, perception of market dominance in Romania deteriorated from 3.9 in 2007 to 3.6 in 2017 and is worse than in the Czech Republic or Poland. Perceptions of competition intensity, on the other hand, have improved somewhat, from 4.6 to 4.9 in the same period, but are substantially worse than in the Czech Republic, Poland, or the Slovak Republic.

An economy with restricted competition tends to be less productive than others. Poorly designed product market policies may affect the degree of competition between firms, which in turn limits their incentives to maximize efficiency, innovate, and increase productivity. Regulations can raise barriers to market entry and rents and generate market frictions and adjustment costs. These, in turn, can hamper productivity growth by increasing slack (Vickers 1995), reducing efficiency in resource reallocation (Restuccia and Rogerson 2007), and discouraging technology adoption and innovation (Aghion and Griffith 2005).[3]

Governments can distort the level playing field through regulations as well as through direct participation in markets. In this respect, it is key to understand whether government interventions affect (i) the possibility of market entry or exit (such as exclusive rights to supply, limitations on the number of suppliers, or interventions that significantly raise the costs of new firms to enter the market); (ii) the market conditions to compete among firms, either through direct restrictions (such as price or product regulation) or by reducing the incentive for firms to compete strongly; and (iii) the ability of consumers to shop between firms and exercise consumer choice (Office of Fair Trading 2009).

Using the OECD product market regulation (PMR), this chapter finds that the degree to which Romania's formal regulations restrict competition has decreased over time, but restrictions in certain areas remain. Formally and despite improvements, regulatory restrictiveness in Romania remains above that of some of its CEE neighbors and the average for OECD or EU-15 countries.[4] The state still has a significant footprint in the economy, beyond network industries. The state's involvement in business operations also takes the form of command-and-control regulation and the few remaining price controls in the energy, professional services, third-party motor vehicle insurance, and retail sectors. Barriers to entry and rivalry are associated with licenses and permits in services. These impose unnecessary administrative burdens on businesses and may be affecting contestability and efficient market functioning.

An important caveat is that the PMR measures officially adopted regulations and do not capture implementation and enforcement—and in Romania the gap between laws on the books and their application may be significant (World Bank 2018). This implies that competition in product markets may be more constrained than the level implied by the PMR.[5] Yet even only considering regulations on the books, a simulated scenario in which Romania implements procompetition reforms that would reduce regulatory restrictiveness in the network and services sectors suggests a potential additional increase of 0.22 percentage points to the observed GDP growth in 2017, all else being equal.

BENCHMARKING PRODUCT MARKET REGULATIONS

To identify and benchmark regulatory restrictiveness in Romania, the analysis relies on existing information on PMR. The OECD–World Bank Group dataset provides information on PMR across 70 OECD and non-OECD countries.[6] The PMR indicator includes three pillars: (i) state control, (ii) barriers to entry and rivalry (also known as barriers to entrepreneurship), and (iii) barriers to trade and investment (box 2.1).

The PMR indicators assess the extent to which public policies promote or inhibit market forces. Each of the areas addressed within the PMR methodology sheds light on specific restrictions of the regulatory framework, both economywide and in key sectors of the economy, such as electricity, gas, telecom, postal service, transport, water, retail distribution, professional services sectors, and others, such as administrative requirements for business start-ups, treatment of foreign parties, governance of public-controlled enterprises, or antitrust exclusions and exemptions. The economywide PMR methodology is useful for pinpointing rules that are likely to restrict competition.

The analysis uses the latest PMR round for Romania from 2013 and includes Romania's performance projection based on information updated in 2017. The latest PMR dataset compiles the most recent data available for each country, which includes 2013 data for 47 countries (all OECD countries included) and most recent data (from 2014 to 2017) for 23 World Bank Group–OECD countries. Although the most recent official information available for Romania corresponds to 2013, updated information as of 2017 is included in the analysis, and relevant indicators and scores have been simulated based on the 2017 information. To analyze regulatory restrictiveness in Romania, four neighboring countries are used as comparators: the Czech Republic, Hungary, Poland, and the Slovak Republic. Additional benchmarks include the OECD average, the average of EU member states prior to 2004 (EU-15),

BOX 2.1

Product market regulation methodology: Economywide score

PMR indicators form a comprehensive and internationally comparable set of indicators that measure the degree to which policies promote or inhibit competition in areas of the product market where competition is viable. PMR indicators are useful to monitor the regulatory achievements of monitored countries and to evaluate the effectiveness of policies introduced over the years. Moreover, they have been widely used to help policy makers create a clear picture of regulations in different countries, with the objective of identifying gaps in regulations and/or room for improvements.

The indicators rely on information collected through the OECD's regulatory indicators questionnaires. The figure B2.1.1 summarizes how the economywide score is calculated (numbers in parentheses represent weights). First, the answers are coded into objective information (scores range from 0 to 6, with 6 being the worst). Second, scores of individual regulations are aggregated into subsequently broader regulatory areas from "lower-level indicators" (18 areas) to "intermediate indicators" (7 areas), and finally the three "subindicators." The three subindicators are averaged to calculate the overall PMR score.

Initially built by the OECD for its members and the OECD-plus countries (47 countries total), in partnership with the World Bank Group, the dataset has since been extended to 20 additional countries.

The PMR indicators are designed to reflect regulations that have the potential to restrict competition in

FIGURE B2.1.1

Economywide PMR methodology

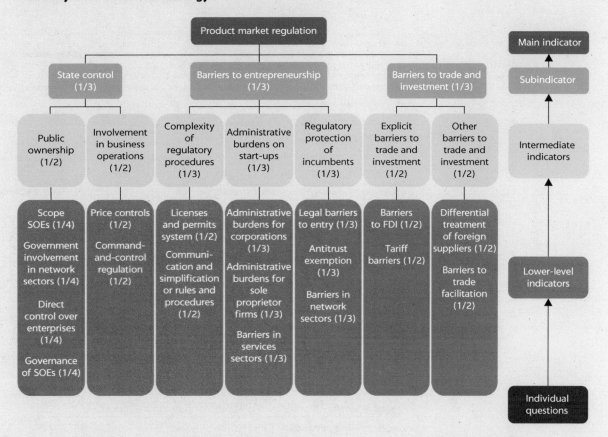

Source: Adapted from Koske, I., et al. (2015), "The 2013 Update of the OECD's Database on Product Market Regulation: Policy Insights for OECD and Non-OECD Countries", OECD Economics Department Working Papers, No. 1200, OECD Publishing, Paris, https://doi .org/10.1787/5js3f5d3n2vl-en.
Note: FDI = foreign direct investment; PMR = product market regulation; SOE = state-owned enterprise.

continued

Box 2.1, *continued*

areas where competition is viable. They have a number of features that make them useful not only for analysis but, more important, for policy advice, since they allow one to pinpoint specific policies that hamper competition. The PMR indicators are focused on enacted policies and not on outcomes, implying that they are "objective" in that they are not based on opinion surveys. Finally,

PMR indicators focus on regulatory measures that affect the economy at large and can therefore be considered as comprehensive measures of regulatory restrictiveness. PMR indicators are not designed to capture informal regulatory practices nor the effective enforcement of regulations, since they are only concerned with formal compliance with a number of criteria.

the total sample average (average of 70 PMR countries), and the average of the top 5 performing countries for each corresponding subindicator analyzed.

Overall, the regulatory framework in Romania, insofar as it appears "on the books," is less restrictive than the total sample average but is more restrictive than that of the OECD and EU-15 countries. Considering the projected PMR score based on the 2017 information (figure 2.1), Romania's overall PMR score would have marginally improved between 2013 and 2017, which implies that, unless other countries would have worsened their performance in four years, Romania's regulatory restrictiveness would be higher than that of the Czech Republic, Hungary, and the Slovak Republic.

The overall restrictiveness of regulations in Romania is mainly associated with state control of the economy and several remaining barriers to entry and rivalry. This indicates persistent state presence in the economy through SOEs in markets where private sector participation and competition are typically viable (such as energy generation and transport). In relative terms, Romania's regulations appear to be more restrictive than the total sample average in the case of state control regulations. Regarding barriers to entry and rivalry, Romania exhibits a less restrictive regulatory framework than the total sample average, but it is still more restrictive when compared to the EU-15 and OECD averages. Conversely, on the barriers to trade and investment, Romania outperforms almost all 70 analyzed countries and positions itself among the top 10 performers in this category.

REGULATIONS WITH ECONOMYWIDE EFFECTS

State control

Despite the slight progress observed in 2017, the extent of state control in Romania is greater than in most comparators. In 2013, Romania was placed among the bottom third of countries for restrictiveness of state control. Based on 2017 data, Romania has improved its position to the middle third of the distribution of countries. In 2017, persistent public ownership is the main driver of high regulatory restrictiveness, together with state involvement in business operations (figure 2.2).

The state's involvement in business operations is still significant, mainly due to the use of command-and-control regulation (figure 2.3). Command-and control-regulation assesses the extent to which the government uses coercive as opposed to incentive-based regulation. According to the PMR, in Romania, such regulatory restrictiveness is mainly associated with the lack of guidance to the regulators on using alternatives to traditional regulation. In addition, there are existing state liabilities for losses of the railways company.

FIGURE 2.1

Product market regulation in Romania and comparator countries

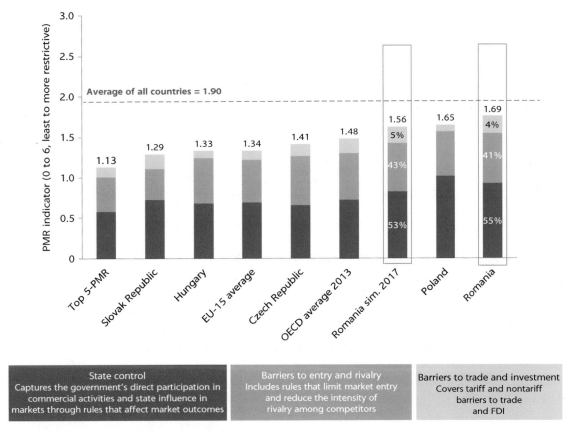

Source: Product Market Regulation (PMR) indicators (database), OECD-World Bank, Washington, DC, https://datacatalog.worldbank.org/dataset /markets-and-competition-oecd-wbg-pmr-indicators-selected-non-oecd-countries-2013-2018.

Note: The top five performers in the overall PMR indicator are the Netherlands, the United Kingdom, Austria, Denmark, and New Zealand. The figure shows 2013 information unless otherwise indicated. EU-15 = for list of countries see Note 4 on page 20; FDI = foreign direct investment; OECD = Organisation for Economic Co-operation and Development; PMR = product market regulation; sim. = simulated results.

FIGURE 2.2

Restrictiveness of state control regulation in Romania and comparator countries

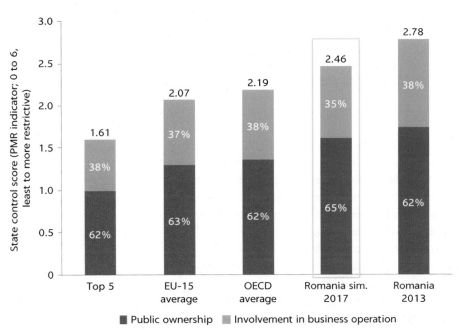

Source: Product Market Regulation (PMR) indicators (database), OECD-World Bank, Washington, DC, https://datacatalog.worldbank.org /dataset/markets-and-competition-oecd-wbg-pmr-indicators-selected-non-oecd-countries-2013-2018.

Note: The top five performers in the state control pillar are the Netherlands, the United Kingdom, Estonia, Austria, and Peru. The figure shows 2013 information unless otherwise indicated. EU-15 = for list of countries see Note 4 on page 20; OECD = Organisation for Economic Co-operation and Development; sim. = simulated results.

FIGURE 2.3
Romania: State control indicator composition

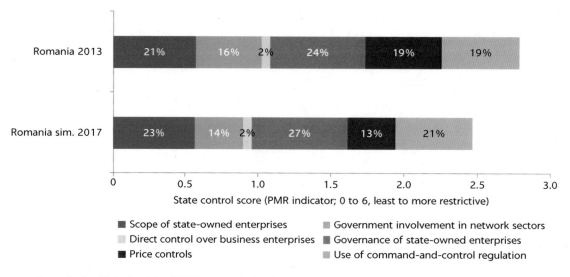

Source: Product Market Regulation (PMR) indicators (database), OECD-World Bank, Washington, DC, https://datacatalog.worldbank.org /dataset/markets-and-competition-oecd-wbg-pmr-indicators-selected-non-oecd-countries-2013-2018.
Note: sim. = simulated results.

Price controls are also in place in the energy, retail (tobacco and pharmaceutical products), professional services, and third-party motor insurance sectors.[7] For example, end-user and wholesale price regulation in the electricity and gas markets have been reintroduced despite their elimination during past reforms. Cigarettes sellers are required to submit in advance their intended retail prices to the Ministry of Finance. Once a certain retail price is communicated to the Ministry of Finance, it becomes a fixed price. In the case of pharmaceuticals, maximum prices for drugs for human use are set by order of the Minister of Health.[8] Additionally, the government sets maximum levels of the insurance premium for the mandatory motor third-party insurance.[9] Price controls may be used for justifiable reasons, but they may distort market outcomes where price competition exists, increase costs of competing, or even induce collusive outcomes. Price ceilings can lead to reductions in supply or shortages that would harm consumers rather than be beneficial to them and may reduce quality or innovation. Minimum prices, on the other hand, prevent more efficient firms from competing on the price dimension. Generally, to promote either social or economic goals through price regulation, the government should be able to differentiate products and services that could be supplied by private players under prevailing market conditions from those markets that are characterized by natural monopolies and require long-term tariff control. In cases where competition is limited because of regulations or other government interventions, it would typically be more effective to find less distortive alternatives to those regulations than to control prices.

Barriers to entry and rivalry

Barriers to entry and rivalry remain relatively high in Romania compared to the EU-15 and OECD averages (even when accounting for the simulated 2017 score), affecting contestability and efficient market functioning. The regulatory restrictiveness is mainly explained by still significant administrative burdens on start-ups (which contribute almost half of the restrictiveness score in this pillar), followed by complex regulatory procedures and regulatory protection to incumbents (figure 2.4).

The licenses and permits systems impose unnecessary burdens on business and may be preventing entry in various markets (figure 2.5). Burdens are associated with the lack of single contact points (so-called one-stop shops) for obtaining information on notifications and licenses and issuing or accepting notifications and licenses.

FIGURE 2.4

Regulatory barriers to entry and rivalry in Romania and comparator countries

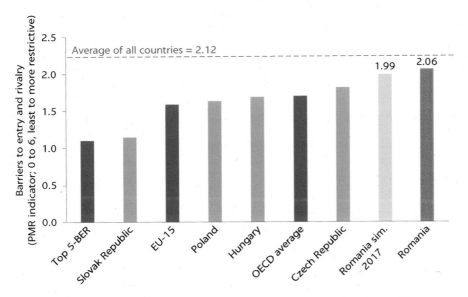

Source: Product Market Regulation (PMR) indicators (database), OECD-World Bank, Washington, DC, https://datacatalog.worldbank.org/dataset/markets-and-competition-oecd-wbg-pmr-indicators-selected-non-oecd-countries-2013-2018.
Note: The top five performers in the pillar of barriers to entry and rivalry are Ukraine, the Slovak Republic, New Zealand, the Netherlands, and Italy. The figure shows 2013 information unless otherwise indicated. BER = barriers to entry and rivalry; EU-15 = for list of countries see Note 4 on page 20; OECD = Organisation for Economic Co-operation and Development; PMR = product market regulation; sim. = simulated results.

FIGURE 2.5

Romania: Regulatory barriers to entry and rivalry indicator composition

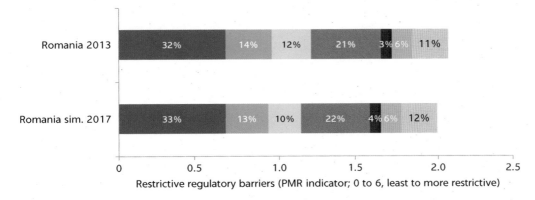

- Licence and permits system
- Administrative burdens for sole proprietor firms
- Communication and simplification of rules and procedures
- Barriers in network sectors
- Administrative burdens for corporations
- Barriers in services sectors
- Antitrust exemptions

Source: Product Market Regulation (PMR) indicators (database), OECD-World Bank, Washington, DC, https://datacatalog.worldbank.org/dataset/markets-and-competition-oecd-wbg-pmr-indicators-selected-non-oecd-countries-2013-2018.
Note: sim. = simulated results.

Rivalry might also be hindered by barriers in service sectors (road freight, retail trade, and professional services), administrative burden to corporations, and some incumbent protection (due to barriers in network sectors) (figure 2.5). In terms of administrative burdens to corporations, for example, there are 31 procedures an entrepreneur must complete in the preregistration and registration stage of the start-up process in Romania, much higher than the 13 procedures required in the Slovak Republic and 9, 11, 16, and 16 procedures corresponding to the averages of the EU-15, OECD, four CEE comparators, and PMR sample, respectively. In the preregistration stage alone, entrepreneurs in Romania must fill out 16 of the 21 forms or steps identified in the PMR (compared to the 5.6 average of top 5 performers).[10] Likewise, to register a public limited company, entrepreneurs need to contact five or seven public or private bodies in the preregistration and registration stages, respectively, which is higher than the comparator CEE average (3.25 and 2.25, respectively), the EU-15 averages (1.3 and 2.3, respectively), and the top five performer averages (1.2 and 1.0, respectively).

Barriers to trade and investment

The Romanian regulatory framework is one of the least restrictive for trade and investment (figure 2.6). Romania is within the top 10 performers globally. Nevertheless, there are remaining regulatory barriers to competition that may require further attention, notably, the different treatment of foreign suppliers and barriers to trade facilitation. Specific restrictions are related to cabotage in road freight, participation of foreign firms in tenders for government transport contracts, and regulators not being required to use internationally harmonized standards and certification procedures in business services (legal, engineering, and architecture).

FIGURE 2.6

Regulatory barriers to trade and investment in Romania and comparator countries

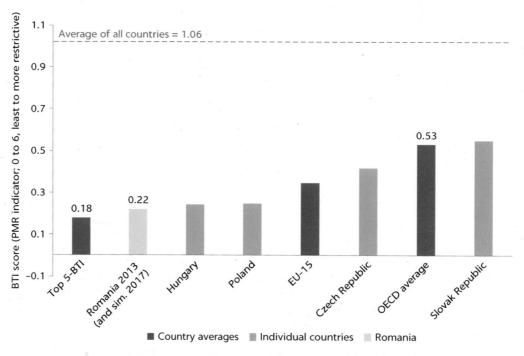

Source: Product Market Regulation (PMR) indicators (database), OECD-World Bank, Washington, DC, https://datacatalog .worldbank.org/dataset/markets-and-competition-oecd-wbg-pmr-indicators-selected-non-oecd-countries-2013-2018.
Note: The top five performers in the BTI pillar are the Netherlands, Belgium, Australia, the United Kingdom, and Finland. The figure shows 2013 information unless otherwise indicated. BTI = barriers to trade and investment; EU-15 = for list of countries see Note 4 on page 20; OECD = Organisation for Economic Co-operation and Development; sim. = simulated results.

SECTOR-SPECIFIC REGULATIONS

Network sectors

Remaining regulatory restrictions to competition in network industries may affect market outcomes. The network sector regulation indicator reveals that Romanian regulations are less restrictive than those in Poland, the OECD, and total averages, but still above the average of the EU-15 and other comparators. Accounting for 2017 information, a slight deterioration in the regulatory restrictiveness is observed (figure 2.7).

Romania shows relatively high regulatory restrictiveness in road freight and air transport. Restrictive regulations in these sectors explain a significant portion of the overall restrictiveness of the network sector regulation score (figure 2.8). Regulatory constraints in the road service sector are entirely explained by entry regulations, whereas public ownership stands as the main driver of restrictive regulation in the other sectors, particularly in the airline,[11] rail,[12] post,[13] and telecom[14] sectors. Across network sectors, except for electricity, restrictive regulations would have remained unchanged or become slightly more restrictive between 2013 and 2017.

It is noteworthy that, in the case of electricity, the improvement since 2013 is based on the information "on the books" at the end of 2017 and is associated with the full deregulation of end-user prices. It does not consider the more recent reinstatement of price regulation in 2018. Top performers tend to show more regulatory restrictiveness in postal and rail sectors and have regulations that are the least restrictive in airline, telecom, and road sectors. Similarly, across EU-15 countries, regulations governing air services and telecom are on average the least restrictive.

FIGURE 2.7

Regulations in network sectors (energy, telecom, and transport): Overall score in Romania and comparator countries

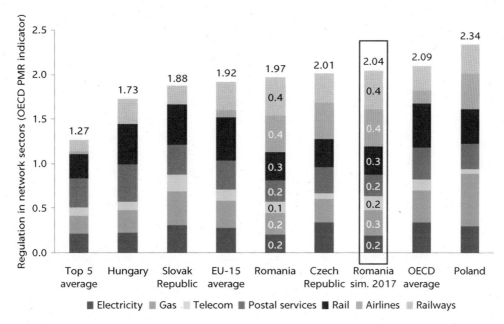

Source: Product Market Regulation (PMR) indicators (database), OECD-World Bank, Washington, DC, https://datacatalog.worldbank.org/dataset/markets-and-competition-oecd-wbg-pmr-indicators-selected-non-oecd-countries-2013-2018. *Note:* OECD PMR score = from 0 (nonrestrictive) to 6 (very restrictive). The top five performers in the overall score of regulation in network sectors are the United Kingdom, Germany, Peru, the United States, and Australia. The figure shows 2013 information unless otherwise indicated. Total average includes most recent (2014–17) information from non-OECD members. EU-15 = for list of countries see Note 4 on page 20; OECD = Organisation for Economic Co-operation and Development; sim. = simulated results.

FIGURE 2.8

Restrictive regulations in network sectors

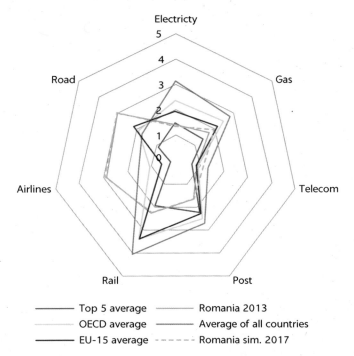

------- Top 5 average   ------- Romania 2013
------- OECD average   ------- Average of all countries
------- EU-15 average   - - - - - Romania sim. 2017

Source: Product Market Regulation (PMR) indicators (database), OECD-World Bank, Washington, DC, https://datacatalog.worldbank.org/dataset /markets-and-competition-oecd-wbg-pmr-indicators-selected-non-oecd -countries-2013-2018.
Note: The top five performers in the overall score of regulation in network sectors are the United Kingdom, Germany, Peru, the United States, and Australia. Averages are calculated based on most recent data (2014–17) available from non-OECD countries (the top five average includes 2014 information for Peru). EU-15 = for list of countries see Note 4 on page 20; OECD = Organisation for Economic Co-operation and Development; sim. = simulated results.

Road freight

Regulatory requirements in road freight services may increase logistics costs. Road services are of substantive importance for logistics in Romania, given that 71 percent of the inland freight cargo volume is mobilized by roads (OECD 2016). Restrictive regulation may be increasing transportation costs of final goods and services. Indeed, Romania appears to have one of the most restrictive road freight sectors, with restrictions entirely associated with entry regulation. Several entry requirements for registration (licenses and permits) could be streamlined to minimize additional entry costs and encourage firms to gain economies of scale. To establish a national road freight business, operators need, among other things, to obtain a license (other than a driving license) or permit (of limited duration, for 10 years) from the competent authorities (Romanian Road Authority and the State Inspectorate for Road Transport Control); to notify the government (regulatory agency) and wait for approval before they can start operation; to register in a transport trade register; to appoint a transportation manager, who requires a training certificate; and to ensure that each driver must have a Certificate of Transporting Cargo, obtained after a course and passing an exam.

Subnational regulation may be imposing extra burdens on the freight business. As pointed out by OECD (2016), local municipalities are imposing extra taxes for the usage of national roads that lie on their territory and of local roads. In addition, the lack of transparency and of an effective payment system would have been adding additional restrictions.

Road freight sector regulation leaves room for discretional entry decisions that may protect vested interests and affect the level playing field. Decisions on entry of new operators may consider criteria different than technical or financial fitness or compliance with public safety. Thirty percent of PMR countries explicitly do not allow for such flexibility into entry decisions in the sector. In Romania, on the other hand, professional bodies or representatives of trade and commercial interests[15] are involved in specifying or enforcing entry regulations. In contrast, the Slovak Republic and most of the PMR (64 percent), OECD (57 percent), EU-15 (53.3 percent), and all top five performers[16] do not allow professional bodies or trade representatives to intervene in entry decisions. These regulations may not only open opportunities for "discretion" in entry decisions, they also discriminate and protect vested interests and therefore may encourage the formation of collusive agreements.

Retail trade

Although regulations in the retail trade sector are less restrictive than in the EU-15 and OECD, there is still room for improvement. Licenses and permits are important to guarantee minimum requirements and quality standards. However, in Romania, requirements may be imposing an unnecessary burden on entry and increase the costs to compete. Companies in the retail trade that operate in traditional or online retail markets are subject to the general conditions, formalities, and procedures applicable to any company. Companies operating in specific retail sectors in Romania are also subject to additional requirements. For instance, in the clothing business, licenses and permits are always required in Romania, as opposed to 53 percent of PMR countries, 57 percent of OECD countries, and 60 percent of EU-15 countries, with the least restrictive countries, such as Bulgaria, Latvia, and Sweden, not having such requirements. Moreover, in Romania, the notification to authorities to establish a new retail clothing outlet is mandatory, in contrast to 50 percent of PMR countries, 49 percent of OECD, and 40 percent of EU-15 countries. None of the top five countries[17] with the lowest restrictiveness in the retail sector have this notification obligation for the clothing or food businesses.

Romania has regulations that impose a relative ban on entry or expansion of business activities and that constrain strategic options to compete in retail markets. Most of the PMR countries and all top five performers do not apply restrictions on sales below costs (beyond a prohibition of predatory pricing) and constraints on sales promotions. Restrictions on sales promotions are not a common practice, either. Among the CEE comparator countries, only the Czech Republic and the Slovak Republic apply restrictions on sale discounted pricing, while only Poland applies constraints to sales promotions. In Romania, sales below cost are prohibited or restricted by a prohibition of predatory pricing.[18] Likewise, sales promotions are restricted to appear within a particular period of the year.[19] Romania is one of a handful of countries, together with France and Italy, that apply both restrictions on discounts and sales promotions (figure 2.9 and figure 2.10).

FIGURE 2.9

Are there any special regulations prohibiting or restricting sales below costs beyond a prohibition of predatory pricing?

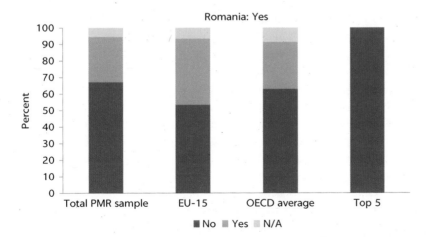

Source: Product Market Regulation (PMR) indicators (database), OECD-World Bank, Washington, DC, https://datacatalog.worldbank.org/dataset/markets-and-competition-oecd-wbg-pmr-indicators-selected-non-oecd-countries-2013-2018.
Note: Including 70 PMR countries. The top five performers are Rwanda, Bulgaria, Latvia, Paraguay, and Sweden. The figure shows 2013 information unless otherwise indicated. Total average includes most recent (2014–17) information from non-OECD members. EU-15 = for list of countries see Note 4 on page 20; N/A = not applicable; OECD = Organisation for Economic Co-operation and Development; PMR = product market regulation.

FIGURE 2.10

Are sales promotions restricted to appear within a particular period of the year?

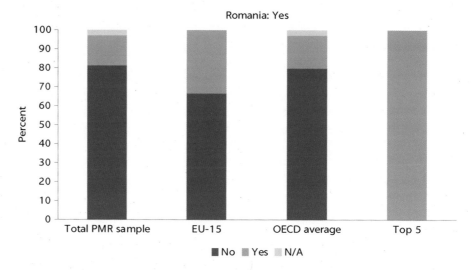

Source: Product Market Regulation (PMR) indicators (database), OECD-World Bank, Washington, DC, https://datacatalog.worldbank.org/dataset/markets-and-competition-oecd-wbg-pmr-indicators-selected-non-oecd-countries-2013-2018.
Note: Including 70 PMR countries. The top five performers are Rwanda, Bulgaria, Latvia, Paraguay, and Sweden. The figure shows 2013 information unless otherwise indicated. Total average includes most recent (2014–17) information from non-OECD members. EU-15 = for list of countries see Note 4 on page 20; N/A = not applicable; OECD = Organisation for Economic Co-operation and Development; PMR = product market regulation.

Professional services

Despite past reforms, Romania still has restrictive entry regulation for accountants, lawyers, engineers, and architects that can limit the incentives to compete and increase the costs to do business, especially for downstream users (box 2.2).

All four regulated professions are granted a high number of tasks with exclusive or shared exclusive rights. In the cases of engineers and architects, Romania grants 10 and 9 tasks, respectively, compared to only 4 on average in the EU-15.

Burdensome *accreditation* requirements apply to lawyers and engineers, which, unlike accountants and architects that need licensing by professional bodies only, are required to undertake additional licensing by state and public authorities.

Romania is one of the few countries that require *double licenses* to lawyers and engineers. None of the EU-15 countries have double licensing requirement—from their professional body and from the state authority—for engineers, and only Belgium requires lawyers to have a double licensing.

Additional restrictions in the form of a mandatory *professional examination* are applied to lawyers, accountants, and architects. Only five EU-15 countries require mandatory examination for architects; these are Austria, France, Greece, Italy, and the U.K. Accountants are also required to have two years of higher education (in addition to a three-year college degree) to enter the profession. This requirement is present only in 20 percent of EU-15 countries and in Hungary.

A compulsory two-year relevant *practice* to become a full member of the profession is applied to lawyers, accountants, and architects. This regulation is quite common in the case of accountants and lawyers (93 percent and 80 percent, respectively, across EU-15 countries). However, the compulsory relevant practice regulation is less common in the case of architects, and more than half the EU-15 countries do not require it—for those that do, less than two years (on average) is required.

BOX 2.2

Tackling entry restrictions in professional services in Romania

Since 2000, the Romanian Competition Council (RCC) has been very active in eliminating regulations governing professional services, noting that such regulations were deemed to distort competition conditions. The RCC identified several barriers to entry or operation in these markets, notably (i) the obligation of membership of a professional association; (ii) restrictions on the number of service providers in certain areas or based on demography, including restrictions on the number of interns; and (iii) ownership restrictions.

In Romania, any professional service provider is obliged to be member of a professional association, but the entry process entails shortcomings that create distortions. To enter any professional service (such as lawyers), a certain set of qualifications is required, but these should not be excessively burdensome, should be transparent and nondiscriminatory, and should provide an appeal mechanism in case of rejections. Such qualifications are mostly related to education, specialized training, experience, and specific exams. A public body or a professional association certifies conformity with these entry criteria. In practice, existing professional associations are favorable to maintaining the membership obligation on the ground that it guarantees a certain level of professionalism and service quality. Nevertheless, obtaining an authorization to practice a certain professional service has not always been targeted toward ensuring high service quality, mainly because (i) other criteria than the ones mentioned above are often applied, (ii) the verification of entry qualifications is not duly done, and (iii) sometimes certain candidates are favored even if they are not the most qualified, while discrimination among certain categories of candidates still exists. Moreover, for certain

professions, only one professional association is allowed by law to operate in the market, while the management of such associations is ensured by its members, who also decide on entry of new members. Therefore, ensuring the independence of management boards is key to removing any entry barrier and may be achieved by ensuring that the board members are not part of the same profession.

Furthermore, the existence of restrictions on the number of service providers in certain areas or based on demography generates unnecessary price increases. For example, the deontological code governing the notary profession considered that opening a notary office in the close proximity (in the same building or within a distance of 50 meters) of an existing notary office was anticompetitive, especially without notifying the latter. Another discriminatory practice stems from the fact that certain notary offices provide only high-priced services, while other services at a lower value are provided by other offices. Other restrictions are related to the obligation for a newly authorized professional service provider to undertake an internship period and be supervised by a senior member of the profession. This further entailed distortions associated with (i) discriminatory treatment among interns based on gender, (ii) lengthy internship periods, in addition to low levels of remuneration, and (iii) limitations on the maximum number of interns supervised by senior experts. Acknowledging that the existence of excessive restrictions to entry may limit competition in the market among professional service providers, leading to higher tariffs and limited choice for consumers, the RCC advocated for and intervened to eliminate existing quantitative restrictions in many cases, such as notaries.[a]

a. For extensive background and information see Romanian Competition Council annual reports, http://www.consiliulconcurentei.ro/en/publications/annual-reports.html.

Another restrictive regulation consists of *compulsory chamber membership* that in Romania is applied to accountants, lawyers, and architects. This entry process seems to engender several shortcomings, creating distortions. Although this regulation applied to lawyers exists in 80 percent of EU-15 countries, 40 percent of EU-15 countries do not apply it to architects. Moreover, none of the top five least restrictive countries[20] apply it to architects. (Only Denmark requires chamber membership for lawyers, and the U.K., for accountants).

Conduct regulation is more restrictive for lawyers compared to the other professions.

Price controls, which may have distortive effects on markets, are applied to lawyers (binding minimum and maximum prices), engineers, and architects (nonbinding but recommended price guidelines). In the case of legal services, prices are set by the national Union of Romanian Bars—with which all regional bars are affiliated—and approved by the Ministry of Justice. Price controls may incentivize collusive agreements, and indeed that is what was observed and sanctioned in the case of notaries (lawyers) in Romania. Across the PMR countries, price regulation of these professions is not the standard. For engineers and architects, prices are typically not regulated (as is the case in 61 percent and 57 percent of PMR countries, respectively, and in 70 percent of OECD countries for both professions). Among Romania's neighbors, only Hungary has price regulation for both engineers and architects, and among the EU-15, 80 percent and 70 percent of the countries do not regulate prices of engineers and architects, respectively. Thus, it is worth exploring alternative, less restrictive methods as in the case of accounting services (box 2.3), to provide better information about costs, pricing, and the quality of legal, engineering, and architectural services.

Further, advertising and marketing are restricted for lawyers, which may lead to inefficiencies in the market. The ability of firms to advertise can help improve the quality of professional services and overcome the information asymmetries inherent in this service industry. Although a significant share of the PMR countries restrict this practice for lawyers (56 percent) rather than banning it, almost a third of the sample (29 percent) impose no restrictions to advertising. Across the EU-15 group, the practice is restricted for 67 percent of the countries, while no restrictions exist in Austria, Denmark, Spain, Italy, or Sweden. Likewise, within the top five performers, Finland and the U.K. restrict advertising for lawyers, while Denmark and Sweden do not.

Likewise, the legal form of business is restricted for lawyers (who are not allowed to provide services as public limited companies) and for engineers (who are not allowed to provide services under limited liability partnerships). Across the observed PMR countries, 57 percent of the PMR countries (and 40 percent of the EU-15[21]) and all four CEE comparators apply this regulation to lawyers, but this type of restriction applied to engineers is nonexistent in OECD countries. Moreover, none

---

BOX 2.3

Tackling price regulation and estimating benefits to the service users

The Romanian Competition Council ordered in 2010 the removal of an internal regulation of the Body of Expert and Licensed Accountants of Romania that had been setting minimum and maximum fees in the accounting profession. It was estimated that the consumers of accounting services would benefit from annual cost savings of around US$60 million. These savings represent the estimated aggregated premium that the firms requesting accounting services did not have to pay above market prices (RCC 2011).

In 2018, the RCC sanctioned the Chamber of Suceava and its members for fixing minimum fees above those levels approved by Order of the Minister of Justice. Also, as a result of an investigation it conducted into possible anticompetitive behavior, the National Union of Public Notaries committed to removing competitive constraints regarding minimum fees and individual advertising to attract the clients and recruit staff for the notaries' offices. Likewise, the RCC also sanctioned the Romanian Chamber of Financial Auditors for establishing a minimum fee for providing financial audit services.

Romania's Product Market Regulations | 55

of the top five countries restricts the legal form of business for engineers, and only Denmark, among the top performers, applies it to lawyers.

Interprofessional cooperation is allowed only between comparably licensed professionals for accountants, lawyers, and architects.[22] For the architecture and accountancy professions, most of the countries allow all forms of cooperation (80 percent and 60 percent among OECD countries, and 23 percent and 47 percent of EU-15 countries). In the case of architects, Romania falls among the handful of countries[23] that limit interprofessional cooperation. In contrast, none of the four CEE comparators nor any of the top five countries restrict interprofessional cooperation for architects.

BOOSTING GROWTH WITH PROCOMPETITION REFORMS

Procompetition reforms could be enacted to tackle economywide and sector-specific competition constraints. Table 2.1 proposes a number of policy measures

TABLE 2.1 **Policy options to remove economywide and sector-specific barriers to firm entry and rivalry**

SHORT TERM	MEDIUM TERM
ECONOMYWIDE	
• Streamline burdensome administrative procedures for businesses to facilitate easy market entry. In particular, consider reducing unnecessary requirements applied to entrepreneurs in the preregistration stage of the start-up process.	• Facilitate access to information on notifications and licenses, and access to issuing or accepting notifications and licenses by setting up (at the local level if possible) single contact points and making available the information on such procedures via the internet.
SECTOR-SPECIFIC	
Transport	
• Consider extending cabotage to foreign firms in the road freight market.	• Consider removing unnecessary entry requirements for road freight services that may be excessive (for example, the requirement to notify the government and/or regulatory agency and wait for approval before road freight businesses can start operation).
• Limit interventions by the trade association in the entry decision in road freight services.	• Ensure entry decisions in the road freight sector regulations follow public safety guidelines as well as transparent, neutral, and adequate technical and financial fitness criteria.
Energy	
• Reassess recent legislative changes regarding price controls in gas and electricity sectors for end-user prices and wholesale market for gas.	• Promote regulatory changes that require ownership separation between the production and distribution segments (electricity and gas).
Retail trade	
• Minimize limitations to promotions/discounts that are not classified or cannot be classified within predatory pricing practices in retail distribution. • Promote fierce competition in the retail distribution by lifting restrictions on the timing of sales and promotions.	
Professional services	
• Consider removing excessive and unnecessary entry requirements for professional services (for example, unnecessary membership requirements in professional associations or double licensing from public and professional bodies to lawyers and engineers).	• Review the rationale for shared exclusive rights in all four professional services (legal, accounting, architecture, and engineers). • Review the limitations on the corporate forms for the provision of legal and engineering services. • Reassess the application of minimum and maximum price for lawyers and recommended price guidelines for engineers and architects. • Support the elimination of advertising and marketing restrictions for the legal professional services. Likewise, improve the ability of these professionals to associate and cooperate with other professionals. • Adopt internationally harmonized standards and certification procedures for legal, engineering, and architecture professions to foster competition and secure a minimum level of quality of service.

TABLE 2.2 **Potential effect on GDP of reforms across service sectors**

REFORMS ACROSS ENERGY, TRANSPORT, TELECOMMUNICATIONS, AND PROFESSIONAL SERVICES	EFFECT OF REFORM ON GROWTH IN DOWNSTREAM INDUSTRIES WITH ABOVE-AVERAGE SERVICE INTENSITY			NUMBER OF SECTORS USING THESE SERVICES MORE INTENSIVELY[a]
	ESTIMATED IMPACT ON ADDITIONAL VALUE ADDED[a,b]	EXPECTED IMPACT ON GDP MEASURED AT MARKET PRICES 2017[c]		
		(LEI BILLION)	(US$ BILLION)	
Overall impact	0.22%	1.92	0.47	26

Sources: World Input-Output database, www.IOD.org; World Development Indicators, https://datacatalog.worldbank.org/dataset/world-development-indicators; Barone and Cingano 2011.
Note: GDP = gross domestic product.
a. Calculations based on the input-output table 2014, which includes information on 56 specific sectors. Service-intensive sectors are those with above-average intensity usage of service sectors. Impact calculations are the additional value added as percentage of the GDP at current international prices of 2014, generated by improvements in a specific sector.
b. Following the results of Barone and Cingano (2011), the estimate assumes a multiplier effect of 0.75 percentage points across all the service-intensive sectors due to joint reforms on a selected sector.
c. We assume the structure of the economy remains constant, meaning that the estimated impact of changes in selected sectors on GDP 2014 was the same in 2017.

to boost market competition based on their feasibility and impact in the short and medium terms.

Removing remaining regulatory restraints to competition in service sectors (energy, transport, telecommunications, and professional services) could potentially have a significant impact on growth. Barone and Cingano (2011) suggest that liberalizing regulated input services sectors would generate gains in value-added growth in downstream service-dependent industries in OECD countries. A simulated scenario, in which Romania implements procompetition reforms in the services sectors, would imply a potential addition of 0.22 percentage points to the observed GDP growth in 2017, which would be associated with potential benefits of US$0.47 billion (lei 1.92 billion) additional value added in 2017, all else being equal (table 2.2). It is important to highlight that this is a lower bound figure based on the 2017 regulatory frameworks as they appear on the books (as opposed to in practice).

Gains would be even greater if one were to consider that poor institutional quality may erect barriers to firm entry and growth in otherwise competitive markets. World Bank (2018) points out how, in Romania, institutional deficiencies are often the cause behind a significant gap between officially adopted policies and their implementation. As a result, an unpredictable business environment is a significant challenge to business operations. Although estimates specific to Romania are not available, the literature suggests that poor institutional quality may affect the allocation of productive resources, when entrepreneurs may devote greater efforts to obtaining valuable licenses and preferential market access than to improving productivity.[24] This suggests that addressing systemic institutional failures may compound the impact of procompetition policies.

NOTES

1. This chapter builds on the background paper "Competition and Government Interventions in Romania: An Assessment with Focus on Product Market Regulations and Competitive Neutrality," authored by Georgiana Pop, Tilsa Guillermina Ore Monago, Georgeta Gavriloiu, and Mariana Iootty (Pop et al. 2019).
2. Central and Eastern Europe (CEE) refers to the Visegrad 4: the Czech Republic, Hungary, Poland, and the Slovak Republic.
3. Also see Arnold, Nicoletti, and Scarpetta (2008, 2011), Conway et al. (2006), and Syverson (2004).
4. The EU-15 includes the following countries: Austria, Belgium, Denmark, Finland, France, Germany, Greece, Ireland, Italy, Luxembourg, the Netherlands, Portugal, Spain, Sweden, and

the United Kingdom. OECD countries include: Australia, Austria, Belgium, Canada, Chile, the Czech Republic, Denmark, Estonia, Finland, France, Germany, Greece, Hungary, Iceland, Ireland, Israel, Italy, Japan, Korea, Latvia, Lithuania, Luxembourg, Mexico, the Netherlands, New Zealand, Norway, Poland, Portugal, the Slovak Republic, Slovenia, Spain, Sweden, Switzerland, Turkey, the United Kingdom, the United States.

5. It is worth highlighting that the results in this report are based on the 2013 PMR methodology and therefore do not capture restrictions related to state aid control, regulatory impact assessment, and additional services included in the 2018 PMR methodology that has a broader scope. At the time of the preparation of this report, PMR Indicators for Romania using the 2018 methodology were not available.

6. The methodology and key findings of the PMR for OECD countries are presented in Nicoletti, Scarpetta, and Boylaud (1999), Conway, Janod, and Nicoletti (2005), and Wölfl et al. (2009). The PMR database used for this study includes Australia, Austria, Argentina, Belgium, Bolivia, Brazil, Bulgaria, Canada, Chile, China, the Czech Republic, Colombia, Costa Rica, Croatia, Cyprus, Denmark, the Dominican Republic, Ecuador, the Arab Republic of Egypt, El Salvador, Estonia, Finland, France, Germany, Greece, Guatemala, Honduras, Hungary, Iceland, India, Indonesia, Ireland, Israel, Italy, Jamaica, Japan, Kenya, the Republic of Korea, Kuwait, Latvia, Lithuania, Luxembourg, Malta, Mexico, the Netherlands, New Zealand, Nicaragua, Norway, Panama, Paraguay, Peru, the Philippines, Poland, Portugal, Romania, Russia, Rwanda, Senegal, the Slovak Republic, Slovenia, South Africa, Spain, Sweden, Switzerland, Turkey, Tunisia, Uruguay, Ukraine, the United Kingdom, and the United States.

7. Across the PMR countries, 24 percent of the countries apply price controls to tobacco; 68.6 percent of PMR countries apply price control to pharmaceuticals. (The shares for the OECD group are 26 percent and 74 percent, respectively, while in the EU-15 these shares are 33 percent and 80 percent). Among the CEE comparator countries, all have price regulation over pharmaceuticals, but only the Czech Republic applies it to tobacco.

8. The acts currently in force are Order no. 43/2017 on the maximum prices and Order no. 368/2017 on the methodology for computing the prices and on the approval procedure.

9. See Government Decision no. 826/2016.

10. Except for the Slovak Republic, where entrepreneurs must fill 12 out of 21 PMR identified pre-registration requirements, in the other four top performers such number of requirements falls to five or less: the Netherlands and Italy with 5, Ukraine with 4, and New Zealand with 2.

11. SOE TAROM S.A.

12. SOE CFR Calatori, CFR Marfa, CFR Infrastructura.

13. SOE CNPR–Posta Romana.

14. Radiocom and significant public ownership of Telekom Romania.

15. By 2014, according to OECD (2016), the most important trade associations in the road freight transport sector were the National Union of Romanian Road Haulers, the Romanian Association of International Road Transport, the Federation of Romanian Transport Operators, Transport Heritage Association Europe 2002, Transylvania Road Haulers Association, Road Haulers in Construction Association, Freight Forwarded Association, and the Romanian-Italian Association of Logistics and Management.

16. The top five performers with the lowest restrictive regulations in the road sector are Australia, El Salvador, Nicaragua, Ukraine, and Costa Rica.

17. The top five countries in the retail sector with lowest restrictive regulation are Rwanda, Bulgaria, Latvia, Paraguay, and Sweden.

18. Provisions of Government Ordinance 99/2000 are still in force and provide an interdiction to sell below costs.

19. Government Ordinance 99/2000 provides for the conditions and periods when certain types of promotions can be organized.

20. The top five countries regarding overall restrictive regulation in four regulated professions are Sweden, Finland, the United Kingdom, Denmark, and Ecuador.

21. These countries are Austria, Belgium, Denmark, France, Ireland, and Portugal.

22. Information on the engineering profession is missing, so it is not possible to conclude that such restriction does not apply to this profession.

23. These are Canada, Cyprus, Egypt, France, Luxembourg, the Philippines, Romania, and Tunisia.

24. See, for instance, De Rosa, Gooroochurn, and Görg (2015), Djankov et al. (2002), and Murphy, Shleifer, and Vishny (1993).

REFERENCES

Aghion, P., and R. Griffith. 2005. *Competition and Growth: Reconciling Theory and Evidence.* Cambridge, MA: MIT Press.

Arnold, J., G. Nicoletti, and S. Scarpetta. 2008. "Regulation, Allocative Efficiency and Productivity in OECD Countries: Industry and Firm-Level Evidence." OECD Economics Department Working Paper 616, OECD Publishing, Paris.

———. 2011. "Does Anti-Competitive Regulation Matter for Productivity? Evidence from European Firms." IZA Discussion Paper 5511, Institute for the Study of Labor, Bonn.

Barone, G., and F. Cingano. 2011. "Service Regulation and Growth: Evidence from OECD Countries." *Economic Journal* 121 (555): 931–57.

Conway, P., D. De Rosa, G. Nicoletti, and F. Steiner. 2006. "Regulation, Competition and Productivity Convergence." OECD Economics Department Working Paper 509, OECD Publishing, Paris.

Conway, P., V. Janod, and G. Nicoletti. 2005. "Product Market Regulation in OECD Countries: 1998 to 2003." OECD Economics Department Working Paper 419, OECD Publishing, Paris.

De Rosa, D., N. Gooroochurn, and H. Görg. 2015. "Corruption and Productivity: Firm-Level Evidence." *Journal of Economics and Statistics* 235 (2): 115–38.

Djankov, S., R. La Porta, F. Lopez-De-Silanes, and A. Shleifer. 2002. "The Regulation of Entry." *Quarterly Journal of Economics* 117 (1): 1–37.

Koske, I., I. Wanner, R. Bitetti, and O. Barbiero. 2015. "The 2013 Update of the OECD's Database on Product Market Regulation: Policy Insights for OECD and non-OECD countries." OECD Economics Department Working Paper 1200, OECD Publishing, Paris, https://doi.org/10.1787/5js3f5d3n2vl-en.

Murphy, K. M., A. Shleifer, and R. W. Vishny. 1993. "Why Is Rent-Seeking So Costly to Growth?" *American Economic Review* 83 (2): 409–14.

Nicoletti, G., S. Scarpetta, and O. Boylaud. 1999. "Summary Indicators of Product Market Regulation with an Extension to Employment Protection Legislation." OECD Economics Department Working Paper 226, OECD Publishing, Paris.

OECD (Organisation for Economic Co-operation and Development). 2016. *OECD Competition Assessment Reviews: Romania.* Paris: OECD Publishing.

Office of Fair Trading. 2009. *Government in Markets: Why Competition Matters—A Guide for Policy Makers.* London: Office of Fair Trading.

Pop, G., T. Ore Monago, G. Gavriloiu, and M. Iootty. 2019. "Competition and Government Interventions in Romania: An Assessment with Focus on Product Market Regulations and Competitive Neutrality." Unpublished document, Markets and Competition Global Team, World Bank, Washington, DC.

RCC (Romanian Competition Council). 2011. *Annual Report 2010.* Bucharest: RCC. http://www.consiliulconcurentei.ro/uploads/docs/items/bucket6/id6477/raport_2010_final.pdf.

Restuccia, D., and R. Rogerson. 2007. "Policy Distortions and Aggregate Productivity with Heterogeneous Plants." NBER Working Paper 13018, National Bureau of Economic Research, Cambridge, MA.

Syverson, C. 2004. "Market Structure and Productivity: A Concrete Example." *Journal of Political Economy* 112 (6): 1181–222.

Vickers, J. 1995. "Concepts of Competition." *Oxford Economic Papers* 47 (1): 1–23.

Wölfl A., I. Wanner, T. Koźluk, and G. Nicoletti. 2009. "Ten Years of Product Market Reform in OECD Countries: Insights from a Revised PMR Indicator." OECD Economics Department Working Paper 695/2009, OECD Publishing, Paris. https://www.oecd-ilibrary.org/content/paper/224255001640.

World Bank. 2018. *From Uneven Growth to Inclusive Development: Romania's Path to Shared Prosperity.* Systematic Country Diagnostics. Washington, DC: World Bank.

3 State Ownership and Competitive Neutrality

Romania still has a significant state-owned-enterprise (SOE) footprint, which extends beyond typical SOE network industries. In this context, competitively neutral policies will need to ensure that all enterprises, public or private, domestic or foreign, face the same set of rules. Competitive neutrality gaps exist in the country's regulatory framework, creating an uneven playing field and generating misallocation of resources and anticompetitive practices. Regulatory shortcomings include exemptions from the law on corporate governance,[1] the lack of rules mandating the separation of commercial and noncommercial functions, and the lack of provisions that require SOE investments to show positive rates of return. Implementation also suffers from fragmentation of SOE oversight, inconsistent reporting, lack of clarity in terms of compensation for public service obligations, and lack of full transparency of state aid allocation, especially to SOEs.[2]

Governments justify their direct participation in the economy through a mixture of social and economic goals. Governments generally invoke the control of strategic resources and the improvement of distribution of wealth and power as justifications to participate in economic activities through SOEs. Employment and industrial policies may also be major drivers for developing a large presence of SOEs in the market (Monti 2007, 441–2; van Miert 2000, 1–2; OECD 2005, 9–10). In times of crisis, state ownership is often used to rescue private businesses affected by systemic economic and financial problems (OECD 2009a).[3] Such government bailouts for private firms in critical conditions are carried out for a variety of reasons, including the protection of employment, industrial policy considerations, and other strategic and political motivations (OECD 2009c, 26). However, it is important to ensure that the participation of the government in the economy remains subsidiary to that of the private sector, that is, that the state provides only those goods and services that the private sector cannot provide itself.

Direct state involvement in markets is not in itself problematic, but in Romania there is a particularly significant SOE footprint. Romania has more than 1,500 SOEs and has at least one SOE in 23 out of the 30 sectors tracked in the Organisation for Economic Co-operation and Development (OECD) product market regulation (PMR) indicators. This compares to 12 sectors in the Slovak Republic, 17 in the Czech Republic, 18 in Hungary, and 15 on average in the EU-15.[4] SOE presence goes beyond typical network industries and into sectors and subsectors—such as manufacturing of basic metals, shipbuilding, and accommodation—where state ownership is not necessarily justified by a clear economic or strategic rationale. Furthermore, the government is liable for losses in the railway sector. In the energy sector, it recently reintroduced price regulation and reversed reforms toward full liberalization.

This chapter finds that competitive neutrality (CN) gaps exist in the regulatory framework, creating an uneven playing field. Regulatory shortcomings include exemptions from the law on corporate governance of newly established SOEs, the lack of rules mandating the separation of commercial and noncommercial functions despite legal separation in the railways and the energy sector, and the lack of specific provisions that require SOE investments to show positive rates of return. Implementation also suffers from the fragmentation of SOE oversight across institutions with frequent overlaps, inconsistent reporting of SOE performance, little clarity in terms of compensation for public service obligations, and lack of full transparency of state aid[5] allocation, particularly to SOEs. In some cases, SOE costs seem to outweigh the benefits, as in the case of the airline TAROM.[6] The lack of competitively neutral policies can facilitate anticompetitive practices, which can lead to inefficient market outcomes.

THE SOE SECTOR IN ROMANIA

Romanian SOEs operate under the supervision of various public entities, at central and local levels, and conduct a broad range of economic activities in many sectors, to an extent that goes beyond typical involvement in network industries and/or industries where market failures or strategic policy objectives may justify direct state intervention in the economy through SOEs.[7] For instance, SOEs are present in sectors and subsectors such as accommodation, road infrastructure construction, production of pharmaceuticals, motion pictures, building and repairing ships and boats, and manufacturing of basic and fabricated metals.

Progress has been made in increasing transparency regarding the number and identity of the companies in which the state and the local authorities have holdings exceeding 50 percent, with the list of such companies being available and periodically updated. According to the "Fiscal-Budgetary Strategy for 2019–2021," the number of nonfinancial SOEs having submitted financial statements in 2017 was 1,565 (Romanian Government 2019, 205). Among these, there are 334 SOEs subordinated to central public authorities (hereafter called "central SOEs") and 1,231 local SOEs subordinated to local public authorities. Out of these, 220 central SOEs and 1,096 local SOEs are currently operational, the remaining being in different stages of insolvency, bankruptcy, and dissolution (Romanian Government 2019, 205).

Central SOEs concentrate most of the nonfinancial SOEs' assets and debts, as well as profits and losses. However, the local SOEs tend to show weaker financial indicators, the gross profit–to–gross loss ratio for central SOEs being 6.3, compared to 1.2 for local SOEs. Small and large players can be found at both the local and central government levels. SOEs employed 274,000 persons in 2017, or 4.3 percent of the total employment, declining from 5.4 percent in 2013. By EU and OECD standards, this is average. The share of SOEs in total gross value added has been hovering around 10 percent since 2013 and is fairly constant in real terms. The share of SOEs in total companies' income has recently declined to below 4 percent of total income generated by nonfinancial corporations.[8]

SOEs register diminishing losses and diminishing subsidies while the overall impact on the consolidated budget is positive. The impact of state companies on the budget balance in the European standard ESA10 was positive in 2013–16. The contribution of the top 20 companies consolidated in the central government sector and in the local sector ranged between 0.5 percent of gross domestic product (GDP) in 2014 and 0.2 percent of GDP in 2015–16. The burden of underperforming SOEs on public finances has been decreasing, although performance seems to remain dependent on subsidies, which have declined from 0.78 percent of GDP in 2013 to 0.49 percent of GDP in 2017. Return on equity (ROE) is improving for both local and central SOEs, although, when adjusting for subsidies, only for central SOEs; in 2017, the ROE becomes marginally positive (0.7 percent).

There is high heterogeneity in the performance of SOEs. As in most countries, network industries (transport and energy) dominate the SOE sector. The ministries of economy, energy, and transport, in their top three activities, produce 75 percent of total declared revenues in central SOEs (74 percent net of subsidies) and receive 87 percent of the total subsidies toward the central SOEs. At local level, terrestrial and pipe transportation receives 60 percent of total subsidies. For example, 85 percent of the subsidies paid toward central SOEs go toward the Ministry of Transport, with the CFR Calatori remaining the biggest loss-making company in the portfolio. At the local level, the subsidies for transport in Bucharest cover only 36 percent of the total subsidies to local SOEs. When adjusted for subsidies, the profit of the central SOEs under the ownership of the Ministry of Economy and, especially, the Ministry of Transport fall into negative territory, pushing down overall performance significantly. When adjusting for subsidies, local SOEs fall virtually to negative values in all regions of Romania. This is due to the predominance of transport among the activities of local SOEs.

There is unusual SOE presence in sectors and subsectors such as manufacturing, accommodation, and building and repairing ships and boats, where the probability of having an SOE in comparator countries is relatively low due to market characteristics (figure 3.1). The Romanian state controls at least one firm in all the 10 network sectors (electricity, gas, postal services, railways, air, water, road, and urban transport, heating, and telecommunications), and SOEs are present in at least 13 nonnetwork sectors. SOEs are present in sectors where the private sector and competition are viable. Regarding network industries, an SOE is still the largest firm in fixed-line rail network operation, and the state currently holds 45.9 percent of stakes in the incumbent fixed-line phone service provider, unlike in other countries where private companies have managed to take the lead.

While direct government involvement in the markets is not in itself problematic, from a market outcome point of view, SOEs would require attention in the presence of certain market conditions. By embedding competition principles in policy making, potential distortions from direct state intervention through SOEs, including through state aid and investment incentives, may be minimized. In this respect, the following three factors are key to review:

1. Whether the SOE occupies a significant position in the market

2. Whether regulations or policies protect SOEs from market competition

3. Whether the private sector could provide the services or goods in an efficient manner (see figure 3.2)

ROMANIAN SOES HOLD SIGNIFICANT MARKET POSITIONS

Several SOEs hold significant market shares in their markets,[9] and many operate in markets together with the private sector, which may raise questions about whether private sector participants face a level playing field. As shown in table 3.1, in at least 21 sectors or subsectors in which SOEs are present, they have a market share of

FIGURE 3.1

Probability of an SOE operating in a sector or subsector

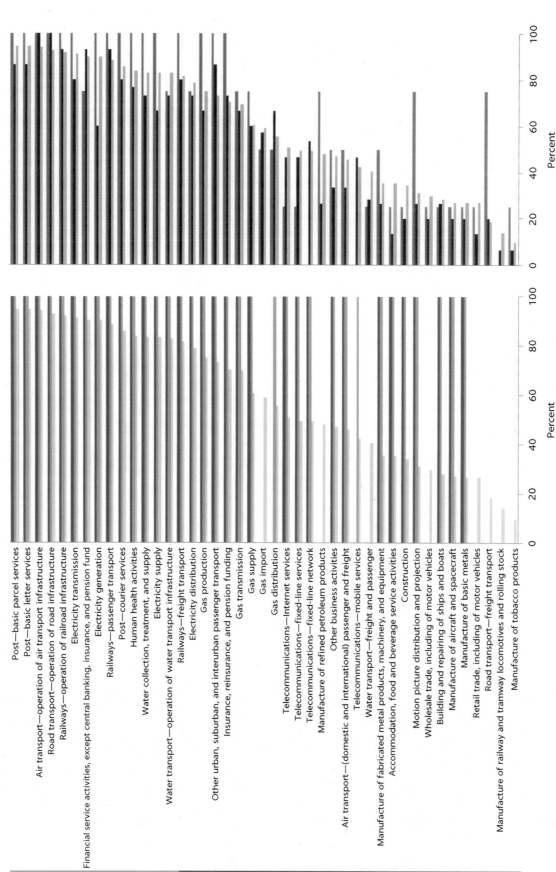

Source: OECD-World Bank Group PMR database, https://www.oecd.org/economy/reform/indicators-of-product-market-regulation/.

Note: Figure shows 2013 information unless otherwise indicated. ECA-4 = the Czech Republic, Hungary, Poland, and the Slovak Republic; EU-15 = for list of countries see Note 4 on page 20; sim. = simulated results.

FIGURE 3.2
Factors related to market position and regulations that may increase the risk of negative effects of SOEs in the market

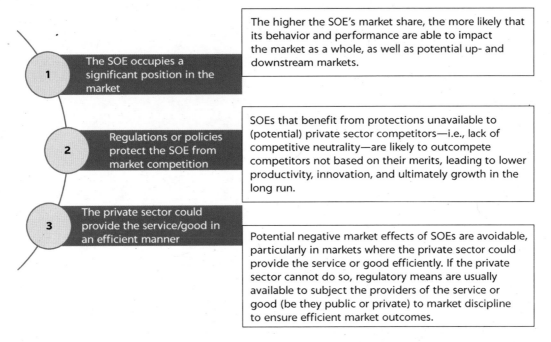

1 — The SOE occupies a significant position in the market — The higher the SOE's market share, the more likely that its behavior and performance are able to impact the market as a whole, as well as potential up- and downstream markets.

2 — Regulations or policies protect the SOE from market competition — SOEs that benefit from protections unavailable to (potential) private sector competitors—i.e., lack of competitive neutrality—are likely to outcompete competitors not based on their merits, leading to lower productivity, innovation, and ultimately growth in the long run.

3 — The private sector could provide the service/good in an efficient manner — Potential negative market effects of SOEs are avoidable, particularly in markets where the private sector could provide the service or good efficiently. If the private sector cannot do so, regulatory means are usually available to subject the providers of the service or good (be they public or private) to market discipline to ensure efficient market outcomes.

Source: Integrated State-Owned Enterprise Framework, Module 1: SOE and the Market (World Bank, forthcoming).
Note: High market shares are not equal to market power and do not automatically translate into a dominant position. It is generally considered that as the significance of any enterprise in its respective market rises—all other things being equal—so does its ability to shape the market. SOE = state-owned enterprise.

50 percent or more. Although the presence of SOEs in infrastructure sectors is not unusual across countries, especially in sectors that require capital-intensive investments (such as electricity transmission), there are other markets in Romania where SOEs compete with private sector players—in at least 11 sectors with SOE presence. While private sector participation is possible in these areas, some form of regulatory intervention (for example, access regulation, and public service obligations and their compensation) is required in the sector or one of its subsectors (for example, electricity transmission) in order for private sector participation to yield optimal market outcomes.

Transport

The Romanian state directly intervenes in the air transport market through TAROM,[10] despite the company's poor financial outcomes over 2007–17. TAROM has been operating at a loss for 10 consecutive years (Romania Insider 2018b). By 2016, with US$11.6 million in losses, TAROM had the country's sixth greatest annual gross loss, representing 3.3 percent of total losses reported by the top 10 SOEs with gross losses (MPF 2017). Moreover, between 2016 and 2017, TAROM more than tripled such losses (to US$42.4 million). In typical market conditions, TAROM would have been unable to cope with the fierce competition from low-cost airlines.[11] By 2017, TAROM owned the third-largest market share for domestic flights (17 percent), and it would have lost market share to low-cost airlines between 2014 and 2016, even when focusing only on the domestic routes it operated at that time. By 2016, seven domestic routes—from Bucharest to Cluj-Napoca, Iasi, Oradea, Sibiu,

TABLE 3.1 **SOE market shares and private sector participation in sectors/subsectors with SOEs**

SECTOR	SOE MARKET SHARE	PRIVATE SECTOR CURRENTLY?	PRIVATE SECTOR POTENTIALLY?
Electricity generation	80% (SOEs aggregated)	Y	Y
Railways passenger transport	>80%–90%	Y	Y
Urban transportation	100% (underground transport), 100% (tram, bus, and trolley transport in Bucharest)	Y	Y
Water transportation (including operation of water transport infrastructure)	100% (seaport infrastructure and navigable channels)	N for port infrastructure	Y*
Construction	100% (road infrastructure construction)	Y	Y*
Mining (coal mining)	>90%	Y	Y
Air transport infrastructure	100%	N	Y*
Railways infrastructure	100%	N (legal monopoly)	Y*
Electricity transmission	100%	N (legal monopoly)	Y*
Electricity distribution	100%	N (legal monopoly)	Y*
Gas production, transmission, distribution, and supply	45% (production), 100% (transmission), 25% (gas supply to nonhousehold consumers)	Y (production and supply)	Y*
Post (basic letter services)	100% (basic letter services)	N (legal monopoly until end of 2019)	Y*
Air safety services	100%	N (legal monopoly)	Y
Water distribution	100%	N (legal monopoly)	Y*
Aerospace manufacturing	100%	N (legal monopoly)	Y
State credit guarantees	100%	N (for state guarantees)	Y
Lottery gambling	100%	N (legal monopoly)	Y
Publishing and printing	100%	N (legal monopoly)	Y
Mining (uranium)	100%	N (legal monopoly)	Y
Mining (extraction of salt)	100%	N (for extraction)	
		Y (products from import sold on the market)	Y
Defense industry (production of weapons)	100% (legal monopoly, national products)	Y (foreign products)	Y
Railways freight transport	36%	Y	Y
Air transport passengers	18%–20%	Y	Y
Shipbuilding	<15%	Y	Y
Financial service activities, banking, and insurance	7.5 % (banking), <5% (insurance)	Y	Y
Television and radio broadcasting	20%–35%	Y	Y
Telecommunications (radio, VPN, and satellite communications)	N/A	N (legal monopoly)	Y
Health care services	…	Y	Y
Services: hospitality	<5% (increasing number of private operators)	Y	Y

Source: Original elaboration based on Product Market Regulation (PMR) indicators (database), OECD-World Bank, Washington, DC, https://datacatalog.worldbank.org /dataset/markets-and-competition-oecd-wbg-pmr-indicators-selected-non-oecd-countries-2013-2018.
Note: Red highlights sectors in which the private sector is currently active but SOEs have a market share of 50 percent or more; yellow highlights sectors in which SOEs have a significant market share without competing with the private sector but in which the private sector could be active; green highlights sectors in which SOEs compete with the private sector without holding significant market shares; for grey sectors market share information was not available. N = no; N/A = not applicable; SOE = state-owned enterprise; VPN = virtual private network; Y = yes; … = not available.
* While private sector participation is possible, some form of regulatory intervention (for example, access regulation) might be required in the sector or one of its subsectors (for example, electricity transmission) for private sector participation to yield optimal market outcomes.

Suceava, Satu Mare, and Timisoara—were operated by TAROM, which accounted for 82 percent of flights and 64 percent of seats (a drop from 97 and 95 percent, respectively, in 2014). Thus, it is important for Romania to reevaluate whether there is a clear economic rationale for TAROM in the market, considering its performance and overall market outcomes. As a comparison, 67 percent of EU-15 countries, and 66 percent of OECD countries (including Hungary and the Slovak Republic), do not have SOEs in air transport (freight and/or passenger services).

Although liberalization of railways started in 1998, the government keeps full control over the separate companies in the three relevant market segments (infrastructure operation, freight services, and passenger services provision) and remains liable for losses by these companies.[12] The government controls (i) CFR (the infrastructure operator), which also raises some concerns on third-party access; (ii) CFR Călători (rail passenger operator); (iii) CFR Marfă (rail freight operator); and (iv) SAAF (company dealing with excess rolling stock to be sold, leased, or scrapped) (Busu and Busu 2015). These publicly owned companies are also subject to special rules concerning the sale of shares or the change of their object of activities (for example, the privatization must be approved by governmental decision). Legal constraints to sales of government stakes do not exist in the freight transport segment in comparator countries such as Hungary and Poland. The Czech Republic has no SOEs in any of these market segments.

In rail freight, there are also concerns about potential anticompetitive market outcomes associated with illegal state aid. Even though SOE CFR Marfă accounts for around 36 percent of the market share, its weak financial fitness combined with allegedly illegal state aid currently investigated by the European Commission raise concerns as to the level playing field. The company would have incurred an annual loss of around US$47 million in 2016 (13.5 percent of the total losses recorded by the top 10 SOEs with largest gross losses) and was the SOE with the second largest gross loss[13] that year (MPF 2017). The recent decision to open an investigation against the granting of state aid of US$406 million (€360 million) to CFR Marfă raises concerns about preferential treatment of the SOEs in the sector. The Netherlands (the top logistics performer) and Denmark do not have SOEs, while Hungary does not have its government as shareholder of dominant companies in the freight segment.

Energy

The government intervenes directly through dominant SOEs in gas production, transmission, and supply, two of which are competitive markets (gas production and supply) and require competitive neutral policies. The government is constitutionally constrained to sell the stakes of Transgaz in the transmission segment. This is similar to what is observed in the Slovak Republic and Poland, although the Czech Republic does not have an SOE in the transmission segment. As a comparison, 53 percent of EU-15 countries and 57 percent of OECD countries either do not have a constraint on the sale of SOE stakes or do not have an SOE in the market segment. The Romanian Ministry of Energy owns 70 percent of Romgaz, one of the two largest companies in the production market and the largest in the supply market; and the Romanian Ministry of Economy owns 58.5 percent of the equity stakes of Transgaz, the only company in the gas transmission market (a market segment with natural monopoly characteristics). It is important to mention that 40 percent of OECD countries (including Hungary) and 40 percent of EU-15 countries do not have government ownership of any firm in gas supply.

Romania delayed end-user price deregulation, and recent legislation introduced wholesale price regulation in the gas sector. Thus, gas prices for household consumers and district heating thermal power plants will remain regulated until 2022.[14] As a reference, 67 percent of EU-15 countries do not regulate prices or regulate only prices of last-resort suppliers. None of the EU-15 countries explicitly regulate gas prices. Recent legislation Emergency Government Ordinance (EGO) 114/2018 reintroduced regulated prices on the wholesale market—consisting of fixed prices for the domestic gas sold by domestic producers to suppliers of end-customers and to producers of thermo energy generated in gas (fire power plants), reversing previous liberalization efforts in the sector (see also chapter 2).

The Romanian state holds stakes in the largest firms of the generation and transmission segments. There is a constitutional constraint on the sale of stakes in the transmission firm Transelectrica.[15] The Ministry of Energy owns 80 percent of Hidroelectrica,[16] the lead company in the generation sector, and the Romanian Ministry of Economy owns a 57 percent equity stake of the Compania Naționala de Transport al Energiei Electrice—Transelectrica, the largest company in electrical transmission. In the supply and distribution segments, the government does not hold equity stakes in the largest or dominant firms. However, the government is a significant shareholder (48.8 percent) of Electrica (which controls three distribution companies: SDEE Muntenia Nord, SDEE Transilvania Nord, and SDEE Transilvania Sud, and one electricity supply company, Electrica Furnizare). There are many players in the electrical supply segment (in 2017, 105 were suppliers with an electricity supply license), and according to the Romanian Energy Regulatory Authority (ANRE), the market is competitive (ANRE 2017).

Although end-user electricity prices are low relative to other European countries, particularly for industrial consumers, the relatively low quality of service might be generating extra costs for business. The frequency of power outages (measured by the System Average Interruption Frequency Index) is relatively significant in Romania. Likewise, businesses may struggle to obtain service due to administrative burdens. In fact, according to the Doing Business report 2019, with 9 required procedures, 174 days, and a very high cost (450 percent of per capita income), Romania ranks 154th among 190 surveyed countries in getting electricity.

Romania had ended price regulation for households in December 2017, but a year later it reintroduced them for the period between April 2019 and February 2022.[17] Moreover, no benchmarking that holds all distributors to the standard of the most efficient distributor is required in determining regulated pricing in electricity and gas. Sixty-two percent of OECD countries and 80 percent of EU-15 countries do not regulate electricity prices (or do it only for prices of last-resort suppliers). (See also chapter 2.)

REGULATIONS AND POLICIES PROTECT SOES FROM COMPETITION

CN suggests that all enterprises, public or private, domestic or foreign, should face the same set of rules. Contacts with the government or government ownership or involvement in the marketplace, in fact or in law, should not confer an undue competitive advantage on any actual or potential market participant. Thus, a CN framework is one (i) within which public and private enterprises face the same set of rules and (ii) where no contact with the state brings competitive advantage to any market participant (OECD 2009b, introduction). It should be noted that none of the CN

FIGURE 3.3

Competitive neutrality gap analysis for Romania

The subsidiary role of the state in the economy: No economic criteria for setting up SOEs

Firm-level principles: Separation of SOE commercial and noncommercial activities

1 Streamlining the operational form of government business

Romania
- Legal separation in the energy sector (between supply and distribution activities)
- Corporate governance rules applicable also to SOEs; however, weak application in practice, especially in recent years

Benchmark
- Legislation requires business separation of SOEs

2 Identifying the costs of any given function

- No cross-cutting rules for separating commercial and noncommercial activities of SOEs
- Overlapping competencies for controlling and monitoring SOEs

- Accounting separation for commercial and noncommercial activities of SOEs
- Clear allocation of competencies exist to monitor and control SOEs

3 Achieving a commercial rate of return

- No requirement for SOEs' investments to show a positive NPV
- Inconsistencies in the reporting of financial and economic performance

- SOEs' commercial operations and investments are required to have positive NPV, market consistent rate of returns, and to be measured based on private sector performance

4 Accounting for public service obligations

- Legislation contains rules on the transparency and criteria in the compensation of PSOs delivered by SOEs, but rules are general and there is weak monitoring and control in practice

- Compensation paid to SOEs for the provision of PSOs is based on transparent accountability and objective criteria

Principles embedded in cross-cutting regulatory frameworks and sectoral policies

5 Regulatory neutrality

Romania
- Newly established SOEs are expressly exempted from the law on corporate governance

Benchmark
- Companies compete on a level playing field
- Sectors where competition is feasible are open to private investment

6 Public procurement

- No preferential access to public procurement procedures

- Market-based competition in public procurement
- Bids/auctions designed to reduce the risks of bid rigging

7 Tax neutrality

- SOEs receive tax exemptions, subsidies, and debt guarantees (also available to private entities)
- All such measures are subject to state aid rules
- However, several instances of state aid to SOEs were found incompatible under the EU state aid rules by the European Commission (acting ex officio or following complaints)

- Tax exemptions, subsidies, and debt guarantees granted following competitive neutrality principles

8 Debt neutrality and outright subsidies

Control of state support measures to SOEs and private sector operators

Level playing field in the market between SOEs and privately owned operators

Source: Original elaboration based on OECD 2012.
Note: NPV = net present value; PSO = public service obligations; SOE = state-owned enterprise.

principles are specific to SOEs. But all of them can pertain to them because the SOEs can benefit from others being prevented from entering markets (and vice versa), the SOEs can enjoy cost and revenue advantages (and disadvantages), and SOEs can benefit from preferential rules or enforcement (and vice versa) (OECD 2018).

A CN gap analysis shows a favorable stance toward procompetition policies, transparency, and accountability of SOEs between 2011 and 2016, followed by several steps back in 2017–18, due to legislative changes and measures affecting the SOEs' competitiveness (figure 3.3).

Overall, the regulatory framework ensures CN, but some gaps remain. SOEs operate under the common set of rules of company law as private companies. Specific rules regarding the roles and functioning of SOEs are provided in the acts enacted by the state for their incorporation. Expanding the application of corporate governance principles to SOEs is key to ensuring an efficient management of public resources and market discipline. SOE performance reporting and monitoring is required by law, and there are no legal exemptions for SOEs on antitrust. State-aid control based on EU norms applies equally to private companies and SOEs, tax neutrality is embedded in legislation, and bankruptcy or insolvency laws generally apply the same way to SOEs as to the private sector operators. However, legislative changes in progress might affect the level playing field in several sectors (see box 3.1).

Gaps in the regulatory framework

SOE governance remains restrictive to competition despite the new rules imposed in 2011, which have been partially reversed (box 3.2). The OECD PMR indicator of SOE

BOX 3.1

The Sovereign Fund for Development and Investments

The Sovereign Fund for Development and Investments (SFDI) was created in November 2018[a] with an initial capital of lei 9 billion (€1.93 billion) with the purpose of financing start-ups and investments in industrial capacities in order to increase job creation and develop the local capital market. SOEs in energy and transport, as well as the forest management company Romsilva, may be included as beneficiaries of this fund.

Although the SFDI objective may be to encourage investment, there are a few concerns related to the transparency of its allocation and market effects. The state's shares in 28 of the most profitable SOEs will contribute to the initial capital of the fund (which can induce certain coordination among these companies and may limit the state's own flexibility in case it decides to privatize some of these SOEs). There are also concerns about the accountability and transparency of the nomination of managers and supervision body of the fund as, under the current draft law, the new fund will be only partially subject to the law on corporate governance. There are concerns about transparency of the fund's activity (for example, the type of projects that will benefit from funding and the selection thereof). Finally, the fund will act in markets where there are already private and even other state-owned operators, which will require increased scrutiny regarding the level playing field.

a. In November 2018, the government approved the Government Emergency Ordinance (GEO) no. 100/ 2018 regulating the general framework applicable to sovereign development and investment funds. According to this legal instrument, sovereign development and investment funds are defined as joint stock companies established under Law no. 31/1990 and are fully owned by the state. Their main activity is financial operations, including the performance of financial investments on their own behalf and account, with cash and in-kind capital contributions, including in the form of shares owned by the state in the companies (including the strategic ones) that fulfil the economic criteria and the requirements for the classification outside the government accounts according to the European Union methodology. Currently, a process to amend GEO no. 100/2018 is under way. After the approval of this amendment, the Ministry of Public Finance will elaborate a draft of Government Decision on the organization and operation of the Sovereign Fund for Development and Investments (SFDI).

BOX 3.2

Corporate governance of Romania's SOEs

Corporate governance rules specific to SOEs were introduced in 2011 through the government's Emergency Ordinance 109/2011. In principle, this ordinance also applies to newly set-up SOEs, as there is no express derogation for the new SOEs in the text of the ordinance. However, in practice, exemptions from the corporate governance law are included in the acts by which certain SOEs were set up or in the acts laying out the conditions for the operation of certain categories of SOEs, such as the investment funds.

Several elements contribute to improved SOE governance, such as establishing a sound legal and regulatory framework for corporate governance, creating proper ownership arrangements for effective state oversight and enhanced accountability, developing a sound performance-monitoring system, promoting financial and fiscal discipline, professionalizing SOE boards, enhancing transparency and disclosure, and protecting shareholder rights in mixed-ownership companies.

The 2011 rules included separation between the ownership and policy-making function of the government; transparency on strategic decisions, related-party transactions, and audited financial information; clarity on public-service obligations versus competitive operations; and professionalization and transparency of board and management nomination and remuneration processes.

Law 111/2016 refined and extended the framework through measures such as a calendar for the selection of board members and for the negotiation of the administration plan; a clear responsibility and sanctioning regime for all the actors (Ministry of Finance, line ministries, board presidents, and general managers); creation of specialized monitoring and implementation units in all line ministries that have SOEs under their ownership and of a dedicated unit in the Ministry of Finance; and rules regarding the remuneration and independence of executives and non-executives and their selection.

Law 111 was amended in 2017 and excluded several strategic key companies from its application. The motivation of this decision, as put forward by the legislators, is that the companies in the list were included in the legislative proposal regarding the creation of the Sovereign Fund for Development and Investments. However, the amendment was declared unconstitutional by the Romanian Constitutional Court. In practice, the application of the corporate governance law was rendered ineffective in many cases, for example by the appointment and repeated renewal of interim board members for four-month periods instead of using the selection criteria and procedures provided for in the law.

---

governance measures the degree of insulation of SOEs from market discipline and of political interference in management. Romania scores 5.25 out of 6 in this indicator, worse than the EU-15 and OECD averages, but also worse than the Czech Republic, Hungary, Poland, and the Slovak Republic.

Despite legal vertical separation in railways infrastructure[18] and energy,[19] there are no rules mandating the separation of commercial and noncommercial functions. In the latter, unconditional and conditional legal separation exists—legal separation between the supply and distribution activities is required for operators having more than 100,000 customers. Vertical separation or unbundling may take different forms and degrees. According to best international practices (ordered from least to most intrusive), figure 3.4 shows the main categories of vertical separation. Each type of business separation also reflects a different degree of regulatory intervention on the shareholder structure of private operators and can be used for achieving different regulatory objectives.

There are no specific provisions requiring SOEs to receive market-consistent rates of returns on the sale of assets, goods, and services or to show a positive net present value. Furthermore, there are no cross-cutting requirements for benchmarking SOE transactions based on transactions carried out by private operators

FIGURE 3.4
Degrees of business separation

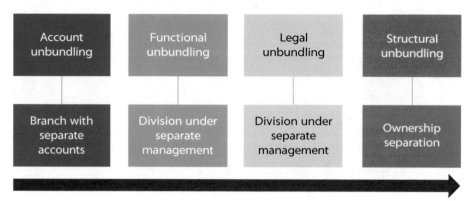

Source: Original elaboration.

in comparable situations. These principles are enshrined in the EU state aid framework directly applicable in Romania; therefore the failure to observe these principles
may trigger prohibition and recovery decisions under EU state aid rules. However,
the effectiveness of control mechanisms exclusively based on the EU state aid law
remedies can be limited due to the length of the European Commission (EC) investigation procedures and to the boundaries of EU state aid rules.

Gaps in implementation

The application of corporate governance rules was uneven, despite progress in
improving transparency and accountability in the management of state participation and in the SOE reorganization, privatization, and postprivatization monitoring since 2011. There were several attempts to exempt many SOEs from the obligations aimed to increase their transparency and the performance of their activities.

The roles of the government vis-à-vis SOEs are fragmented across institutions
with frequent overlaps, which may impact performance and market outcomes. Most
SOEs are still directly managed by line ministries,[20] which risks creating conflicts of
interest and can facilitate political interference in SOEs' management (which may
reduce SOEs' competitiveness and profitability), especially when the existent rules
for the competitive selection of private managers are excluded in case of certain
SOEs. After 2017, the private managers previously selected via competitive procedures were gradually replaced by interim managers, appointed directly, without any
selection procedure. The delays of selection procedures and the repeated renewal of
provisional mandates of interim managers avoided the rules on the appointment of
managers of SOEs.

The inconsistent methodology for reporting on SOE performance and for monitoring prevents comparability and traceability of performance, which need to be
conducted as they are in the private sector in comparable market situations. Since
2016, all SOEs have been required to submit to the Ministry of Public Finance financial and economic indicators, which are subsequently published on the ministry's
website. Since 2011, the ministry publishes annually a report on the activities of
SOEs. Nevertheless, the format and content of such reports varies significantly from
one year to another, which prevents the comparability of data and reduces the transparency of SOEs' activities.

The perception of the overall profitability of the SOE sector in Romania may be distorted by the fact that a reduced number of SOEs with high profits significantly influence aggregate results (RFC 2018, 5). While the average profit margin of SOEs in 2017 was 9.6 percent, the profit margin drops to 1 percent when computed in a scenario that excludes the five best performing SOEs. For comparison, the profit margin of private companies in 2017 was 4.8 percent. SOEs operating in a competitive environment are typically expected to earn rates of return comparable to private businesses over a reasonable period, otherwise private sector competitors can be undercut and crowded out from the market because the SOEs could factor their low profit margins into their pricing decisions.

Increased transparency is required as compensation for public service obligations. When an SOE is entrusted with public service obligations, the rate of return on capital is based on the internal rate of return that the undertaking makes on its invested capital over the period during which it was entrusted to perform public service obligations.[21] Despite the fact that general principles for the compensation to SOEs for the delivery of public service obligations are set by law, the compensation is set in each case by the act through which the public service operation is entrusted. The oversight of how compensations are implemented in practice remains weak. Failure to observe these principles triggers the risk of prohibition or recovery decisions under EU state aid rules. However, as mentioned, the effectiveness of exclusively applying remedies under the EU state aid law can be limited, and there is a need for more increased ex ante and ex post supervision of SOE activities (box 3.3).

SOEs in Romania are recurrent state aid recipients, notably in the railways transport, energy, mining, and chemical sectors. Out of the total state aid given through direct grants and reported to the European Commission between 2007 and 2018, 36 percent was state aid given to SOEs.[22]

Lack of full transparency in the allocation of state aid, notably to SOEs, may be undermining competition.[23] To avoid competition distortions, financial aids and other forms of preferential treatment to enterprises (including to SOEs) must be granted in strict observance of EU state aid rules. However, an increasing number

---

BOX 3.3

State aid in Romania

State support measures (tax exemptions, state guarantees, and subsidies) to SOEs and the private sector are granted in accordance with EU state aid rules. In 2016, subsidies represented 2.7 percent of overall public expenditures, decreasing to 2.2 percent in 2017. Out of total subsidy expenditures, 52 percent were granted for supporting agricultural producers, 36 percent to support public passenger transport by rail, 7 percent for passenger transport via metro, and 3 percent for coal mine preservation or closure.

The state aid granted by the Romanian government is mostly through direct grants and subsidies (98.6 percent), and the rest by tax exemptions, loans, and loans with subsidized interest (1.4 percent). Total state aid (including railway subsidies and agricultural aid) granted in 2017 represented 0.63 percent of GDP. Nonagricultural state aid (excluding railways subsidies) amounted to 0.5 percent of GDP in Romania compared to 0.8 percent for the EU-15 average and 0.7 for the EU-28 average. Across time, the total amount of aid peaked in 2014 (1.22 percent of GDP), followed by a decreasing trend since then. Although Romania is one of the countries with low nonagricultural (not transportation-related) state aid, it is one of the members of the EU with high state spending for environmental protection and energy-saving objectives.

of the investigation procedures initiated by the European Commission against Romania indicate that further efforts are necessary to improve compliance with the state aid rules. The European Commission launched, between 2015 and 2018, 12 state aid investigations, as compared to a total of 7 cases between 2007 and 2014.[24] In 2017–18, four out of five state aid actions considered problematic from a competition point of view by the European Commission involve SOEs, which jointly accounted for a total illegal state aid of US$970 million (€820 million) or 0.45 percent of GDP in 2017. By comparison, the total state aid (including railway subsidies and agricultural aid) granted by the Romanian government in 2017 represented 0.63 percent of the GDP, while the total state aid for the EU countries represented 1.1 percent of GDP (EU-27) in 2017.[25] Examples include the restructuring aid to SOE Complexul Energetic Hunedoara[26] and alleged aid to the rail freight operator SOE CFR Marfă.[27]

ROMANIA LACKS AN ECONOMIC TEST FOR GOVERNMENT INTERVENTION THROUGH SOES

SOEs can be justified by the existence of market failures in which the private sector could or would not provide the service or good in a competitive and efficient manner without some form of government intervention (table 3.2). Market failures are situations in which the market-determined production and allocation of goods and services does not maximize social welfare absent government intervention.

In cases where the private sector could provide the service or good in a competitive and efficient manner, the presence of an SOE is harder to justify. Alternative options available to governments include regulation of natural monopolies, taxes to correct for negative externalities, or subsidies to correct for positive externalities and the presence of public goods. From an economic point of view, SOEs should be employed as a policy tool only once all other regulatory means (such as the provision of incentives to the private sector, regulation of access, or regulation of tariffs) are unsuccessful.

The principle of subsidiarity can help systematize the two roles that the state plays: as an operator in the market through SOEs and as a regulator.[28] This implies that if there are—or could be—private agents able to participate in a market, the state does not need to participate. Instead, it is typically more efficient and effective for the state to act as a regulator. The subsidiarity principle is grounded in economic and social considerations. The state's resources are limited and must be assigned to the most valuable objectives. If private agents are interested and

TABLE 3.2 **Market failures**

MARKET FAILURE	DESCRIPTION	IMPLICATION	EXAMPLES
A natural monopoly	The market can only accommodate one player efficiently.	The private sector often could provide but does not do so in a competitive way without strong regulation, since it would hold monopoly power.	Electricity transmission
Negative externalities	The social costs of provision outweigh private costs of provision.	The private sector overproduces.	Fisheries, water inputs, and use of radio frequency
Positive externalities	Social returns to provision outweigh private returns to provision.	The private sector underproduces, or in the extreme case does not enter and provide the good or service at all if the private returns are not positive.	Road construction to a factory, telecom services, or postal service in remote areas
Public good	There are nonexcludable and nonrivalrous goods or services.	The private sector may not provide the good or service since nonexcludability means a fee cannot be charged for consumption.	Defense, street lighting, and trial of a new seed variety or farming technique

Source: Original elaboration.

capable of supplying goods and services to attend demand in an adequate way, then the best means for the state to intervene is by supervising and controlling the behavior of private agents. Meanwhile, direct intervention of the state should focus on supplying essential goods and services that will not be provided by private agents, in line with a social role driven by distributive and welfare objectives. Some countries have embraced a strictly economic perspective on government participation in the economy. Peru and Chile, for example, have enshrined in their respective constitutions the principle of the subsidiarity role of the state in the economy. In Ireland, SOEs are mainly justified by natural monopolies, market failures, externalities, or equity, objectives that the government reviews periodically.

In Romania, recent events have slowed progress toward liberalization of markets. In the 1990s, Romania initiated an extensive privatization process, which resulted in the state maintaining controlling holdings in a rather limited number of companies. As privatization itself was not sufficient to ensure the overall competitiveness of the Romanian economy, structural reforms were implemented in critical sectors, like energy, with significant steps toward liberalization and improvement of market access, coupled with measures for the improvement of the corporate governance of SOEs. In recent years, progress has slowed, with decisions being adopted without a medium- and long-term strategy. The only major privatization in the past three years has been the sale of viable assets of Oltchim by Chimcomplex, while nonviable assets remained in the ownership of the state.

Romania has no preestablished procedures or economic tests for the creation of new SOEs, and several new SOEs were created in the past five years, including in sectors where there are private operators. It is difficult to justify the existence or creation of additional SOEs in sectors such as travel arrangements, advertising space, parking space, and even taxi services, where private operators are present, as the Bucharest City administration did with the creation of 22 new SOEs.[29]

Several SOEs do not follow a clear justifiable reason under an economic or public policy rationale. In some cases, costs seem to outweigh benefits, as in the case of TAROM. SOE losses strain the government's limited fiscal resources, and the market dominance of SOEs risks crowding out private investment. Thus, rather than constraining SOE presence to sectors that are not attractive for private sector development (due to large positive externalities, natural monopolies, associated to national security, and so forth), many SOEs are involved in sectors and markets where there is no obvious rationale for government participation. Although a detailed analysis could reveal market failures that warrant SOE involvement, the international experience indicates that many sectors in which Romanian SOEs operate—including chemical manufacturing, commercial banking, accommodation, and road infrastructure construction—tend to function efficiently without SOEs, and SOE involvement in these sectors is rarely justified by strategic considerations or development policy objectives.

REDUCING ANTICOMPETITIVE MARKET OUTCOMES

The lack of CN in markets where SOEs have a dominant position may engender anticompetitive practices. Table 3.3 shows four examples from actual antitrust cases in which lack of CN was manifest in a number of ways. These included (i) the prolongation of the legal monopoly over the services falling under the universal services obligation in case of Romanian post (at the beginning of 2019, the legal monopoly granted for the period 2014–18 was extended until the end of December 2019); (ii) the state's regulatory interventions related to SOE activities in the energy industry (for example, new rules enacted by Emergency Government Ordinance (EGO) no. 114/2018 undoing the liberalization of energy markets); and (iii) undue regulatory protection hindering competition in the harbor services market that could otherwise be operated under competitive conditions (for example, towing and piloting services).

Table 3.4 presents a series of solutions designed to ensure competitively neutral markets based on their feasibility and impact in the short and medium terms.

TABLE 3.3 **Examples of competition constraints in markets where SOEs breached the competition law**

CASE	LACK OF COMPETITIVE NEUTRALITY	VERTICAL INTEGRATION OF A DOMINANT SOE LEADING TO POTENTIAL FOR EXCLUSIONARY CONDUCT	LACK OF PROCOMPETITIVE REGULATION	PREVIOUS OR CURRENT PROTECTION LEADS TO DOMINANT MARKET POSITION
Posta Romana (postal services)	✓	✓	N/A	✓
Hidroelectrica (energy)	✓	*	✓	N/A
CN Administratia Porturilor Maritime Constanta (ports)	✓	✓	✓	✓
Electrica (energy)	✓	*	✓	✓

* In these cases, Hidroelectrica and Electrica were found to have engaged in anticompetitive (exclusionary) practices, but these were not the result of vertical integration.
Note: CN = Compania Nationala Administratia Porturilor Maritime SA; N/A = not applicable; SOE = state-owned enterprise.

TABLE 3.4 **Policy options to ensure competitive neutrality of SOEs**

SHORT TERM	MEDIUM TERM
ECONOMYWIDE	
• Undertake competition assessments in selected markets with significant SOE presence to understand their effects on market outcomes. • Pursue reforms on streamlining SOE management and ensure avoidance of conflicts of interest (separation between regulatory and operational functions). • Require that SOEs must achieve a commercial rate of return and show positive net present value. • Ensure transparency with respect to (i) state aid granted to SOEs versus non-SOEs, (ii) the beneficiaries of state aid measures, and (iii) the size of illegal state aid to be recovered and the beneficiaries of such aid, including SOEs and private sector. • Ensure that government interventions in markets follow the principle of the subsidiarity roles of the state in the economy, with a clear economic rationale.	• Minimize the government intervention (at any level) in strategic choices of publicly controlled firms. • Restrict publicly controlled firms to markets where the presence of the state is needed as last resort, and in those sectors where private and public firms coexist, ensure CN. • Require that state equity holdings in publicly controlled firms be managed by an independent entity instead of any ministry connected to the SOE. • Ensure systematic application of the EU state aid rules to SOEs, including control of illegal state aid.
SECTOR-SPECIFIC	
Transport	
• In the airline sector, reassess the economic rationale of SOE participation and ensure CN.	• Consider removing any legal or constitutional constraints for the sale of the stakes held by the government in the railway infrastructure segment.
Energy	
	• Ensure CN between existing SOEs and private firms. • Promote regulatory changes that require ownership separation between the production and distribution segments (see electricity and gas).
Retail trade	
	• Ensure CN between private firms and any public firm and ensure that publicly controlled firms are restricted to markets where the presence of the state is needed as last resort (for example, the pharmaceutical sector).

Note: CN = competitive neutrality; EU = European Union; SOE = state-owned enterprise.

NOTES

1. Even though no express derogations for the newly set-up SOEs are included in the law on corporate governance, in practice, exemptions are included in the normative actions by which new SOEs were established or in the act of laying out the conditions for the operation of certain categories of SOEs (for example, derogations introduced in April 2019 for the sovereign investment and development funds established on the basis of Emergency Government Ordinance (EGO) no. 100/2018).

2. This chapter builds on the background paper "Competition and Government Interventions in Romania: An Assessment with Focus on Product Market Regulations and Competitive Neutrality," authored by Georgiana Pop, Tilsa Guillermina Ore Monago, Georgeta Gavriloiu, and Mariana Iootty (Pop et al. 2019). Inputs based on the unpublished background note "The SOE Sector in Romania," by Geomina Turlea and Constantino Navarro, are also included.

3. For example, in response to the latest financial crisis the European Commission (EC) adapted, in fact, and loosened its rules for restructuring aid given by member states to banks. Further information from the EC may be found at https://ec.europa.eu/competition/state_aid/legislation/temporary.html.

4. The EU-15 includes the following countries: Austria, Belgium, Denmark, Finland, France, Germany, Greece, Ireland, Italy, Luxembourg, the Netherlands, Portugal, Spain, Sweden, and the United Kingdom.

5. State support can take various forms, including tax exemptions, loan guarantees, provision of resources at below market prices, subsidies, and capital injections. While offering government support to private firms or SOEs may help achieve specific goals, it may have a negative impact on competition. If not properly designed, state aid may provide an undue advantage to specific firms and/or reinforce a dominant position, thus facilitating anticompetitive behaviors and/or reducing a firm's incentive to make investments, thus generating market inefficiencies.

6. Some of the losses incurred by TAROM may be attributable to the increased competition from other operators, generally "low-cost" carriers, as well as to the meager revenues associated with the company's commercial activity. However, in 2018, TAROM's market share in the domestic market increased, the first growth in the past five years.

7. Under Romanian law, a company is qualified as an SOE based on control, which may be derived not only from the holding by the state of the majority of shares but also from the existence of special rights granting control over the company.

8. The Fiscal Council Report uses a subsample (916 SOEs) of the Ministry of Finance dataset used in the rest of the document (1,408 SOEs in 2016), based on an expert assessment of the self-declared ownership by the companies. The assessment mostly concerns the local SOEs. Unless otherwise specified, this chapter uses the Ministry of Finance full sample and own calculations based on the respective sample.

9. Such as Hidroelectrica, Nuclearelectrica, and Complexul Energetic Oltenia, accounting together for approximately 70 percent of the market of electricity generation, and Romgaz, with 45 percent market share of the market of production of natural gas, as well as other examples.

10. The Ministry of Transport holds 97.17 percent of the equity shares in the national company Transporturi Aeriene Române C.N. (TAROM). The remaining shares are owned by three companies, two of which are controlled by the Romanian state: 0.09 percent of the shares is owned by SIF Muntenia; 1.26 percent by Regia Autonoma Administratia Româna a Serviciilor de Trafic Aerian (ROMATSA); and 1.48 percent, by Compania Nationala Aeroporturi Bucuresti (the latter two's shareholders are also controlled by the government). See TAROM's website for shareholder information (https://www.tarom.ro/informatii-de-interes-public) and the Ministry of transport for state-controlled companies (http://mt.gov.ro/web14/domenii-gestionate/aerian/domenii-aerian-unitati).

11. Indeed, according to the MPF (2017, 59), the reasons for TAROM's losses were, among other things, with "the company not being able to attract sufficient revenue from the operation of the races and auxiliary activities; a reduction of transport capacity due to the withdrawal of two aircrafts from operation; [...]."

12. The government owns 100 percent of the equity shares of CFR–Călători, CFR–Marfă, and CFR. See the companies' websites: (i) Societatea Națională de Transport Feroviar de Călători (CFR–Călători), http://mt.gov.ro/web14/domenii-gestionate/feroviar/domenii-feroviar-unitati; (ii) Societatea Națională de Transport Feroviar de Marfă (CFR–Marfă), http://mt.gov.ro/web14/domenii-gestionate/feroviar/domenii-feroviar-unitati; and (iii) Compania

Nationala de Cai Ferate (CFR), http://mt.gov.ro/web14/domenii-gestionate/feroviar /domenii-feroviar-unitati.

13. CFR Huneodora with a gross loss of US$211.5 million was the SOE with the largest loss in 2016, accounting for 59.5 percent of the total loss generated by the 10 SOEs with large losses (MPF 2017).

14. Prices have been regulated since 2000. In July 2015, the timeline for phasing out the regulated end-user prices for household customers and for heat producers (only for the quantities of natural gas used to produce heat in cogeneration plants and in thermal power stations for the consumption of the population) was extended until June 30, 2021 (by government Decision no. 488/2015), which then was delayed to 2022. The end-prices for industrial customers (other than heat producers) were fully liberalized by January 2014 (ANRE 2017, 180.)

15. Article 136, paragraph 4 of the Constitution of Romania provides for the inalienability of goods that are public ownership of the state, correlated with article 35 of governmental Decision no. 927/2000 (by which Transelectrica was granted the right to administer certain goods that are public ownership of the state).

16. The remaining 19.94 percent of equity stakes of Hidroelectrica are owned by Fondul Propietatea. According to the Romanian Energy Regulatory Authority (ANRE), by 2017 Hidroelectrica held 24 percent of the market share, closely followed by CE Oltenia. For the distribution of equity shares, see the Hidroelectrica website, https://www.hidroelectrica.ro/Details.aspx?page=29.

17. Changes introduced by EGO 114/2018 as modified in March 2019.

18. Government Emergency Ordinance no. 12/1998 on transportation on Romanian railways and reorganization of National Company of Romanian Railways.

19. Law no. 123 on energy and natural gas, as subsequently amended and supplemented. Published in the *Official Gazette of Romania*, part I, no. 485, 16 July 2012.

20. Although SOEs managed by the relevant sector ministry are observed in 33 percent of all the PMR countries, 20 percent of PMR countries rely on an independent public holding entity.

21. For public service obligations rendered by the SOEs, the European Commission regards a rate of return on capital that does not exceed the relevant swap rate plus a premium of 100 basis points as reasonable.

22. Based on 25 cases, as disclosed by the European Commission.

23. ReGas, the national general registry of state aid, which should include information on all the state aid measures granted in Romania, is not available to third parties (private individuals, professionals, or companies) and can be accessed only by the Romanian Competition Council and the institutions which are involved in granting state aid.

24. There are 12 illegal state aid cases according to the EC. These include seven cases between 2015 and 2016: two cases of state aid to Cluj-Napoca Airport and Wizz Air, and to Târgu Mureş Airport, Wizz Air, and other airlines; three cases that involve Hidroelectrica for alleged preferential tariffs with electricity traders, thermoelectricity sellers, and industrial producers; preferential electricity tariffs for ArcelorMittal Galaţi; and preferential electricity tariffs for ALRO Slatina. There were five cases between 2017 and 2018: aid to Oltchim; aid to Viorel and Ioan Micula; alleged aid to SOE CFR Marfă; aid to SOE CE Hunedoara, and aid for restructuring of SOE National Uranium Company. The European Commission competition cases can be found at http://ec.europa.eu/competition/elojade/isef/index.cfm.

25. For more information, see the European Commission's "State Aid Scoreboard 2018," http://ec.europa.eu/competition/state_aid/scoreboard/index_en.html.

26. For more information, see the European Commission's State Aid Case SA.43785 (2018/C) (ex 2015/PN, ex 2018/NN)—Romania: Restructuring aid to Complexul Energetic Hunedoara, http://ec.europa.eu/competition/elojade/isef/case_details.cfm?proc_code=3_SA_43785.

27. For more information, see the European Commission's State Aid Case SA.43549—Alleged aid to CFR Marfă, http://ec.europa.eu/competition/elojade/isef/case_details.cfm?proc_code=3_SA_43549.

28. When the state acts as a *regulator*, it supervises and controls economic agents, which supply products and services. The state does that through the exercise of legal powers—control regulation—but without directly interfering in the market. When the state acts as an *economic agent*, it assumes a direct participation in the market by supplying goods and services through an SOE.

29. These 22 companies set up in 2017 operate across sectors that include travel arrangements, graveyard administration, leisure activities, "electricity and heat production and supply, public lighting, hospital management, construction, security, advertising space management, infrastructure projects consultancy, road management, parking management, and even taxi

services" (Romania Insider 2018a). See the list of the 22 public companies at "Home Municipal," City of Bucharest, http://www.pmb.ro/institutii/primaria/societati_comerciale/holding_mun _buc.php.

REFERENCES

ANRE (Romanian Energy Regulatory Authority). 2017. *National Report 2016*. Bucharest: ANRE. https://www.ceer.eu/documents/104400/5988265/C17_NR_Romania-EN.pdf /f91e100d-0e28-fd97-2c18-719d1993c1e1.

Busu, M., and C. Busu. 2015. "The Liberalization Process of the Railway Sector in Romania and Some Infringement Case Studies." In *Proceedings of the 9th International Management Conference: Management and Innovation for Competitive Advantage*, edited by I. Popa, C. Dobrin, and C. N. Ciocoiu, 532–40. Bucharest: Bucharest University of Economic Studies.

Monti, G. 2007. *EC Competition Law*. Cambridge, UK: Cambridge University Press.

MPF (Ministry of Public Finance). 2017. *Raport Privind Activitatea Întreprinderilor Publice în Anul 2016 (Annual Report on State-Owned Enterprises 2016)*. Bucharest: MPF.

OECD (Organisation for Economic Co-operation and Development). 2005. *OECD Guidelines on Corporate Governance of State-Owned Enterprises*. Paris: OECD Publishing.

——. 2009a. "Competition and the Financial Crisis." OECD, Paris.

——. 2009b. "State-Owned Enterprises and the Principle of Competitive Neutrality." OECD Policy Roundtables, OECD, Paris.

——. 2009c. "State Owned Enterprises and the Principle of Competitive Neutrality." OECD Policy Roundtables, OECD, Paris.

——. 2012. *Competitive Neutrality: Maintaining a Level Playing Field between Public and Private Business*. Paris: OECD Publishing.

——. 2018. "Experience and Best Practice: Applying the Principles of Competitive Neutrality." World Bank Group–Korean Development Institute SOE Reforms and Shared Prosperity Workshop. Seoul, March 27, 2018.

Pop, G., T. Ore Monago, G. Gavriloiu, and M. Iootty. 2019. "Competition and Government Interventions in Romania: An Assessment with Focus on Product Market Regulations and Competitive Neutrality." Unpublished document, Markets and Competition Global Team, World Bank, Washington, DC.

RFC (Romanian Fiscal Council). 2018. *Analiza performanţei economico-financiare a companiilor de stat din România în anul 2017. (Analysis of the Economic and Financial Performance of State-Owned Companies in Romania in 2017)*. Bucharest: RFC. http://www.consiliulfiscal.ro.

Romanian Government. 2019. *Strategia Fiscal-Bugetară pentru perioada 2019–2021. (Fiscal-Budget Strategy for the Period 2019–2021)*. Bucharest: Romanian Government.

Romania Insider. 2018a. "Private Sector: Bucharest Municipal Companies' Activity Distorts Competition." April 3. https://www.romania-insider.com/coalition-romania-development -municipal-companies.

——. 2018b. "Romanian State-owned Airline TAROM Sees EUR 38 mln Losses in 2017." June 7. https://www.romania-insider.com/tarom-losses-2017-2.

van Miert, K. 2000. "Liberalization of the Economy of the European Union: The Game Is Not (Yet) Over." In *The Liberalization of State Monopolies in the European Union and Beyond*, edited by Damien Geradin. Alphen aan den Rijn, the Netherlands: Kluwer Law International.

World Bank. Forthcoming. *Markets and Competition Policy Assessment Toolkit*. Washington, DC: World Bank.

4 Romania's Human Capital Deficit

This chapter examines the human capital that children in Romania start with, focusing on differences across regions. The analysis uses the Human Capital Index, which measures the amount of health and education that a child born today is expected to achieve by adulthood. There are widespread differences across counties: children living in Bucharest-Ilfov, with the highest human capital indicator, have human capital levels similar to those in Bulgaria or Greece, while those living in the worst performing counties have levels equivalent to those in Tonga or Tunisia. The analysis emphasizes the need to focus on lagging regions and groups to support the next steps of Romania's human development trajectory.[1]

To counteract its demographic challenges, Romania needs to raise the productive potential of children and youth entering the labor market. Romania's workforce is shrinking and aging rapidly, reflecting declining fertility and emigration (figure 4.1). The Romanian education system is currently not equipped to face the challenges that this declining stock of workers places on the labor force. Despite the government's efforts to reduce the rate of early school-leaving (ESL) among 18-to-24-year-olds, it has remained largely unchanged in the past decade. In 2018, the ESL rate in Romania stood at 16.4 percent, the third highest in the EU and slightly above the 2007 rate of 15.9 percent.[2] In addition, the number of tertiary education graduates entering the labor force decreased by nearly 30 percent between 2014 and 2017, further contracting the supply of skilled workforce.[3] These deficiencies of the education system, combined with mass migration, result in an insufficient availability of both medium- and high-skilled workers, in turn contributing to labor market tightening and to unit labor costs rising by almost 10 percent per year since 2016 (EC 2019).

Striking gaps across urban and rural areas as well as across regions of Romania point to the substantial potential to raise human capital to meet the needs of its demographic transition. In 2015, Romania's public spending on nontertiary education accounted for less than 2 percent of gross domestic product, nearly half of the EU-28 average. In 2015, Romania had some of the lowest shares of top performers in the Program for International Student Assessment (PISA) in the world. The difference in PISA 2015 performance among students from the top and bottom socioeconomic quintiles was equivalent to three years of schooling, among the highest in Europe. The contrasts between better- and worse-off students is highly linked to where students live: the majority of bottom quintile students are found in

FIGURE 4.1

Romania's workforce is both shrinking and aging

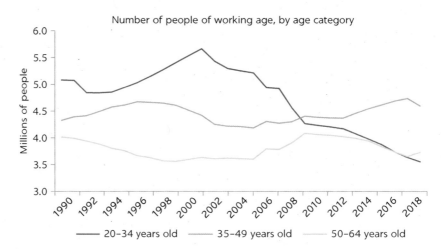

Number of people of working age, by age category

Source: Eurostat (database), European Commission, Brussels, https://ec.europa.eu/eurostat/data
/database.
Note: Eurostat database indicator lfst_lmbpcited, EU/EFTA citizens of working age who usually reside
in another EU/EFTA country.

rural areas, which have a significantly higher incidence of poverty than urban areas. Students in these areas face greater challenges in completing their schooling, with early school-leaving rates in rural areas of 25.4 percent, six times greater than those seen in urban areas (4.2 percent).[4] Regional variations are also marked, ranging from 21.3 percent in the South East region to 8 in Bucharest-Ilfov. These differences signal a strong relationship between a student's socioeconomic background and her educational outcomes.

This chapter highlights the spatial variation in the human capital opportunities that children in Romania start with. To do so, it uses the Human Capital Index (HCI), recently developed by the World Bank (2018b). The index measures the amount of health and the quantity and quality of education that a child born today is expected to achieve by the age of 18, given the risks to poor health and education that prevail in the place where that child currently resides. The analysis will subsequently shift to a more detailed examination of the dimensions of human capital along which the system is underperforming, taking an equity lens to look across regions and by sex. As such, the overall HCI is explored, as well as its three subcomponents, at the NUTS3[5] subnational (county) level. The analysis identifies the dimensions of human capital that are lagging and takes an equity lens to understand the supply- and demand-side factors that can explain why the outcomes and productive potential of children in some regions fall so far behind those of others. A deeper policy diagnosis of the education system that may be linked to these outcome variations is discussed in chapter 5.

The analysis shows widespread differences in the HCI across counties and highlights those counties that have fallen behind the most in terms of the human capital accumulation of their children. There is also a marked relationship between the HCI and county-level poverty rates (World Bank 2016): children born in poorer counties are expected to be less productive than they would have been even if they received full health and a complete education.[6] The years of schooling a child born today can expect to achieve by the age of 18, given the current enrollment rates that prevail in the county where the child lives, significantly decrease in all counties when adjusted by the quality of education. In general, quality of education explains low HCI performance across the board, while years of schooling drives most of the HCI differences seen between counties. Finally, large inequities in the HCI exist between rural counties and better-off and more densely populated urban ones, mainly driven by differential access to quality education. The relationship between a child's educational prospects, her socioeconomic background, and the locality in which she is born is linked to the high intergenerational persistence of educational attainment. Reducing these inequalities in access to basic health and education opportunities will likely translate into lower income inequality and poverty in the years to come and allow Romania's children to achieve their full productivity potential in adulthood.

MEASURING ROMANIA'S HUMAN CAPITAL

The Human Capital Index[7]

The World Bank Group's HCI, launched in October 2018, measures the amount of health and the quantity and quality of education that a child born today is expected to achieve by the age of 18, given the risks to poor health and poor education that prevail in the country where that child currently resides. The HCI follows the trajectory of a child born today from birth to adulthood by integrating five indicators grouped into three components of the HCI (figure 4.2).[8]

The first component of the HCI measures whether children survive from birth to five years of age. This component of the HCI captures a very unfortunate reality: not all children born today will be alive when human capital starts to accumulate through formal education. As such, the subcomponent is measured as the complement of the under-5 mortality rate.

The second component of the HCI refers to learning-adjusted expected years of schooling, which combines both the quantity and the quality of formal education. There is ample consensus regarding the indicators to be used for measuring both elements. The quantity of education is measured as the number of years of schooling a child born today can expect to achieve at the age of 18, given the current enrollment rates that prevail in the country where the child resides. Expected years of schooling are adjusted by repetition rates. The maximum possible value for the expected years of schooling would be 14 if a child starts preschool at four years of age.

The quality of education is measured using harmonized test scores in units of the Trends in International Mathematics and Science Study (TIMSS) testing program. For this, a harmonization effort was followed using international student achievement tests from several multicountry testing programs (Patrinos and Angrist 2018). These scores include the three major international testing

FIGURE 4.2
The HCI is based on three components

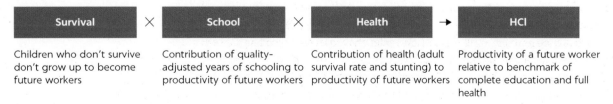

Source: The Human Capital Project (World Bank 2018a).
Note: HCI = Human Capital Index.

programs—TIMSS, the Progress in International Reading Literacy Study, and PISA—as well as the major regional testing programs. Learning-adjusted expected years of education are obtained by multiplying expected years of education by the ratio of harmonized test scores to 625, which corresponds to the TIMSS benchmark of advanced achievement.[9]

The third component of the HCI refers to health. Unlike for education, there is less consensus regarding the indicators to be used to capture the expected health outcomes experienced by a child born today. The HCI uses two indicators as proxies for health outcomes. The first one is the adult survival rate, which is measured as the share of 15-year-olds who survive to age 60 and which captures a range of health outcomes that a child born today would experience in adulthood, given the current health situation in the country. The second indicator is one minus the stunting rate (that is, one minus the share of children under five years of age who are below normal height for their age). Stunting captures the risks of good health faced by children born today, which have serious consequences in adulthood. Stunting rates are not available for all EU countries (including Romania) and therefore are ignored in the present analysis.

The indicator reduces human capital to a single summary metric. However, all the components of the HCI have an intrinsic value that makes them difficult to combine in an index. To do so, the five indicators in the three components are first converted into their corresponding contribution to future productivity relative to a benchmark, and then they are combined into a single HCI by multiplying all survival, health, and education contributions to future productivity. Health and education are converted into productivity units using rigorous evidence on returns to health (0.65 for the case of adult survival rate and 0.35 for nonstunting rates) and education (0.08). For the case of under-5 survival rate, the productivity conversion is straight: children who do not survive until they enter formal education never become productive adults. As such, expected productivity is reduced by a factor equal to the infant survival rate.

The HCI is measured relative to the benchmark situation of full health (no stunting and 100 percent adult survival rate) and complete education potential (14 years of high-quality formal education by 18 years of age). As such, the HCI ranges between 0 and 1. An HCI equal to x means that, if current health and education condition persists, the productivity as an adult worker of a child born today will be a fraction x of what she could be in the benchmark situation of full education and health.

ESTIMATING THE SUBNATIONAL HCI FOR ROMANIA

The main objective of this analysis is to highlight spatial variation in human capital opportunities that children in Romania start with. To do so, we follow the proposed methodology for the World Bank's HCI to estimate the same index at the county (NUTS3) level in Romania. This section presents the conceptual framework on how to measure the components across regions of the country. The source of the information used to estimate the subnational HCI is described in annex 4A.

The survival rate of children under five years of age is measured as the complement of the under-5 mortality rate. Mortality rates come from Romania's National Institute for Statistics 2017 Tempo dataset, available at the national and county levels.

Assuming a child begins preschool at age 4, the expected years of schooling are defined as the sum of enrollment rates, by age, from 4 to 17 years of age. As such, the indicator ranges from 0 to 14 years. The enrollment rate used in this study is the repetition-adjusted total net enrollment rate.[10] Enrollment numbers come from National Institute for Statistics 2017 Tempo dataset, while repetition numbers come from 2014–19 Integrated Education Information System (SIIIR). Both enrollment and repetition data are available at the national and county level, and the data are broken down as well for urban-rural and boy-girl categories. However, the net enrollment rates are calculated based on two registries from the Tempo dataset: (i) residential population (linked to children's home address) and (ii) enrollment registry (linked to children's school address). Combining these figures for Bucharest yields net enrollment rates higher than 100 percent, mainly because children from Ilfov—the predominantly rural county surrounding Bucharest—are likely to be attending schools in Bucharest. To address this issue, the Bucharest and Ilfov counties are grouped together as one throughout the analysis.[11]

To enable the subnational analysis of harmonized test scores, this analysis draws on data from the 2014–19 SIIIR that, again, are broken down for national and county levels as well as for urban-rural and boy-girl categories. The national examination is taken in the eighth grade and includes math and the Romanian language. The two test scores are first averaged, then converted into TIMSS units—which correspond to approximately an average of 500 and a standard deviation across students of 100 points—and finally scaled up to match the mean PISA score in Romania (452).

Finally, the adult survival rate is estimated based on the prevailing patterns of death rates by age in the country. The number of deaths come from the National Institute for Statistics 2017 Tempo dataset and are available at the national and county level and for urban-rural and boy-girl categories. The probability of being nonstunted is not computed, due to the lack of relevant data.

LAGGING THE REST OF THE EU

Romania's HCI score is lowest in the EU.[12] Figure 4.3 presents the HCI scores for Romania and all EU countries. As can be seen, the HCI varies significantly among EU countries, with poorer member states performing lower on average.[13] Romania's score is the lowest of the EU countries. According to the HCI, given the current education and health conditions in Romania, a child born in the country is expected to be 60 percent as productive as an adult as she could be if she received complete education and full health.

Looking at the subcomponents of the HCI, Romania lags behind other

FIGURE 4.3

Romania's HCI score is the lowest among EU countries, 2017

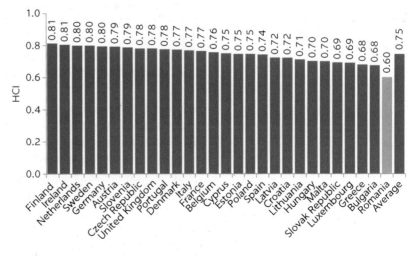

Source: The Human Capital Project (World Bank 2018a). Data are available at www.worldbank.org /humancapital.
Note: EU = European Union; HCI = Human Capital Index.

FIGURE 4.4

Subcomponents, in particular education, are also low compared with other EU countries, 2017

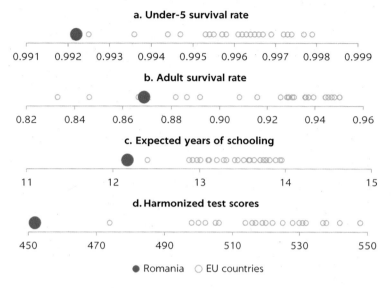

a. Under-5 survival rate

0.991   0.992   0.993   0.994   0.995   0.996   0.997   0.998   0.999

b. Adult survival rate

0.82   0.84   0.86   0.88   0.90   0.92   0.94   0.96

c. Expected years of schooling

11   12   13   14   15

d. Harmonized test scores

450   470   490   510   530   550

● Romania   ○ EU countries

Source: The Human Capital Project (World Bank 2018a). Data are available at www.worldbank.org/humancapital.
Note: EU = European Union.

EU countries. Figure 4.4 shows the distribution of all subcomponents for Romania and the rest of the EU countries in 2017. As can be observed in panel a of the figure (figure 4.4, panel a), differences among EU member states in child survival rates are relatively small, ranging from about 99.2 percent in Romania to about 99.8 percent in Slovenia and Finland. Although Romania is at the lower end of the distribution of EU countries, the difference represents an incremental loss to human capital productivity of about 0.8 percent relative to the benchmark situation of 100 percent child survival rate.

Greater variability is observed in adult survival rates in the EU, which range from around 83 percent in Lithuania to about 95 percent in Italy (figure 4.4, panel b). The adult survival rate in Romania is about 87 percent, one of the lowest among all EU countries. By using the share of 15-year-olds who will survive to 60 years old as a proxy for health, the potential productivity of a child born in Romania in 2017 would be about 92 percent of what it would be if she received full health.[14]

Romania is also at the bottom of the distribution of EU countries in terms of learning-adjusted expected years of education (figure 4.4, panels c and d). Expected years of schooling range from around 12 years in Romania to about 14 years in France, while harmonized test scores range from about 452 in Romania to about 548 in Finland. Combining the results for expected years of schooling (as a proxy for the quantity of education) and harmonized test scores (as proxy for its quality) reveals that the amount of human capital that a child born in Romania in 2017 will accumulate by the age of 18 translates to a productivity level of about 66 percent of what it would be if she received a full education.[15]

REGIONAL DISPARITIES ARE DRIVEN BY EDUCATION, MORE HUMAN CAPITAL FOR GIRLS, AND A WIDE URBAN-RURAL DIVIDE

There is a marked variability among all counties, even within the four macro and eight development regions. Figure 4.5 shows the overall HCI at the county level in Romania, grouped by macro (NUTS1 level) and development (NUTS2 level) regions.[16] A child born in Cluj county, located in the North West development region of the macroregion 1, is expected to be 65 percent as productive as an adult as she could be if she received full health and education. Meanwhile, a child born in Satu Mare, located in the same macro and development region, is expected to only be 53 percent as productive when compared to the benchmark. These differences are more pronounced between the counties located in different macro and/or development regions. For instance, a child born in Bucharest-Ilfov, located in macroregion 3, is expected to be 68 percent

FIGURE 4.5
Marked disparities in human capital exist across counties within Romania, 2017

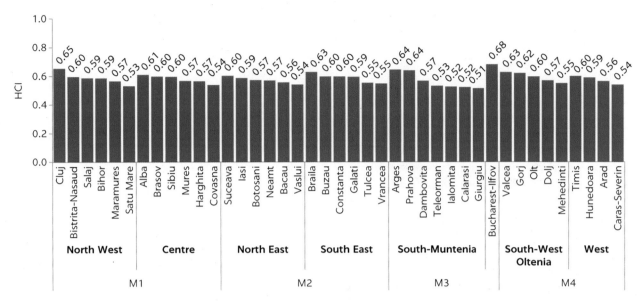

Sources: 2017 Tempo dataset, National Institute for Statistics, Bucharest, http://statistici.insse.ro:8077/tempo-online/#/pages/tables/insse-table; 2014–19 SIIIR (Integrated Information System of Education in Romania) dataset, Ministry of Education, Bucharest.
Note: M1, M2, M3, and M4 are macroregions 1, 2, 3, and 4, respectively. HCI = Human Capital Index.

as productive as an adult as she could be if she received full health and education, a productivity almost 20 percent higher compared to a child born in Giurgiu located in the development region of South-Muntenia also in the macroregion 3.

Children born in poorer counties are expected to be less productive than they would be if they received full health and education. Figure 4.6 presents the county-level HCI score and poverty rate using the national relative poverty line in 2011. A regression analysis reveals a high negative correlation between the poverty rate and the accumulation of human capital. For instance, Bucharest-Ilfov, the richest development region, with only 5 percent of its population living below the poverty line, has the highest HCI score (0.68), comparable to that of Bulgaria and Greece (0.68). On the other end, Botosani, the poorest county with about 44 percent of its population living below the poverty line, has one of the lowest HCI scores (0.57), comparable to that of Armenia (0.57), Kuwait (0.58), and the Kyrgyz Republic (0.58). Giurgiu has the lowest HCI score (0.51) among all counties in Romania, comparable to that of Tunisia (0.51), Tonga (0.51), and Kenya (0.52).

The HCI score in most of the counties is lower than that of Bulgaria, the country at the lower end of the HCI distribution among all EU countries, after Romania. Figure 4.7 shows the distribution of the overall HCI and all its subcomponents for all the counties within Romania, as well as for Bulgaria and Finland, the lowest and highest HCI among all EU countries, respectively. Except for Bucharest-Ilfov, the rest of the counties had a lower HCI than Bulgaria (0.68) in 2017 (figure 4.7, panel a).

Most of the counties within Romania have higher under-5 survival rates than Bulgaria, although the differences between counties are relatively small. In Romania, the survival rate of children under the age of 5 ranges from around 98.7 percent in Botosani to about 99.5 percent in Bucharest-Ilfov (figure 4.7,

FIGURE 4.6

There is a high negative correlation between HCI and poverty rates between counties

a. HCI by county, 2017

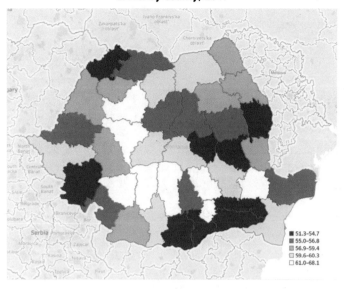

■ 51.3–54.7
■ 55.0–56.8
▨ 56.9–59.4
▫ 59.6–60.3
□ 61.0–68.1

b. Poverty rate by county, 2011

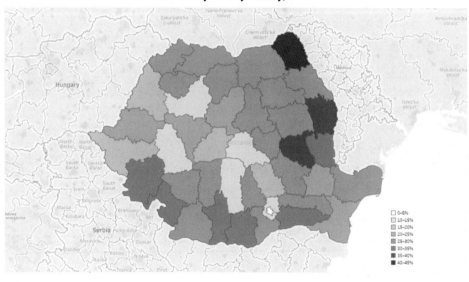

□ 0–5%
▫ 10–15%
▨ 15–20%
▨ 20–25%
■ 25–30%
■ 30–35%
■ 35–40%
■ 40–45%

c. Correlation between 2017 HCI and 2011 poverty rate

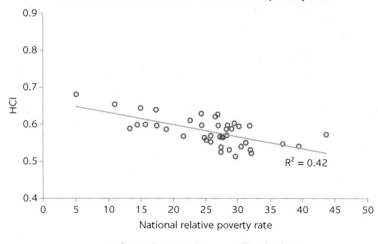

$R^2 = 0.42$

HCI (y-axis)

National relative poverty rate (x-axis)

○ Romanian counties ⸺ Fitted values

Sources: 2017 Tempo dataset, National Institute for Statistics, Bucharest, http://statistici.insse.ro:8077/tempo-online/#/pages/tables/insse-table; 2014–19 SIIIR (Integrated Information System of Education in Romania) dataset, Ministry of Education, Bucharest; and World Bank 2016.
Note: The figure examines the relationship between county level poverty rates (x-axis), using the national at risk of poverty threshold from 2011 and HCI indicators (y-axis). The blue circles represent county level poverty and HCI indicators. HCI = Human Capital Index; R^2 = R-squared.

panel b). This implies an incremental loss to productivity of about 0.7 percent for a child born in Botosani county compared to a child born in Bucharest-Ilfov region.

Adult survival rates present greater variability, and many of the counties perform better than Bulgaria. The share of 15-year-olds who will survive to the age of 60 ranges from around 81.5 percent in Vaslui to about 90.1 percent in Valcea (figure 4.7, panel c). As such, the potential productivity of a child born in Vaslui in 2017 is about 5 percent lower compared to Valcea.

Education largely explains the low HCI score across all counties. As can be seen in panels d and e of figure 4.7, the learning-adjusted expected years of schooling in all Romanian counties is lower than that in Bulgaria. In 2017, learning-adjusted years of education ranged from about 7.0 years in Giurgiu to around 10.2 years in Bucharest-Ilfov. These results imply that the potential productivity of a child born in Giurgiu is about 16 percent lower than that of a child born Bucharest-Ilfov.

There are large learning gaps with great variability across counties. Figure 4.8 presents the learning-adjusted expected years of education by county in 2017. The horizontal axis shows the expected years of education, while the vertical axis adjusts these expected years of schooling according to the quality of the education received. All dots are below the 45-degree line, which means that quality of education negatively affects learning. All these learning gaps are large, and the analysis points to a marked variability among all Romanian counties. For instance, a child born in Harghita, the county with the largest learning gap, is expected to complete about 12.5 years of schooling by age 18. However, this would be equivalent to about

FIGURE 4.7

Education explains low performance at the county level

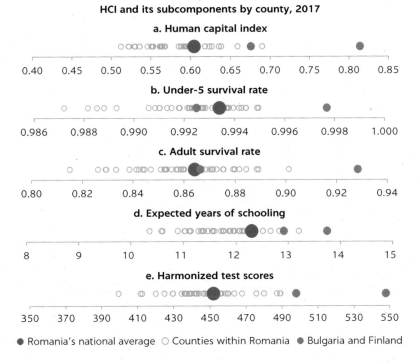

HCI and its subcomponents by county, 2017

a. Human capital index

| 0.40 | 0.45 | 0.50 | 0.55 | 0.60 | 0.65 | 0.70 | 0.75 | 0.80 | 0.85 |

b. Under-5 survival rate

| 0.986 | 0.988 | 0.990 | 0.992 | 0.994 | 0.996 | 0.998 | 1.000 |

c. Adult survival rate

| 0.80 | 0.82 | 0.84 | 0.86 | 0.88 | 0.90 | 0.92 | 0.94 |

d. Expected years of schooling

| 8 | 9 | 10 | 11 | 12 | 13 | 14 | 15 |

e. Harmonized test scores

| 350 | 370 | 390 | 410 | 430 | 450 | 470 | 490 | 510 | 530 | 550 |

● Romania's national average ○ Counties within Romania ● Bulgaria and Finland

Sources: 2017 Tempo dataset, National Institute for Statistics, Bucharest, http://statistici.insse.ro:8077 /tempo-online/#/pages/tables/insse-table; 2014–19 SIIIR (Integrated Information System of Education in Romania) dataset, Ministry of Education, Bucharest.
Note: HCI = Human Capital Index.

FIGURE 4.8

Expected years of schooling decrease in all the counties when adjusted for quality of learning, and there is high variability in the reduction

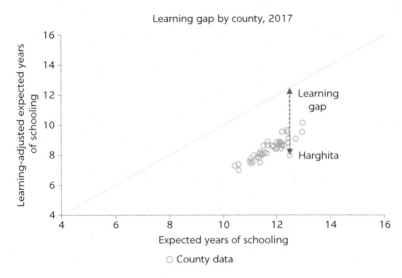

Learning gap by county, 2017

Sources: 2017 Tempo dataset, National Institute for Statistics, Bucharest, http://statistici.insse.ro:8077/tempo-online/#/pages/tables/insse-table; 2014–19 SIIIR (Integrated Information System of Education in Romania) dataset, Ministry of Education, Bucharest.

8 years when expected years of education are adjusted for quality, which represents a learning gap of about 4.5 years. On the other end, Braila has the lowest learning gap. Expected years of schooling decrease from about 12.2 years to an equivalent of around 9.6 years: a learning gap of about 2.6 years.

In every county in Romania, the HCI gap is mainly driven by learning-adjusted years of education. Figure 4.9 presents a decomposition that sheds light on the relative contribution of every component (child survival, health, and education) to the productivity gap in every county. The loss of productivity due to Romania's performance on health indicators (child and adult survival rates) is quite similar among counties: on average, about 8 percent. Harmonized test scores explain most of the gap in all the counties. On average, the productivity loss due to low quality of education is around 22 percent, and it ranges from 18 percent in Braila to about 29 percent in Harghita, the counties with the lowest and highest learning gaps, respectively. Finally, the contribution of the expected years of schooling to the HCI gap is greater for counties with lower HCI; the HCI gap would have remained fairly constant if expected years of education were at the HCI frontier of 14 years in all counties.

A simulation exercise suggests that significant investment in education is needed—an average of 2.1 quality-adjusted years of schooling—for most counties to reach the HCI levels of Bucharest-Ilfov. Figure 4.10 shows the change in learning-adjusted expected years of education that is required to close the

FIGURE 4.9

The gap with respect to full health and education is driven mainly by test scores

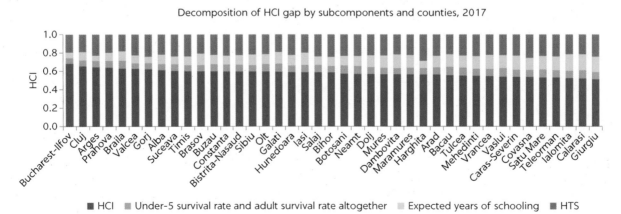

Decomposition of HCI gap by subcomponents and counties, 2017

■ HCI ■ Under-5 survival rate and adult survival rate altogether ■ Expected years of schooling ■ HTS

Sources: 2017 Tempo dataset, National Institute for Statistics, Bucharest, http://statistici.insse.ro:8077/tempo-online/#/pages/tables/insse-table; 2014–19 SIIIR (Integrated Information System of Education in Romania) dataset, Ministry of Education, Bucharest.
Note: The figure shows the Shapley decomposition of the HCI gap (the difference between the actual HCI and the full health and education hypothetical situation). HCI = Human Capital Index; HTS = harmonized test scores.

gap with Bucharest-Ilfov, the highest HCI in the country (figure 4.5). On average, more than 2 quality-adjusted expected years of schooling are needed. These results vary from county to county. For instance, Giurgiu would require about 3.5 years of additional learning-adjusted years of education to catch up with Bucharest-Ilfov. On the other hand, Cluj would require about half a year of quality-adjusted years of education to close that gap.

Girls have higher human capital than boys. The HCI can be divided into girls and boys whenever data on all subcomponents of the HCI are available. In Romania, the productivity of girls is about 6 percent higher than that for boys (World Bank 2018a). This is also true for all counties within Romania. Figure 4.11

FIGURE 4.10

On average, more than two years of additional schooling is required to close the gap with Bucharest-Ilfov

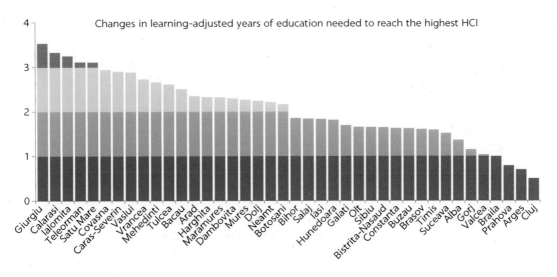

Sources: 2017 Tempo dataset, National Institute for Statistics, Bucharest, http://statistici.insse.ro:8077/tempo-online/#/pages/tables/insse-table; 2014–19 SIIIR (Integrated Information System of Education in Romania) dataset, Ministry of Education, Bucharest.
Note: HCI = Human Capital Index.

FIGURE 4.11

Adult survival rates explain most of the gender gap

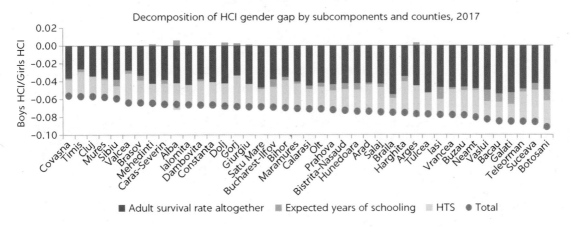

Sources: 2017 Tempo dataset, National Institute for Statistics, Bucharest, http://statistici.insse.ro:8077/tempo-online/#/pages/tables /insse-table; 2014–19 SIIIR (Integrated Information System of Education in Romania) dataset, Ministry of Education, Bucharest.
Note: The figure shows the Shapley decomposition of the HCI gap (the difference between girls' HCI and boys' HCI). HCI = Human Capital Index; HTS = harmonized test scores.

FIGURE 4.12

The Human Capital Index is positively correlated with the level of urbanization of counties

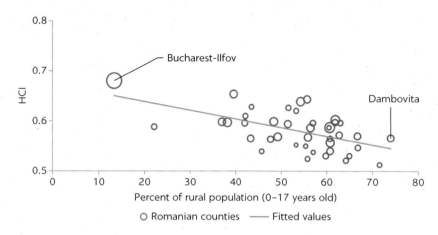

○ Romanian counties — Fitted values

Sources: 2017 Tempo dataset, National Institute for Statistics, Bucharest, http://statistici.insse.ro:8077/tempo-online/#/pages/tables/insse-table; 2014–19 SIIIR (Integrated Information System of Education in Romania) dataset, Ministry of Education, Bucharest.
Note: The size of the bubbles represents the total population (0–17 years old) in every county. HCI = Human Capital Index.

presents a decomposition that allows us to understand the contribution of every HCI subcomponent (adult survival rate, expected years of schooling, and harmonized test scores)[17] to the HCI gender gap. Girls' HCI is higher than boys' HCI in all counties: about 7 percent, on average. HCI gender gaps are more prominent in adult survival rates; 15-year-old girls are more likely than boys to survive to age 60 in all counties. The same happens with learning-adjusted expected years of schooling, mainly because girls are doing better in test scores. However, gender gaps due to expected years of schooling and test scores are relatively lower than those of survival rates. As such, health accounts for most of the gender gap in all counties. On average, the gender productivity gap due to gender differences in health outcomes is about 4.2 percentage points, while it is about 2.6 percent due to harmonized test scores.

Children born in more rural counties are expected to be less productive in adulthood than they would be if they were born in more urban ones. Large inequities in access to basic health and education opportunities exist between urban and rural areas of Romania. Figure 4.12 shows the HCI index and the level of urbanization of every county, defined as the percentage of the rural population ages 0 to 17 years old. There is a negative correlation between the HCI and the percentage of rural population (R^2=0.30); the HCI is considerably lower for more rural counties. For instance, Bucharest-Ilfov is the most urban development region of the country, with only about 15 percent of its population ages 0 to 17 years old residing in rural areas, and has the highest HCI (0.68). On the other end, Dambovita is the least urban county in Romania, with around 74 percent of its population ages 0 to 17 years old residing in rural areas, and has one of the lowest HCI (0.57).

Inequality of opportunities is a problem also in terms of the number of children who lack access to basic health and education services. While the Bucharest-Ilfov region HCI performs remarkably better on the spectrum, it only accounts for a small share of total population ages 0–17 years in the country (about 11 percent). The other 90 percent of children are almost evenly distributed in the rest of the counties, further alerting to inequities in access to quality public services and the likely productivity and income gaps later in life.

Harmonized test scores, the subcomponent that explains most of the HCI gap (see figure 4.8), are also highly associated with the level of urbanization of the Romanian counties. Figure 4.13 shows average harmonized test scores by county in rural and urban areas. Scores in urban areas are much higher than in rural areas in all counties in Romania. For instance, the rural area in Harghita has the lowest average harmonized test score (377), contrasting with the urban areas in Braila and Iasi that have the highest harmonized test scores (507). Similarly, harmonized test scores in the Bucharest county are on par with those in Iceland; the rest of urban Romania has

FIGURE 4.13

Harmonized tests scores are higher in urban areas

HCI by areas and county, 2017

Source: 2014–19 SIIIR (Integrated Information System of Education in Romania) dataset, Ministry of Education, Bucharest.
Note: M1, M2, M3, and M4 are macroregions 1, 2, 3, and 4, respectively. B-I = Bucharest-Ilfov; HCI = Human Capital Index.

a slightly lower performance (similar to that of Ukraine), while rural Romania as a whole has similar test scores to those of Senegal.

More interestingly, some rural areas have higher scores than some urban areas in other counties, even within the same macro and development regions. For instance, average harmonized test scores in the rural area of Prahova (454) are higher than the average harmonized tests scores in the urban area of Giurgiu (446).

Although disparities in health indicators are not a leading driver of regional variation in the HCI, regional discrepancies in some indicators can be seen. Average life expectancy at birth differs between urban and rural areas, with variations observed between regions: for example, the rural-urban difference in the West region is 0.8 years, compared to three years in Bucharest-Ilfov. Infant mortality (under-1 mortality) also differs across regions, ranging from 6.0 to 6.5 per 1,000 births in Bucharest and Cluj compared to highest rates of 16.0 and 19.4 per 1,000 births in in Mehedinți and Salaj, respectively. In several counties (Cluj, Buzau, Dolj, Constanta, Salaj, and Vrancea), infant mortality rates in rural areas are as high as two to three times the rate in urban ones.

Access to public health services varies between urban and rural areas, contributing to variation in health care outcomes between areas. A slightly larger share of the rural than urban population is not covered by public health insurance, with 21 percent uninsured compared to 18 percent of urban residents. Similarly, of the 211 local public administration authorities that do not have a local family physician practice, over 90 percent are rural. The coverage of medical care providers also varies significantly between urban and rural areas, with urban areas having a density of 0.73 family doctors per 1,000 residents and rural areas having 0.5 per 1,000. Finally, the Roma population (about 5 percent of the country's total population) is less likely to be enrolled with a family medicine practice; up to 9 percent of Roma are not registered with a family physician, which is double the rate in the general population. The combination of these factors implies that rural areas have a significantly lower supply of family physicians than urban areas, contributing to geographic disparities in access to basic health care and, thus, human capital opportunities.

The strong relationship between the HCI, poverty rates, and the level of urbanization of every county is clearly mirrored in other assessments showing that the background of students plays a fundamental role in their education outcomes—and particularly more so in Romania than in other EU countries. The low spending on essential public services, most notably education, means that a child's background has a pivotal impact on her human capital outcomes (World Bank 2018a). Romania was found to have the 22nd highest level of intergenerational persistence of education among 189 countries—implying that a student's final educational achievement is highly linked to her parents', limiting the role that education plays as a great equalizer of opportunities.[18] Furthermore, we see that children who are more likely to live in poor and rural locations are more likely to leave school early (World Bank 2019). The combination of these two factors alerts us to the notion that the Romanian education system is struggling to provide equal opportunities to children of different backgrounds.

In chapter 5, the analysis focuses in on the factors that feed into the large disparities in learning outcomes across regions and urban and rural areas. Significant investment in education is needed in most of the counties to reach HIC levels in Bucharest-Ilfov: more than two years of quality-adjusted years of schooling on average (see figure 4.9). Chapter 5 proposes a set of additional policy solutions aimed at closing the gaps between areas and counties and at reducing the high degree of intergenerational persistence of education in the country. We do this by looking at learning through a framework developed in the 2018 *World Development Report* (World Bank 2018b), notably examining school inputs and the situation faced at a system level as well as by learners, teachers, and school management.

ANNEX 4A: HUMAN CAPITAL INDEX FOR ROMANIA: DATA AND METHODOLOGY

The HCI results from aggregating contributions of survival, health, and education to future productivity relative to the situation of full health and complete education, as follows:

$$\text{HCI} = (1 - \text{U-5 SR}) * e^{\phi\left(\text{EYS}*\frac{\text{HTS}}{625}-14\right)} e^{\gamma(\text{ASR}-1)},$$

where *HCI* refers to Human Capital Index; *U-5 SR* and *ASR* refer to under-5 survival rate and adult survival rate; *EYS* refers to expected years of schooling; *HTS* refers to harmonized test scores; ϕ is the return to education; and γ is the return to health (using ASR). The benchmark for complete education is 14, for full education is 1, and for harmonized test score is 625.

Data used

Table 4A.1 presents the data sources by HCI component.

TABLE 4A.1 **Data sources**

COMPONENT	DATA SOURCE
Under-5 survival rate	2017 Tempo dataset, National Institute for Statistics, Bucharest, http://statistici.insse.ro:8077/tempo-online/#/pages/tables/insse-table
School enrollment	2017 Tempo dataset, National Institute for Statistics, Bucharest, http://statistici.insse.ro:8077/tempo-online/#/pages/tables/insse-table
Test scores	2014–19 SIIIR (Integrated Information System of Education in Romania) dataset, Ministry of Education, Bucharest
	2015 PISA for scaling up National Examinations
Adult survival rate	2017 Tempo dataset, National Institute for Statistics, Bucharest, http://statistici.insse.ro:8077/tempo-online/#/pages/tables/insse-table
Additional analysis	2011 Poverty map for county-level poverty rates, The Human Capital Project (World Bank 2018a) for country-level Human Capital Index, 2014–19 Integrated Education Information System for repetition rates

HCI at the national level

Table 4A.2 replicates the national HCI in Romania and its subcomponents, using data at the county level and comparing results with those of the Human Capital Project (World Bank 2018a).

TABLE 4A.2 **Comparative data**

COMPONENTS	HUMAN CAPITAL PROJECT			OWN NATIONAL ESTIMATES		
	TOTAL	BOYS	GIRLS	TOTAL	BOYS	GIRLS
Human Capital Index	0.60	0.58	0.63	0.59	0.56	0.63
Under-5 survival rate	0.992	0.991	0.993	0.993	0.993	0.993
Adult survival rate	0.869	0.818	0.922	0.864	0.812	0.921
Expected years of schooling	12.2	12.1	12.2	11.9	11.8	12.0
Harmonized test scores	452	448	456	452	437	466

Note: The National Institute for Statistics 2017 Tempo dataset does not disaggregate under-5 mortality rates by gender at the county level. Therefore, girls' and boys' under-5 survival rates in the table are equal to county averages.

HCI at the subnational level

Table 4A.3 presents the HCI and its subcomponents at the national and subnational level.

TABLE 4A.3 **HCI breakdown by administrative components**

MACROREGIONS, DEVELOPMENT REGIONS, AND COUNTIES	HCI	U-5 SR	ASR	EYS	HTS
TOTAL	0.59	0.993	0.86	11.9	452
Macroregion 1	0.59	0.993	0.87	11.9	445
North West	0.59	0.993	0.87	11.9	449
Bihor	0.59	0.994	0.87	12.2	434
Bistrita-Nasaud	0.60	0.992	0.87	12.1	451
Cluj	0.65	0.995	0.89	12.4	487
Maramures	0.57	0.992	0.86	11.4	443
Satu Mare	0.53	0.993	0.83	11.1	425
Salaj	0.59	0.990	0.86	12.3	439
Centre	0.58	0.993	0.87	11.8	441
Alba	0.61	0.994	0.88	12.1	459
Brasov	0.60	0.993	0.88	11.7	463
Covasna	0.54	0.992	0.86	11.4	412
Harghita	0.57	0.994	0.87	12.5	400
Mures	0.57	0.993	0.87	11.5	440
Sibiu	0.60	0.994	0.88	11.8	456
Macroregion 2	0.58	0.993	0.85	11.8	451
North East	0.57	0.993	0.84	11.8	448
Bacau	0.56	0.993	0.83	11.4	449
Botosani	0.57	0.989	0.84	12.0	442
Iasi	0.59	0.994	0.85	11.5	468
Neamt	0.57	0.995	0.83	12.0	438
Suceava	0.60	0.993	0.87	12.4	444
Vaslui	0.54	0.995	0.82	11.3	436
South East	0.59	0.992	0.85	11.9	457
Braila	0.63	0.992	0.85	12.2	489
Buzau	0.60	0.995	0.85	12.2	454
Constanta	0.60	0.992	0.87	12.2	449
Galati	0.59	0.992	0.84	11.7	476
Tulcea	0.55	0.993	0.83	11.5	437
Vrancea	0.55	0.990	0.86	11.0	438
Macroregion 3	0.61	0.994	0.87	12.1	465
South-Muntenia	0.58	0.993	0.86	11.6	450
Arges	0.64	0.995	0.88	13.0	460
Calarasi	0.52	0.989	0.83	10.6	437
Dambovita	0.57	0.993	0.88	11.2	448
Giurgiu	0.51	0.994	0.84	10.6	413
Ialomita	0.52	0.993	0.84	10.4	437
Prahova	0.64	0.993	0.87	12.4	480
Teleorman	0.53	0.994	0.84	11.1	420
Bucharest-Ilfov	0.68	0.995	0.89	13.0	489

continued

TABLE 4A.3, *continued*

MACROREGIONS, DEVELOPMENT REGIONS, AND COUNTIES	HCI	U-5 SR	ASR	EYS	HTS
Macroregion 4	0.58	0.993	0.87	11.9	444
South-West Oltenia	0.59	0.993	0.87	12.0	448
Dolj	0.57	0.994	0.86	11.6	442
Gorj	0.62	0.993	0.88	12.7	447
Mehedinti	0.55	0.993	0.86	11.4	430
Olt	0.60	0.993	0.85	12.0	460
Valcea	0.63	0.991	0.90	12.4	456
West	0.58	0.993	0.87	11.8	440
Arad	0.56	0.994	0.85	11.6	436
Caras-Severin	0.54	0.990	0.86	11.0	430
Hunedoara	0.59	0.994	0.87	11.9	449
Timis	0.60	0.993	0.88	12.2	443

Note: ASR = adult survival rate; EYS = expected years of schooling; HCI = Human Capital Index; HTS = harmonized test scores; U-5 SR = under-5 survival rate.

NOTES

1. This chapter is authored by Leonardo Lucchetti, Reena Badiani-Magnusson, Zohar Ianovici, with contributions from Vincent Belinga.
2. Eurostat indicator edat_lfse_14, "Early Leavers from Education and Training by Sex and Labour Status," http://appsso.eurostat.ec.europa.eu/nui/show.do?dataset=edat_lfse_14&lang=en.
3. Eurostat indicator educ_uoe_grad02, "Graduates by Education Level, Programme Orientation, Sex and Field of Education," http://appsso.eurostat.ec.europa.eu/nui/show.do?dataset=educ_uoe_grad02&lang=en.
4. Eurostat indicator edat_lfse_30, "Early Leavers from Education and Training by Degree of Urbanization," http://appsso.eurostat.ec.europa.eu/nui/show.do?dataset=edat_lfse_30&lang=en.
5. Nomenclature of Territorial Statistics (NUTS) is a geocode standard for subdivisions of a country for statistical purposes. NUTS3 in Romania reflects counties and the municipality of Bucharest.
6. *Full health* refers to a situation where there is no stunting and where all children survive to the age of 60, while *complete education* refers to receiving 14 years of high-quality education by the age of 18.
7. This section largely relies on Kraay (2018) and World Bank (2018b).
8. Annex 4A presents a technical description of the HCI.
9. LAEYS = EYS * (HTS / 625), where LAEYS is the learning-adjusted expected years of schooling, EYS are expected years of schooling, and HTS are harmonized test scores.
10. The order of preference used by the HCI project is as follows: total net enrollment rates (TNER) > adjusted net enrollment rate > net enrollment rate > gross enrollment rate. See World Bank (2018b) for more details.
11. Total net enrollment rates (TNER) are slightly higher than 100 percent for three individual one-year age groups: (i) 101.1% for those who are 14 years of age, (ii) 100.8% for those who are 15 years of age, and (iii) 102.6 for those who are 17 years of age. However, all these TNER become lower than 100 percent once they are adjusted for repetition rates.
12. This section relies on data from the World Bank (2018b).
13. The R^2 of regressing the HCI in figure 4.3 on poverty rates (using a \$15 per day poverty line in 2011 purchasing power parity) is 0.62.
14. The productivity loss due to health is $e^{\gamma \text{ASR}(0.87-1)} = e^{0.65(0.87-1)} = 0.92$, where $\gamma_{\text{ASR}} = 0.65$ is the return to health measured using the adult survival rate (Kraay 2018).
15. The productivity loss due to education is $e^{\phi(12.17 * 0.72 - 14)} = e^{0.08(12.17 * 0.72 - 14)} = 0.66$, where $\phi = 0.08$ is the return to education (Kraay 2018); 12.17 are the repetition-adjusted expected years of education; and 0.72 is the average PISA score divided by the TIMSS benchmark of advanced achievement (625).

16. The HCI and its subcomponents at the macro and development region levels, as well as at the county level, are shown in annex 4A. The annex also shows the comparison of the national human capital index using county-level data in figure 4.4 with those produced by the Human Capital Project (World Bank 2018a).

17. The National Institute for Statistics 2017 Tempo dataset does not disaggregate under-5 mortality rates by gender at the county level. However, gender differences are small at the national level (see HCI numbers at the national level in annex 4A). Therefore, we assigned county averages to both girls and boys and did not assess the contribution of infant survival to the gender gaps at the subnational level.

18. Narayan et al. (2018) estimated international mobility for persons born in the 1940s–80s. The figures mentioned here refer to international mobility of persons born in the 1980s.

REFERENCES

EC (European Commission). 2019. *Country Report Romania 2019: Including an In-Depth Review on the Prevention and Correction of Macroeconomic Imbalances.* European Commission Staff Working Document 27.2.2019, SWD (2019) 1022 final. Brussels: European Commission.

Kraay, A. 2018. "Methodology for a World Bank Human Capital Index." Policy Research Working Paper 8593, World Bank, Washington, DC.

Narayan, A., R. Van der Weide, A. Cojocaru, C. Lakner, S. Redaelli, D. Gerszon Mahler, R. G. N. Ramasubbaiah, and S. Thewissen. 2018. *Fair Progress? Economic Mobility across Generations Around the World.* Equity and Development. Washington, DC: World Bank.

Patrinos, H. A., and N. Angrist. 2018. "Global Dataset on Education Quality: A Review and an Update (2000–2017)." Policy Research Working Paper 8592, World Bank, Washington, DC.

World Bank. 2016. "Pinpointing Poverty in Romania." Poverty in Europe Country Policy Brief, World Bank, Washington, DC. https://openknowledge.worldbank.org/handle/10986/23910.

——. 2018a. *The Human Capital Project.* Washington, DC: World Bank.

——. 2018b. *World Development Report 2018: Learning to Realize Education's Promise.* Washington, DC: World Bank.

——. 2019. "Romania Equity Brief." World Bank, Washington, DC.

5 Closing Learning Gaps in Primary and Secondary Education

Chapter 5 examines challenges that have exacerbated gaps in education outcomes across and within regions in Romania. Changes are taking place, but learning gaps in primary and secondary education persist. These can be seen clearly between urban and rural areas, across regions, and across social groups. Proposed solutions focus on enhancing the role of the four determinants in the learning process outlined by the World Development Report 2018 *(World Bank 2018a). Changes are needed at two levels: at the systems level, where reforms and legislative changes involve high-level stakeholders, and at the learning center level, where teachers and school managers are implementers of agreed-on policy actions that affect learners and the use of school inputs. An improvement in funding allocation can help bridge inequities more efficiently.*[1]

To sustain its current fast-paced economic growth, Romania needs to promote inclusive development through equal access to high-quality education. A better-educated labor force can more easily adapt to the rapid global changes in markets, new technologies, and demographics. High-quality education and learning are linked to good employment outcomes, higher earnings, improved social and economic mobility, and lower levels of poverty. Moreover, the future performance of any economy intrinsically depends on the level of preparation of its future workforce and, therefore, of its students (Hanushek and Woessmann 2012). At the student level, achievement is related to economic and social progress, and high-quality education improves inclusive development (Rindermann and Thompson 2011).

In recent decades, the Romanian government has made progress in the education sector by strengthening institutions, encouraging better teaching practices, changing school curricula, and improving students' evaluations (Kitchen et al. 2017). However, implementation challenges and relatively limited funding have slowed or halted progress altogether. There are no global solutions to fix education systems, but examples of proven programs, services, and policies in other countries can provide a roadmap on how to address bottlenecks.

The *World Development Report 2018: Learning to Realize Education's Promise* (WDR) (World Bank 2018a) offers a framework for analyzing the Romanian education system that places student learning at the center. The WDR learning framework shows that improving learning outcomes can occur by intervening at both a systems level and the school level through four entry points: students, teachers, school managers, and school inputs. Such an approach is relevant for three reasons. First, the WDR's holistic approach sheds light on promising entry points in the learning process that involve not only students and teachers but also other relevant inputs and actors. As Romania currently implements several reforms involving these different actors, an integrative approach that looks at several school-level components allows for consideration of the most effective solutions and how integrated solutions leverage each other. Second, the WDR emphasizes that student assessments and actions should be analyzed based on evidence of how students learn. In this regard, for Romania there are accessible annual statistical reports with detailed data on students, school facilities, public financing, teachers, and national and international student assessments. Third, at a systems level, shifts in legislation, funding, and institutional practices may be needed to enhance education systems and to produce a positive change in learning outcomes. On this, the WDR suggests identifying the key actors and aligning them to overcome technical and political barriers (see box 5.1).

In recent decades, Romania has made significant progress in modernizing its education system. The Organisation for Economic Co-operation and Development (OECD) and the European Commission note that Romania has focused on strengthening institutions, encouraging formative teaching practices, promoting a competency-focused school curriculum, and improving school evaluations (Kitchen et al. 2017). In addition, the Ministry of National Education has recently presented the Education Is Uniting Us vision to set general objectives for each compulsory

---

BOX 5.1

Conceptual framework from the *World Development Report 2018*

The conceptual framework presented in the *World Development Report 2018* (WDR) (World Bank 2018a) includes strategies and suggestions for the roles of actors critical to achieve progress in the education system. It emphasizes the need to prioritize *learning* and not just schooling. The framework identifies three strategic policy responses to improve educational outcomes:

1. *Assess learning*, using well-designed student assessments.

2. *Act on evidence* of how students learn.

3. *Align actors* to make the whole system work for learning.

These strategies are interdependent. For example, setting priorities without appropriate metrics can mislead resource allocation, hamper innovation, and lead to a gridlock of the political process.

The framework also conceptualizes four proximate *determinants of learning* and their critical role in the success of the education system. The WDR notes that the four elements that drive the learning experience are learner preparation, teacher skills and motivation, school

management and governance, and availability of relevant school inputs (figure B5.1.1).

FIGURE B5.1.1

WDR determinants of learning

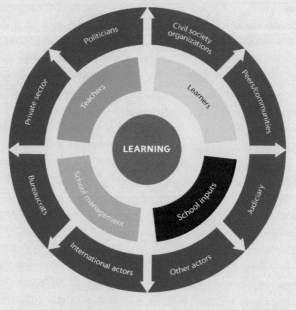

Source: World Bank 2018a.

education cycle, promoting changes in the preuniversity education cycles, as well as in the assessment and evaluation of students. An accompanying effort in official data collection has helped to inform policy makers, researchers, and other stakeholders. The ministry has put in place data compliance policies and penalties for schools to safeguard the production of timely annual statistics reports. However, implementation challenges and underinvestment have stalled progress in key areas, while systematic disparities in quality and equity in education remain significant.

For over a decade, at least two laws (2005 Quality Law and 2011 Education Law), consultation efforts (2016's Educated Romania), and government visions (2018's Education Is Uniting Us) have promoted principles of equality, decentralization, and involvement of different stakeholders in the education system. The European Union (EU) has played a major role in Romanian reforms through framing and funding for implementation. However, these promising changes did not achieve full completion, as some of the major changes introduced in the 2011 Education Law were reversed.

Romania still struggles to support high-quality learning for all its students. While top-performing students have comparable abilities to their peers in the EU and OECD countries, low-performing disadvantaged students lack the foundational competencies required to transition effectively into the workforce and for lifelong learning. The education system shows a high degree of socioeconomic segregation that results from severe urban-rural disparities in funding, school infrastructure, and teacher quality. Funding per capita is not currently serving the needs of students and schools in disadvantaged communities, especially those in rural areas (MLFSPE 2016). Rural schools have lower student achievement scores, higher levels of early school-leaving (ESL), and lower enrollment at the primary and secondary levels compared to their urban counterparts. Roma children face high levels of marginalization and segregation, leading to worse educational outcomes and training opportunities. Disadvantaged children, disproportionately found in rural areas or belonging to an ethnic minority, are also at a higher risk of being out of school.

LEARNERS: PERFORMANCE IS CHARACTERIZED BY SYSTEMIC GAPS AND DISPARITIES

School segregation, performance gaps, and ESL characterize the learning environment of Romanian students. First, school social segregation and marginalization drive students to attend schools with children and young people of the same socioeconomic status, lowering potentially positive peer effects and biasing teachers' expectations of students. Second, wide performance gaps in several key foundational competencies and subject areas (math, reading, and science) have shown little progress over the years, placing Romania behind other comparable countries. Third, high rates of ESL are closely related to poverty, with differences evident both between urban and rural areas and by socioeconomic status. Several of these regional and subnational differences are outlined in more depth in chapter 4.

Poverty and school segregation in schools are major drivers of the education gaps. Poorer students attend lower-quality schools, have fewer resources, and have less-motivated and less-experienced teachers. Among disadvantaged students, Roma children face high levels of marginalization and segregation, leading to worse education, employment, training opportunities, and overall well-being (UNICEF 2011).

Student performance in reading is low by both international and national standards. About 40 percent of 15-year-old students have low reading and numeracy proficiency according to the 2015 Program for International Student Assessment

(PISA).[2] This rate is almost double the EU average (23 percent). Consistently low literacy proficiency affects the efficiency of learning and postgraduation productivity. Romanian students lag those in other EU countries by about 1.5 years, and the gap in Romania between the top and bottom quintile's PISA scores is among the highest in the EU. In 2012, students enrolled in urban schools scored 59 points higher in mathematics than their peers in rural schools, equivalent to a year and a half of additional education. This gap is half a year larger than the average urban-rural gap in OECD countries. Using national grade eight examinations, 4 in 10 (41 percent) students get low scores (receiving a grade of 6.0 or lower), while only 2 in 10 (17 percent) get high scores (a grade of 8.5 and above). Looking across urban and rural areas, we see again that rural children are falling behind, with 59 percent of rural children scoring low, compared to 28 percent of urban children.

Mathematics performance has one of the largest urban-rural divides in learning outcomes. Consistent with international assessments, national evaluations show wide performance gaps between rural and urban students. Results from the 2018 grade eight national student evaluations show that the percentage of low-performing students in rural schools was close to 80 percent, compared to 45 percent for urban schools.[3] The urban-rural gap in math for low-performing students is 35 percentage points and for the high-performing students the difference is 15 percentage points, in both cases favoring urban students. This equates to a 50-percentage-point cumulative performance gap between urban and rural students.

Top-performing schools are mostly located in urban areas, a large proportion of which are in Bucharest. The proportion of top-performing students in Romania (measured through 2015 PISA scores)[4] is 5 percent in reading, 9 percent in math, and 2 percent in science, the lowest in the EU. There is also a divide in school completion among vulnerable populations and minority groups. In 2011, only 9 percent of Roma children completed secondary education, compared to 54 percent of non-Roma children (EU FRA 2014).

Regional differences show significant underachievement among disadvantaged students. This has widened the gap between the top and bottom income quintiles and between urban and rural regions. In 2016, the percentage of students with poor learning results in urban schools was less than half that found in rural schools. Only about 1 percent of high-performing schools[5] are in rural areas, compared with 83 percent of the country's low-performing schools. A high proportion of top-performing schools are in Bucharest (18 out of 31), followed by counties in the Carpathian arc and the Moldova region.[6]

High rates of ESL portray inefficiencies in the school system. ESL refers to students who leave the system without completing the eighth grade. Romania is moving away from the EU 2020 ESL target of 11.3 percent. In 2013, the overall ESL rate was 17.3 percent and by 2017 it reached 18.1 percent. Relative to the EU average, most rural regions and small towns in Romania show high levels of ESL, with rural areas having the highest rates among all, as shown in figure 5.1. No overall gender gaps are observed on early leaving, except among the Roma population. As part of the EU 2020 Strategy, and the 2011 Education Law change, the government is addressing ESL by reaching out to the most at-risk groups in marginalized communities and in rural areas, setting targets, and monitoring.

Teachers who are placed in hard-to-staff areas frequently have to manage high student absenteeism, which is often a consequence of health issues or insufficient care at home. This situation is complicated by findings that poor families have their child allowances suspended

FIGURE 5.1

Early school leaving in lower middle school (percent of total) in Romania, 2017

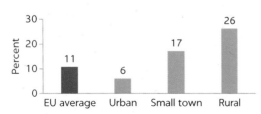

Sources: World Bank 2018b, 2018c.
Note: Data for EU average are for 2016. EU = European Union.

following several unexplained absences (UNESCO 2017). Overall, students in rural areas, from socioeconomically disadvantaged backgrounds, or those who speak a foreign language at home are more likely to underperform in the education system (World Bank 2018c).

TEACHERS: CHALLENGES IN RECRUITMENT, DEPLOYMENT, AND MOTIVATION

Recruitment of teachers in Romania remains a challenge. Very few university graduates complete programs in education—3.8 percent in Romania compared to 10.4 percent in Germany and 13.8 percent in Poland. Once students reach master's level, only 3.3 percent of graduates elect to specialize in education, compared to 34 percent in business, administration, and law collectively. Education science graduates who reach the doctoral level in Romania represent just 0.9 percent of all fields of study, compared to 1.8 percent in Germany and 1.7 percent in Poland (World Bank 2017). Teacher recruitment is a routine problem across primary and secondary education. According to the World Bank (2017), both primary and secondary school teachers are required to teach for one year, pass a written examination, and complete an on-the-job assessment to become professionally licensed. Despite the requirements, some primary school teachers are accepted into the profession with only a pedagogical high school degree, because schools need to fill posts and the pool of qualified applicants is highly unequal across regions.

Recruitment in rural areas is not effective. The current merit-based allowance system rewards teachers whose students achieve exceptional results in assessments and competitions. Consequently, there is a reluctance to remain in schools with low-performing students, so disadvantaged schools struggle to attract and maintain high-quality teachers. The 2011 Education Law considered decentralizing teacher-hiring practices, but this process has not yet happened, and current recruitment methods are not responsive to school needs. In addition, there are scarce resources and limited budgets for teacher training. A 2011 Teaching Staff Statute introduced a mentorship project (teachers teaching other teachers), but, by 2016, an evaluation by the OECD found that this project had not been implemented nationally, as mentor and mentee teachers remain burdened with administrative work and other responsibilities.

Schools in challenging contexts require incentives to staff schools. For example, some countries provide a higher basic salary, housing support, subsidized education, and monetary bonuses for teachers who work in difficult situations. In Romania, these hard-to-staff schools grant teachers a monetary bonus that changes depending on the challenge. For teachers who work in isolated areas, the salary increase is up to 20 percent of base salary; teachers working with special needs students receive a 15 percent increase of base salary; and schools in prisons offer up to a 15 percent increase of base salary. However, the process to determine the status of a hard-to-staff school is discretionary, while the monetary incentives to work in remote, isolated, or rural areas are insufficient to attract talented teachers.

Teachers' salaries are not aligned with hard-to-staff schools. Hence, working with low-achieving students in underresourced settings is not appealing, as it requires more effort without the equivalent compensation. This practice likely exacerbates urban-rural gaps. Low-performing counties have a high share of substitute teachers who serve a high proportion of vulnerable students in challenging school contexts. In addition, teacher mobility is low. It takes an average of 40 years of experience to move from the lowest to the highest pay grade (compared to an OECD average of 24 years).

Teachers in Romania receive relatively low salaries compared to other EU countries, despite recent increases, and compensation structures are not linked to performance to improve broad-based results in the classroom (figure 5.2). Romanian teachers' average annual salary is equivalent to 44 percent of the gross domestic product (GDP) per capita, as compared with 80 percent of GDP per capita on average in other European countries. Even though teachers' salaries have gradually increased over the past two years (by about 50 percent), they remain comparatively low.

There are seldom consequences for not meeting professional development requirements, although teachers are expected to meet requirements of 240 hours of training every five years. There are also concerns that the professional development activities are not well aligned with teachers' needs (OECD, forthcoming).

Although teacher evaluations are conducted regularly, there is no standardized system for promotions, which tend to occur predominantly on an ad hoc basis (World Bank 2017). Teachers are also required to pass an examination to be promoted. While examinations can be effective in determining teachers' knowledge, they provide limited insight into the practical side of teaching, including the use of modern pedagogical methods to address students' diverse learning styles. An associated issue is that promotions are linked only to salary increases and not to an extension of the teacher's roles and responsibilities, limiting opportunities for personal and professional growth—and for student learning (OECD, forthcoming).

Although Romania developed occupational teaching standards in 1999, their implementation has not been compulsory, and they were not updated in 2011 after the Education Law was introduced; they have become outdated. Since joining the EU in 2007, the country has taken steps toward improving the quality of education through efforts to tackle ESL, encourage lifelong learning, and improve tertiary and vocational education. Teachers' professional development is seen as being a critical element of this, but the implementation of teaching standards has proven more challenging than originally envisaged. By updating, implementing, and monitoring relevant occupational standards for teaching, Romania could take a large step forward in professionalizing teaching (OECD, forthcoming).

FIGURE 5.2

Annual gross salaries for full-time teachers in lower secondary education (2018 purchasing power parity euros)

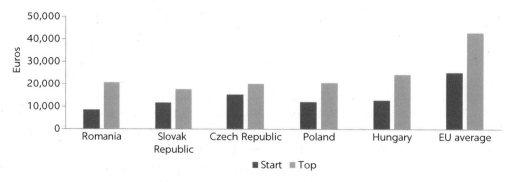

Source: Original elaboration using data from EC, EACEA, and Eurydice 2018.
Note: EU = European Union.

SCHOOL MANAGEMENT: DRIVING TOWARD GREATER PROFESSIONALIZATION

School-based management in Romania today presents a mixed outlook. In other OECD countries, school leaders are expanding their roles into shaping the quality of teaching and learning in their schools, while school leaders in Romania currently retain a largely administrative role. The country has not yet developed professional standards for school leaders, only a list of the skills expected of individuals who apply for school leadership positions. Although partial measures to professionalize the appointment of school principals and school inspectors have improved monitoring and accountability processes in school management, much work remains to be done to prepare school principals for a career in effective school leadership.

School boards in Romania include teachers, local authorities, and parents. The school board has direct responsibilities related to the school budget execution, the school-based institutional development plan, and the school-based curriculum. However, the school principal oversees most tasks related to school administration and relations with the community, teachers, and students. Principals face a wide array of tasks that include teacher evaluations, guidance for curriculum and teaching tasks, representing the school at community meetings, encouraging student discipline, and hiring and dismissing teachers. However, most receive no formal training in ensuring the proper use of resources or supporting teachers and curriculum development. In addition, there are limited incentives for good managerial performance, relevant preparation, and professional development opportunities for principals.[7] Some principals are responsible for multiple schools, which challenges their ability to oversee school improvement and to be optimal managers and leaders. Currently, school leadership relies more on administration than on pedagogical leadership.

To be eligible to become a principal, a teacher must be a member of the National Group of Experts in Educational Management, which requires completion of a 60-credit education management course. In 2011, an education reform introduced merit-based competitions for school leadership positions and school inspectors to bring transparency to the roles. Although implementation barriers delayed the use of these merit-based open contests, by 2016 candidates for the positions of principal, general inspector, and deputy principals competed across counties. As part of the process of becoming a school principal, candidates had to submit a curriculum vitae, perform well in a knowledge-based examination, and undergo an interview. As a complement to this reform, an additional legislative change was passed to consolidate anticorruption monitoring processes in the education system (Kitchen et al. 2017). While there are no formal large-scale evaluations, qualitative evidence shows some promising results.

Like teachers, school leaders are required to complete 240 hours of professional development within a five-year cycle. In 2013, a large majority (87.5 percent) reported having participated in some form of professional development within the past year. However, during field visits for the *OECD Reviews of Evaluation and Assessment in Education: Romania,* principals reported that they did not feel sufficiently supported to address administrative problems or legal issues, nor did they have enough access to professional development of pedagogical approaches to meet school needs or address students' diverse needs effectively (OECD, forthcoming).

SCHOOL INPUTS: SKEWED FUNDING MECHANISMS AND ALLOCATIONS

Romania devotes the smallest share of GDP to education of any European country, and the lowest share of its national budget. Figure 5.3 shows Romania's public spending on nontertiary education is low compared to other EU countries.

Public finance is not bridging urban-rural inequities. The funding formula is not directing more resources to schools with the most vulnerable students. Under the current per student allocation formula, urban schools overcrowd their classrooms to receive more money, since funds are issued on a per student basis, while rural schools with lower enrollment rates receive fewer resources. Thus, it costs more to provide education for children in Romania's poorer counties than in richer counties. The costing methodology uses a correction factor, but it does not always compensate for the low enrollment in rural schools or the proportion of vulnerable students at certain schools. The main consequence of this imbalance is that rural schools end up having lower budgets, worse infrastructure, and lower-quality inputs. This unequal allocation of resources exacerbates the urban-rural divide.

Both unequal resource allocation and the structure of funding mechanisms have far-reaching consequences. Current funding mechanisms, which favor schools in densely populated areas over less populated rural ones, partially explain the divergence in education outcomes. The low allocation of government funds to education requires schools to operate in survival mode, with little to no investment in modernization of facilities or innovative teaching methods possible. Low salaries offered to teachers make it difficult to attract qualified and young talent, particularly to rural schools, where the percentage of vulnerable students is higher. Furthermore, because a significant share of the funding mechanism is covered by local municipalities, richer localities are better positioned to support their local schools than poorer ones. Thus, although the funding allocation formula does differentiate between rural and urban schools,[8] it is still not effective in assuring equality of educational opportunity. Of specific concern is the lack of an incentive structure in the formula to promote and reward improvements in education outcomes and student learning.

FIGURE 5.3

Public expenditure on education by education level as percentage of GDP in the EU, 2015

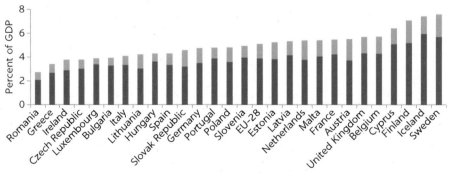

■ Total nontertiary (levels 0–4) ■ Tertiary education (levels 5–8)

Sources: EU 2018, 8; Eurostat (database), European Commission, Brussels, https://ec.europa.eu/eurostat/data/database.
Note: EU-28 = for list of countries see Note 3 on page 20; GDP = gross domestic product.

A recent study found that high-performing schools have a significantly higher expenditure per teacher and students per school, while low-performing ones have a larger share of substitute teachers and vulnerable students (World Bank 2018b). In total, 98 percent of the 115 high-performing schools in the country are in a large urban area in 31 out of the 41 counties in Romania. These results imply that disparities in schools' performance are related to the capacity of individual schools to correct for general low funding by overcrowding classrooms and/or supplementing public funds with local contributions.

School-related expenses constrain school attendance. In 2014, 47.3 percent of parents living in rural areas mentioned financial constraints as the main reason for their children not continuing into upper secondary education. While households of formal workers allocate an average of 56 euros per child for school-related expenses, households of informal low-income workers allocate about 3 euros per child. Among disadvantaged families, school fees and other school-related expenses increase the opportunity cost of sending children to school and therefore affect enrollment, continuation, and completion. The costs of school participation also contribute to the gap between the top and bottom deciles.

School infrastructure needs upgrading. A lack of libraries and learning spaces affects both urban and rural schools. However, rural areas have more than twice as many schools without library facilities: 70 percent of students lacking adequate library facilities attend rural schools. Similarly, the absence of science laboratories and appropriate physical exercise spaces are observed at a much higher rate in rural schools, compared to urban schools. Students with disabilities are further challenged by having limited access to suitable infrastructure facilities. As part of the development of national targets for Europe 2020, a National Strategy for Infrastructure Investments in Education Institutions is under development. European-level monitoring systems are expected to complement this and other strategies in the education system. Funding and implementing the infrastructure strategy will be both a challenge and an opportunity to improve the learning environment, especially in rural schools.

IMPROVING SCHOOL PERFORMANCE IN ROMANIA: SUGGESTED POLICY ACTIONS

Investing in human capital development through education policy has been a growing priority for governments and society. To tackle challenges in education, interventions and policies have centered on broadening access and improving learning. Most interventions in this sector can be categorized under two types: *incentives-based* interventions, aiming to reduce barriers to access, and *instructional* interventions, aiming to improve learning and enhance education curriculum delivery (Plaut et al. 2017). Figure 5.4 shows the goals for both types of policy actions and their expected education outcomes. In Romania, given the prevalence of regional gaps and lagging subnational regions, it is relevant to review interventions that focus on increasing access to education to

FIGURE 5.4

Policy actions and interventions in education: Goals and outcomes

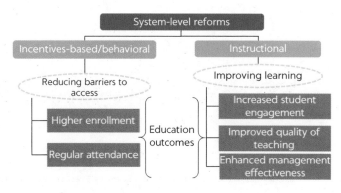

Source: Adapted from Plaut et al. 2017.

understand how to reduce initial disparities: that is, leveling the playing field to improve conditions that are conducive to learning for all students.

Using figure 5.4, one can identify a range of possible education policy actions to tackle the key educational challenges in Romania, especially at the service-delivery level. A detailed description of the examples is available in a technical note that accompanies this report. The examples draw on experiences from around the world. Although it is beyond the scope of this chapter to present the full detail of these examples, table 5.1 outlines options for consideration and further investigation. It should be emphasized that the level of impact reported in the table is highly associated with the design, implementation arrangement specificities, and the context under which the reviewed interventions took place. It is plausible that similar interventions might achieve different outcomes when designed, funded, and/or implemented more effectively, or when paired with other school-based or system-level reforms as part of an integrated reform package.

In table 5.1, the four determinants of student learning are found in the top row, relevant outcomes are found in the following row, and different types of interventions are classified into four categories of impact: positive, promising, unclear, and little to no impact, as reported in the literature. Outcomes for learners are divided

TABLE 5.1 Examples of education policy actions to address determinants of learning

	LEARNERS			TEACHERS AND SCHOOL MANAGEMENT		SCHOOL INPUTS	
	Attendance, absenteeism, graduation	Enrollment	Student achievement	Student attendance, student achievement	Teachers' and school managers' outcomes	Parental involvement	Student achievement
Positive impact	• Student mentoring • School meals • Targeted information on benefits of education • Conditional cash transfers	• Targeted information on benefits of education • Cost reduction	• School meals • Student mentoring	Teacher training on socioemotional skills	N/A	Use of technology: text messages with school content	N/A
Promising	School tracking and flexible remediation for catch-up	N/A	• Curriculum focused on socioemotional skills • Class reduction	N/A	N/A	Home computers	Communication through text messages with school content
Unclear impact	N/A	N/A	School vouchers	N/A	• Teachers' professional development • School-based management interventions	N/A	• Classroom computers • Incentives to read books
Little to no impact	School tracking alone	N/A	Targeted information on benefits of education	• School-based management interventions • Teacher incentives to attend high-need schools	Teacher pay incentives	N/A	N/A

Note: These selected interventions took place in OECD countries and other European countries, including Romania. All interventions in the background paper (De la Cruz Toledo, E., A. Sava, M. Moarcas, N. Butcher, and A. Valerio. "Closing Learning Gaps in Primary and Secondary Education." Unpublished paper.) had enough robust information on access or learning outcomes to allow for their classification. Some interventions described in the technical note are not included in the table if the outcome measures do not include at least one student-related outcome. Note also that the level of impact reported in this table is directly associated with the design and implementation specificities of the interventions reviewed. It is plausible that similar interventions can achieve better outcomes if designed, targeted, and/or implemented more effectively. N/A = not applicable.

into two types: access (attendance, absenteeism, graduation, and enrollment) and learning (student achievement). For teachers and school management, two outcome measures are used: attendance and learning outcomes. For school inputs, the outcome measures include parental involvement and learning outcomes.

Although there are few interventions with a direct impact on student achievement, compared to other schooling outcomes, interventions that have an impact on learning are seldom implemented in isolation. In fact, interventions that affect access and retention outcomes have an important indirect effect on learning by creating conditions and preparing students for more and better learning. In urban areas, where schools tend to have more qualified teachers, better school infrastructure, and a higher proportion of top-performing schools, relevant suggested interventions should focus on improving student achievement. In rural areas, basic needs should also be covered, and interventions that address ESL, enrollment, and attendance can be stepping-stones to reducing education gaps more effectively.

In the following material, we provide more information on a few policy actions drawn from the examples of educational polices, which, as a package, might have the strongest potential to tackle the country's most pressing educational challenges.

Review current school funding mechanisms to ensure that finances are directed to those schools and students that need it most. The chapter analysis has presented a picture of an education system characterized by significant geographical and related disparities. Despite this, the current funding allocation mechanisms linked to numbers of students and the way in which funds are allocated by local municipalities means that those schools and students most in need of funds typically receive the lowest allocation. Researchers that sampled schools in a disadvantaged area in Romania found that nearly half of them had insufficient funds to cover their needs, and that families or local government ended up compensating the shortfalls (Fartușnic et al. 2014). Thus, there is a need to adjust the school funding formula in ways that put more resources into the lowest-performing schools and the lagging regions, both to meet the needs of students and to incentivize better teachers to teach at those schools. The per student funding formula can be revised, setting a higher unit cost for rural schools (or schools with different types of disadvantages). In addition, block grants could be designed and used to attract teachers in hard-to-staff areas or to strategize how to reduce ESL. Some OECD countries use so-called compensatory programs to provide additional resources to schools with a high proportion of disadvantaged students. An example of this practice is found in the Dutch education system, where schools receive block grants based on the educational background of students' parents and/or the school's location; schools can also receive a targeted grant to tackle specific issues (OECD 2016). International financial institutions and private investors can also complement funding gaps with access to resources, instruments, and knowledge to provide a more integrated investment environment (World Bank 2018b). A revision of funding allocation, along with increasing school-level authority and accountability to assign discretionary funding to improve learning, will bring more equity to the education system and can bridge urban-rural gaps.

Implement a more flexible approach to teacher development and appraisal that focuses on improving teaching performance and the students' learning experience. This type of policy approach could motivate teachers and help increase their retention in rural areas. This in turn could play a major role in improving learner performance and reducing high rates of ESL. While there are several important efforts under way in Romania to improve the teaching profession and classroom teaching practices, there is a need to sustain implementation efforts, integrate them with other actions that are implemented at the school level, and evaluate their performance over time to scale the practices that offer the best evidence to boost learning. Examples of programs to improve teacher classroom practices include coaching, classroom observation methodologies, and classroom management techniques. Danielson's Framework for Teaching, for example, groups teaching techniques into four domains: planning and preparation, classroom environment, instruction, and professional responsibilities.

- *Planning and preparation* entails showing knowledge of content and pedagogy, selection of student goals, and assessment of student learning.

- *Classroom environment* focuses on encouragement of respect and rapport, founding a culture of learning, and managing classroom procedures and student behavior.

- *Instruction* includes use of questioning and discussion to engage students, provide feedback to students, and show flexibility and responsiveness.

- *Professional responsibilities* include communication with families, reflection on teaching, and showing professionalism.

These four components are evaluated through a four-point scale (unsatisfactory, basic, proficient, or distinguished). Each component contributes in equal parts to a global score for teaching performance (Danielson and McGreal 2000). Teachers in the United States, Chile, the United Kingdom, and Quebec use this approach to enhance professional practice. The advantage is that it incorporates the need to encourage student learning through feedback, questioning and discussion, and other techniques, while also placing importance on professionalism and a culture of respect and learning in the classroom. Moreover, the fact that all the elements are rated in an equal-weight system reinforces the holistic nature of the method. In Romania, the current appraisal process for career progression (examinations and inspections) does not encourage a multistage career path. As teachers progress, they are rewarded with salary increases but are not encouraged to take on new roles or responsibilities, which does not motivate teachers to improve their skills or to be open to new job responsibilities, representing a missed opportunity to use teachers' skill sets to improve student learning. This policy action could thus help teachers develop their teaching practice and be more engaged with learners as well as with the community, attracting high-caliber candidates into the profession.

Consider introducing student mentoring programs to reduce ESL and develop socioemotional skills. While allocating greater resources to low-performing schools and introducing more effective approaches to teacher development, appraisal, and deployment are essential to resolving disparities in school and student performance, there is also strong evidence of the need to accompany this with interventions that tackle additional challenges encountered by students from disadvantaged backgrounds. In addition to developing foundational skills, socioemotional skills are essential to build long-lasting human capital and job-related skills. Romanian employers consistently identify socioemotional skills as among the most important skills in new hires and have reported that students lack tolerance, self-management, problem solving, teamwork, and communication skills (World Bank 2018c). An example of a program intervention with robust impacts is the Becoming a Man (BAM) student mentoring program implemented in Chicago, United States. The program showed significant reductions in crime and improvements in academic and behavioral outcomes for relatively low expenditure.

Programs like this one have been found to motivate students to stay in school and reduce ESL, while also improving teacher-learner relationships and developing students' socioemotional skills, which are valuable not only in the labor market but also in daily life.

Incorporate stakeholder consultations into educational reform efforts to build consensus, ensure buy-in during implementation, and enable more rapid scale-up and long-term sustainability. In Romania, there have been many promising strategies and policy proposals to improve system performance and the learning experience in the classroom. However, implementing these proposals has been slow, in part due to a volatile political environment and a lack of continuity in policy implementation. Without policy vision and sustained progress that cuts across inevitable shifts in political leadership, long-term education reforms cannot occur and learning outcomes will not improve. Institutional capacity could improve by involving all relevant stakeholders in the development, implementation, and accountability of policy solutions. It is critical to align policy reforms and solutions toward a single overarching goal: learning for all.

Finally, it is imperative to act on evidence, such as international and national student assessment results, to hold stakeholders accountable to achieving learning for all. At the *school level,* school managers and teachers have first-hand knowledge of the bottlenecks at their own learning centers, so there is significant value in engaging them. At the *systems level,* a stakeholder consultation process on education policy implementation could be established. For example, in Canada, the creation of an Education Partnership Table provided a forum to engage teachers, unions, and organizations involved in teachers' continuing education in the creation of new education policies. Table members provided their perspective on the issues discussed, but also agreed to find solutions to foreseeable challenges. In parallel, the minister of education committed to gather input and feedback from members of this partnership to be included in the policy development process. Stakeholders then committed to consensus building with the government. This process contributed to the informed development of education policies (Kitchen et al. 2017). Such a consensus-building policy action could help enhance the roles of school managers and their interaction with high-level officials, while also having a positive effect on subsequent implementation and long-term sustainability in Romania. Selected policy recommendations are provided in table 5.2.

TABLE 5.2 Policy options to close learning gaps in primary and secondary education

SHORT TERM	MEDIUM TERM
SYSTEMWIDE	
Funding	
Review current school funding mechanisms to ensure that finances are directed to those schools and students that need them most.	Introduce dynamic changes in the school funding formula to incentivize learning and close the gaps across regions. This will require improvements in the system's monitoring and evaluation system to track results, make decisions, and hold stakeholders accountable to achieving learning outcomes.
Institutional development	
Incorporate stakeholder consultations into educational reform efforts to build consensus, ensure buy-in during implementation, and enable more rapid scale-up and long-term sustainability.	• Use information, including international and national student assessment information, as well as evidence to hold the system and stakeholders accountable to achieving student learning. • Track progress of program interventions through systematic efforts to measure program impacts. Having robust evidence can help programs survive through short political cycles.

continued

TABLE 5.2, *continued*

SHORT TERM	MEDIUM TERM
SCHOOL-LEVEL	
Teachers	
Design and implement a more flexible approach to teacher development and appraisal that focuses on improving teaching performance and the students' learning experience.	• Upgrade the teaching profession using innovative teacher recruitment, motivation, and development practices that recognize teachers as valued professionals. • Introduce a system that links professional development to student performance and offer coaching to teachers who are at the beginning of their careers or who need to upgrade their practices to be in line with changes in curricula and modern teaching methods that engage students meaningfully in their learning journey.
Students	
Consider introducing student mentoring programs to reduce early school leaving and develop socioemotional skills.	• Introduce a system that provides schools with the ability to plan school-level improvements that are tailored to the teaching force and diverse needs of the student populations they serve. • Offer systematic support to school leaders and teachers to ensure that relevant training and guides are available to prepare school staff on methodologies that can engage students meaningfully, especially students from vulnerable groups and disadvantaged homes who endure multiple constraints. Recognize schools and groups of teachers who make substantive progress in improving student outcomes and student learning.

NOTES

1. This chapter is authored by Elia De la Cruz Toledo, Alina Sava, Mariana Moarcas, Neil Butcher, and Alexandria Valerio.
2. Measured through PISA test scores, 38.5 percent of 15-year-old students are below basic proficiency in science, 38.7 percent are below proficiency in reading, and 39.9 percent are below proficiency in mathematics.
3. Performance in mathematics is based on scores from the grade eight national examination; low performers have scores of 0 to 5.99, medium performers have scores of 6.0 to 8.49, and high performers have scores of 8.5 to 10.
4. Top-performing students are those with scores greater than or equal to 625 in the PISA.
5. High-performing schools are defined as those having an average grade of 8.5 or more on the 8th grade national examination.
6. For further details, refer to the Vulnerability Index in World Bank (2018b, 29).
7. There is only one award for high achievement in management, and it is limited to 16 percent per county.
8. The variables used in the per student formula, and their weight and composition, are neither clear nor transparent (World Bank 2018b). The value of standard cost used for per capita financing is established and published annually, but the methodology to calculate this cost is not transparent.

REFERENCES

Danielson, C., and T. L. McGreal. 2000. *Teacher Evaluation to Enhance Professional Practice.* Alexandria, VA: Association for Supervision and Curriculum Development.

EC (European Commission), EACEA (Education, Audiovisual and Culture Executive Agency), and Eurydice. 2018. *Teachers' and School Heads' Salaries and Allowances in Europe—2016/17.* Eurydice Facts and Figures. Luxembourg: Publications Office of the European Union. https://eacea.ec.europa.eu/national-policies/eurydice/sites/eurydice/files/teacher_and_school_head_salaries_2016_17.pdf.

EU (European Union). 2018. *Eurostat Regional Yearbook. 2018 Edition.* Luxembourg: Publications Office of the European Union. https://ec.europa.eu/eurostat/documents/3217494/9210140/KS-HA-18-001-EN-N.pdf/655a00cc-6789-4b0c-9d6d-eda24d412188.

EU FRA (European Union Agency for Fundamental Rights). 2014. *Education: The Situation of Roma in 11 EU Member States. Roma Survey–Data in Focus.* Luxembourg: Publications Office of the European Union. https://fra.europa.eu/sites /default/files/fra_uploads/fra-2014-roma-survey -dif-education-1_en.pdf.

Fartușnic, C., B. Florian, S. Iosifescu, and O. Măntăluță. 2014. *Financing the Pre-University Education System Based on the Standard Cost: A Current Assessment from the Equity Perspective.* Bucharest: UNICEF Romania.

Hanushek, E. A., and L. Woessmann. 2012. "Do Better Schools Lead to More Growth? Cognitive Skills, Economic Outcomes, and Causation." *Journal of Economic Growth* 17 (4): 267–321.

Kitchen, H., E. Fordham, K. Henderson, A. Looney, and S. Maghnouj. 2017. *Romania 2017.* OECD Reviews of Evaluation and Assessment in Education. Paris: OECD Publishing.

MLFSPE (Ministry of Labor, Family, Social Protection, and the Elderly). 2016. *National Strategy on Social Inclusion and Poverty Reduction 2015–2020.* Bucharest, Romania: MLFSPE.

OECD (Organisation for Economic Co-operation and Development). 2016. *Netherlands 2016: Foundations for the Future.* Reviews of National Policies for Education. Paris: OECD Publishing.

———. Forthcoming. *Romania.* OECD Reviews of Evaluation and Assessment in Education. Paris: OECD Publishing.

Plaut, D., M. Thomas, T. Hill, J. Worthington, M. Fernandes, and N. Burnett. 2017. "Getting to Education Outcomes: Reviewing Evidence from Health and Education Interventions." In *Child and Adolescent: Health and Development,* 3rd ed., edited by D. A. P. Bundy, N. de Silva, S. Horton, D. T. Jamison, and G. C. Patton, vol. 8, chap. 22 , 307–24. Washington, DC: World Bank.

Rindermann, H., and J. Thompson. 2011. "Cognitive Capitalism: The Effect of Cognitive Ability on Wealth, as Mediated through Scientific Achievement and Economic Freedom." *Psychological Science* 22 (6): 754–63.

UNESCO (United Nations Educational, Scientific and Cultural Organization). 2017. *Global Education Monitoring Report: Accountability in Education—Meeting Our Commitments.* Paris: UNESCO.

UNICEF (United Nations Children's Fund). 2011. *The Right of Roma Children to Education: Position Paper.* Geneva: UNICEF. https://www.unicef.org/eca/sites/unicef.org.eca/files/2017-11/Roma _Position_Paper_-_June12.pdf.

World Bank. 2017. "Romania: Teachers." SABER Country Report 2017. World Bank, Washington, DC.

———. 2018a. *World Development Report 2018: Learning to Realize Education's Promise.* Washington, DC: World Bank.

———. 2018b. *Romania Public Finance Review: Enhancing of Public Spending in Pre-University Education.* Washington, DC: World Bank.

———. 2018c. "Romania Systematic Country Diagnostic: Background Note—Education." World Bank, Washington, DC.

6 Romania's Skills Challenge

Chapter 6 explores the skills supply system in Romania and its labor market demands. It documents several skills mismatches and gaps that are preventing Romania from achieving the economic growth and transformation it requires to respond to changing global circumstances and demographic challenges. It identifies opportunities to tackle these challenges, highlighting the potential to introduce a precision training framework to promote continuous skills development. It concludes by presenting a series of possible policy actions to overhaul the country's skills-development system.[1]

Given the rapid pace of transformation and disruption of global economies driven by technological development, Romania needs to invest in the right skills and training models to keep pace with the rapid change in technology and markets. Countries at the economic frontier are forward looking, have robust economies, are open to investment and technology, and have competitive, well-matched workforces. But the frontier is an ever-moving target, and keeping up with it requires ongoing strategic investments in human capital. Striving for the frontier requires the right skills and training models that allow individuals, firms' employees, and countries' workforces to update their skills frequently and efficiently to meet changing needs.

A declining population, extensive emigration, and low labor force participation, especially for women, reduce the quantity of skills available in Romania. Between 2000 and 2017, Romania's population fell from 22.8 million to 19.6 million, and it is expected to continue falling. Romania's labor force participation, at 66 percent, is the lowest in the European Union (EU), in part due to weak participation of women in the labor market. Between 3 million and 5 million Romanians currently live and work abroad. Romanian working-age emigrants in countries of the Organisation for Economic Co-operation and Development (OECD) may exceed 2.6 million (UN-DESA and OECD 2013), representing over 76 percent of Romanian emigrants and around 20 percent of the Romanian total working population. The share of highly educated emigrants among total emigrants was also high, at 23 percent, as of 2010 (World Bank 2018).

The education and training system is struggling to provide the skills the country needs.[2] A disconnect between employers, workers, and education and training providers results in a lifelong learning system in which the various actors act in isolation. According to the EU *National Strategy for Life Long Learning 2015–2020* (EC and Eurydice 2019), expanding lifelong learning in Romania will require resolution of information asymmetries, improved incentives to entice more people to participate in education and training, and adequate capacity and resources for such training to take place (EC and Eurydice 2019).

There is significant evidence of skills mismatches in the Romanian labor market. A high proportion of people with tertiary education are either overeducated for their occupations (vertically mismatched) or working in a sector that does not match their field of education (horizontally mismatched). Growing job vacancy rates indicate a shortage of matched labor supply, while automation of production processes has started driving demand for higher levels of cognitive skills, and jobs involving routine application of procedural knowledge are shrinking. Most enterprises are not providing continued vocational training, and there is limited evidence of strong partnerships between state agencies and the private sector for skills development. These gaps create opportunities to develop new models and approaches. Together with educational reform, the Precision Training Framework provides a strong conceptual model for Romania to follow.[3]

MULTIPLE CAUSES FOR SKILLS MISMATCHES

Skills mismatches can be used to identify a general imbalance between the skills of the workforce and labor market demand. The following types of mismatches are commonly identified: *skill shortages*, where the demand for a certain skill exceeds the supply; *qualifications mismatches*, where the qualification (type or curriculum) is different from that required to perform the job adequately; *overqualification/ overeducation* or *underqualification/undereducation*, where the level of education is higher or lower than is required; and *skill gaps*, where the type or level of skills is different from that required to perform the job adequately. Such mismatches might lead to loss of productivity, particularly where employers are forced to place lower-skilled workers in skilled positions. Skill requirements are also changing rapidly because of technological advancements and international competition.

While skills gaps are a key factor contributing to mismatches in the labor market, job shortages, information asymmetries, and sociocultural conceptions are equally relevant. Skills gaps refer to inadequacies in the quantity, quality, and types of skills available in the workforce, while job shortages refer to the insufficiency of job opportunities for working-age individuals with different types of skills. Mismatches are also influenced by information asymmetries that prevent employers and workers from establishing mutually desirable job matches and by sociocultural conceptions that translate into biases in hiring practices.

QUANTITY OF GENERAL EDUCATION

Romania's pool of potential and actual workers is relatively less educated than in the rest of the EU, with significant regional disparities. In 2017, only 15 percent of Romania's working-age population had completed tertiary education, while 27 percent had less than upper secondary education, both significantly worse that the EU average (figure 6.1). Within the country, the North East and South East regions had both the highest shares of population with less than upper secondary education, at 36 and 33 percent, respectively, and the lowest shares of population with tertiary education, at 10 and 11 percent, respectively. On the other extreme, Bucharest-Ilfov is the most educated region, with only 14 percent of its working-age populationhaving less than upper secondary education level. Bucharest-Ilfov also has the highest share of its working-age population with a tertiary education (33 percent).

FIGURE 6.1

Romania's working-age population is relatively less educated than international peers; Bucharest-Ilfov is the most educated region in the country

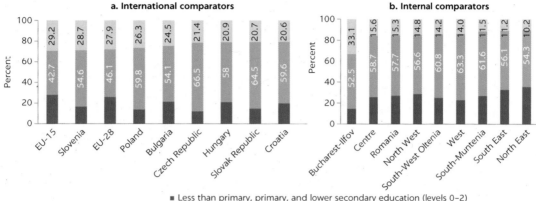

Source: EU 2018, 8.
Note: EU-15 = for list of countries see Note 4 on page 20; EU-28 = for list of countries see Note 3 on page 20.

LEVELS OF SKILLS

Romania has many overeducated workers in low-skilled, blue-collar occupations. However, the country's proportion of undereducated workers in high-skilled, blue-collar occupations exceeds both its peers and the EU average. In comparison with its peers,[4] Romania's high-skilled and low-skilled, white-collar occupations are broadly well matched by workers with the right education level. For low-skilled blue-collar occupations, however, Romania has a substantial proportion of overeducated workers (more than two-thirds). In high-skilled, blue-collar occupations, 36 percent of workers are undereducated, which exceeds both its peers and the EU average of 29 percent.

Conversely, a significant proportion of workers in high-skilled, white-collar and high-skilled, blue-collar jobs in suburban and rural areas are undereducated. Although the situation had improved between 2012 and 2017, 34 percent and 46 percent of workers in high-skilled, white-collar jobs in suburban and rural areas still have only upper secondary or postsecondary education, so are undereducated for their occupation. In addition, about 28 percent and 46 percent of workers in high-skilled, blue-collar jobs in suburban and rural areas are undereducated. Meanwhile, up to 83 percent of workers in low-skilled, blue-collar jobs in cities are overeducated compared to 64 percent in rural areas.

A significant share of female workers in high-skilled, blue-collar jobs are undereducated compared to males. There is no significant gender gap between levels of education and occupations for workers in high-skilled and low-skilled, white-collar jobs. However, in 2017, around 45 percent of female workers in high-skilled, blue-collar jobs had lower than an upper secondary level of education, compared to 31 percent among male workers. Both male and female workers in low-skilled, blue-collar jobs are significantly overeducated.

In summary, there is extensive evidence of vertical mismatching across different occupations within each skill level. As figure 6.2 illustrates, technicians and associate

FIGURE 6.2
Vertical skill mismatching by all occupations, 2017

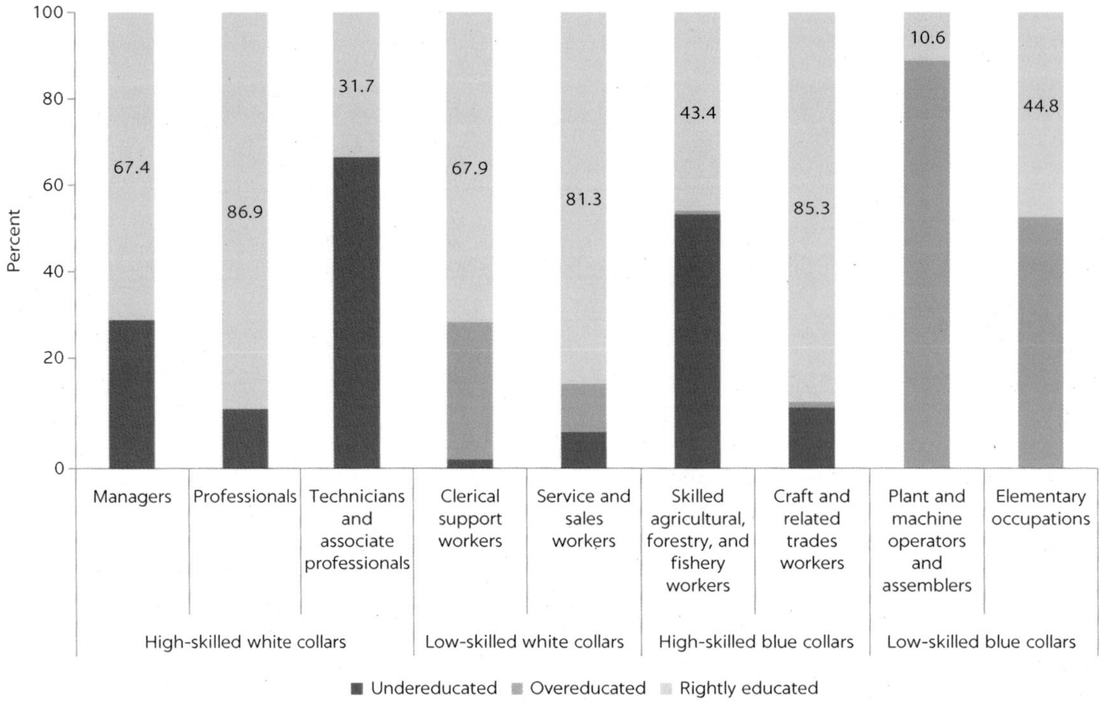

Source: Eurostat (database), European Commission, Brussels, https://ec.europa.eu/eurostat/data/database.

professionals, skilled agricultural workers, and all low-skilled, blue-collar workers are the occupations with the most vertical mismatches.

QUALITY OF EDUCATION

Chapter 5 provided clear evidence of challenges in the formal education system at primary and secondary levels. For the purposes of this chapter, the following issues are worth highlighting briefly:

• *Romanian workers between ages 19 and 28 lag EU peers in foundational skills proficiency.* Although they have improved, Romania's Program for International Student Assessment (PISA) scores in mathematics, science, and reading are substantially lower than the EU average (OECD 2016b).

• *About 50 percent of the 2006 student cohort currently in the labor market had low reading and numeracy proficiency, compared to approximately 20 percent in the EU.* Romanian students are, on average and in broad terms, one-and-a-half years of schooling behind students across the EU.

• *Results for the national assessment in grade 8, a test of accumulated foundational skills, show an increasing share of low-performing students moving into the upper secondary level.*

• *An increasing proportion of students, especially in the technological class profile, complete upper secondary education and enter the labor market without participating in the baccalaureate assessment, making it difficult to evaluate their skills proficiency.* Proportionally, rural areas represent up to 27.6 percent of these students, compared to 8.2 percent in urban areas. Students from the technological class profile provide the greatest cause for concern, as about 20.6 percent (against only 3.2 percent in the humanities) did not participate in the national baccalaureate assessment.

- *An assessment of literacy skills of Romanian technical and vocational education and training (TVET) and university students conducted by the World Bank (2017) indicated that they score low by international standards.* An estimated 90 percent of TVET students fail to reach the level needed to get full value from study at the tertiary level or to satisfy the demands of jobs in the labor market.

- *Employers strongly believe that current employees, students, and graduates entering the labor market lack key socioemotional skills.*

- *Employer perceptions of a lack of technical or job-related skills among employees stem in part from an outdated education and training system.* Many employers view the secondary and tertiary curricula as too abstract, with little focus on practical application or problem solving. Teaching methods are also described as outdated, with a focus on memorization rather than application, problem solving, and team cooperation.

SKILLS SPECIALIZATION

A very small proportion of tertiary education graduates, from all fields of study, are unemployed or inactive. However, as figure 6.3 illustrates, a relatively high proportion of people with tertiary education in some fields are either overeducated for their occupations or working in a sector that does not match their field of education. While most people from all fields are employed, relatively high proportions of employees (more than a third) with tertiary education graduated in services; business and administration; sciences, mathematics and statistics; and social sciences and journalism are overeducated given their occupations. Meanwhile, high

FIGURE 6.3

High proportion of employees with a tertiary education level in some fields are either vertically or horizontally mismatched

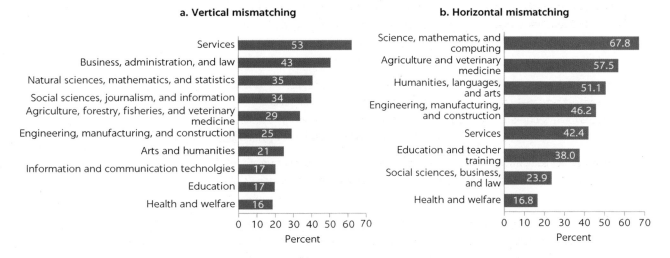

Sources: Vertical mismatching: Labor Force Survey micro data based on National Institute of Statistics, http://www.insse.ro/cms/en; horizontal mismatching: Eurostat (database), European Commission, Brussels, https://ec.europa.eu/eurostat/documents/7884615/8088533/Horizontal+Skills+Mismatch+Rate+by+FoE.xlsx.

proportions of specialists in information and communication technologies (ICT); sciences, mathematics, and statistics; agriculture and veterinary medicine; and arts and humanities are working in a sector not matching their fields of education. Only health and welfare as well as education tend to be appropriately matched, whether vertically or horizontally.

ECONOMIC ACTIVITY AND LABOR DEMAND

In recent years, Romania experienced stronger economic growth than the EU average and new EU member peers, but employment growth has remained sluggish. Between 2012 and 2017, Romanian real gross domestic product grew on average at 4.5 percent annually, twice the rate of the EU. However, employment growth stood at only 0.3 percent, below the EU and peer averages due to a shortage of labor supply as reflected in increasing vacancy rates.

The job vacancy rate has doubled in Romania on aggregate and has increased across all regions in the past several years. Between 2012 and 2017, the job vacancy rate at the national level has doubled from 0.6 percent to 1.3 percent. The vacancy rate increased in all of Romania's eight regions, with the West region experiencing the largest increase of 1.1 percentage points where the vacancy rate passed from 0.6 percent to 1.7 percent.

Across all regions, high-skilled white-collar and low-skilled blue-collar occupations are the most difficult occupations to fill, except in Bucharest-Ilfov. High-skilled white-collar occupations (managers, professionals, and technicians and associate professionals) and low-skilled white-collar occupations (clerical support workers and service and sales workers) contributed almost 80 percent of the total vacancy rate in Bucharest-Ilfov in 2017, indicating that Bucharest's main challenge is to fill high-skilled position occupations (figure 6.4). Meanwhile, in other regions, the most difficult occupations to fill are high-skilled, white-collar and low-skilled, blue-collar occupations (plant and machine operators and assemblers and elementary occupations). While the demand for high-skilled labor is mostly for new jobs, the demand for low-skilled workers is for replacement purposes.

FIGURE 6.4

Contributions to total vacancy rates by region, 2017

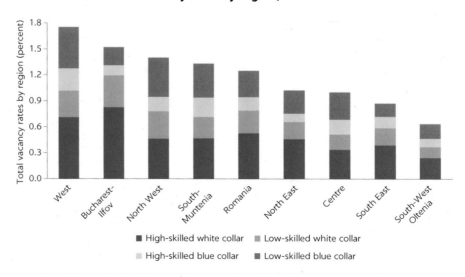

Source: Eurostat (database), European Commission, Brussels, https://ec.europa.eu/eurostat/data/database.

Across economic activities, some sectors also face a significant challenge in filling open positions. Transportation and storage, ICT, manufacturing, administrative support services, and professional, scientific, and technical activities are among the fastest-growing sectors, but they face a shortage of labor supply. In 2017, vacancy rates varied between 1.0 percent for administrative support services and 1.3 percent for ICT. The less dynamic sectors in services like human health and services; arts, entertainment, and recreation; public administration; and finances and insurance had the highest vacancy rates, reaching 2.8 percent for health and human services and 3.3 percent for public administration.

THE CHANGING NATURE OF WORK

Automation has started to change the demand for skills and has led to changes in production processes. Technology is increasing the premium on nonroutine cognitive skills, including critical thinking and sociobehavioral skills, such as managing and recognizing emotions that enhance teamwork. Technology is disrupting the demand for three types of skills in the workplace in the following ways: (i) demand for nonroutine cognitive and sociobehavioral skills appears to be rising in both advanced and emerging economies; (ii) demand for routine job-specific skills is declining; (iii) and payoffs to combinations of different skill types appear to be increasing. These changes show up, not just through new jobs replacing old jobs, but also through the changing skills profile of existing jobs (World Bank 2019a).

Automation of production processes has started driving demand for higher levels of cognitive skills, while jobs involving routine application of procedural knowledge are shrinking (figure 6.5). This suggests that the Romanian economy is particularly vulnerable, as it currently has a disproportionate share of routine types of jobs in the manufacturing, ICT, and agriculture sectors, and most of Romania's labor force (55 percent) is in blue-collar occupations (figure 6.6).

FIGURE 6.5

Jobs in Romania have become intensive in cognitive skills, 1998–2014

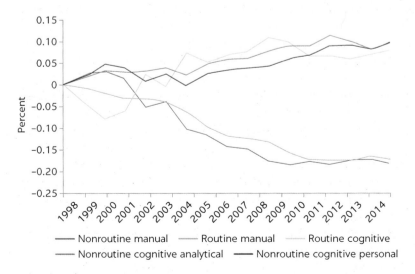

Source: Hardy, Keister, and Lewandowski 2016.

FIGURE 6.6

Romania labor demand is shifting toward high-skilled workers

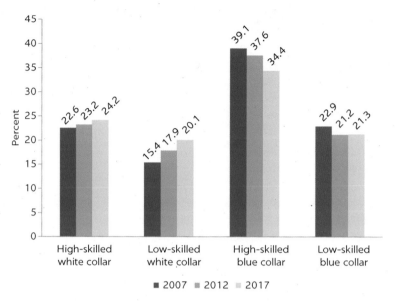

Source: Eurostat (database), European Commission, Brussels, https://ec.europa.eu/eurostat/data/database.

ASYMMETRY OF INFORMATION

Low and relatively inefficient public spending on active labor market policies (ALMPs)[5] contributes to scattered and poor access to information about labor market opportunities. ALMPs are meant to link the large pool of untapped labor force to the labor market, especially the youth population, whose unemployment rate exceeds 20 percent. However, in 2016, Romania spent about 0.02 percent of gross domestic product on ALMPs, well below the 0.4 percent average in the EU. As a result, only 5.3 percent[6] of unemployed people looking for a job participated in ALMPs compared to an EU average of about 20 percent. Not surprisingly, close to 10 percent (two times the rate of 2008) of the inactive population aged 25–59 in 2017 reported feeling discouraged about seeking employment since they "think there is no work available for them," despite increasing vacancy rates. Although ALMPs often serve heterogenous populations and program offerings tend to vary in quality and effectiveness, well-targeted, designed, and implemented programs nonetheless can make a positive difference in improving labor market attachments.

Likewise, a reported lack of transparency that characterizes recruitment in public administration and state-owned enterprises (SOEs) is detrimental to equality of opportunities and skills matching. The Romanian public sector accounts for nearly 18 percent of the labor force.[7] Unfortunately, weak human resources management in the public sector, including asymmetric information regarding employment opportunities, hampers skills matching (World Bank and NACS 2017). According to a recent analysis carried out by the National Agency of Civil Servants in 2015, recruitment in the central and local public administration is characterized by limited information on duties, remuneration, and promotion prospects, as well as lack of clarity regarding the competencies required (NACS 2015). Similar concerns have been raised regarding the politicization of recruitment and retainment of employees in SOEs (Marrez 2015).

Extensive use of temporary recruitment of managerial positions in the public administration and absence of centralized management and monitoring of contract-based staff contributes to asymmetry of information and deters skills matching. In 2017, over 20 percent of all managerial positions in the public sector were filled with temporary recruitments, which are exempted from formal and transparent selection procedures (World Bank and NACS 2017). With no centralized performance management or monitoring of contract-based staff, it is hard to verify the extent to which this type of recruitment adheres to productive skills matching.

Unfavorable perceptions that Romanian citizens have regarding fairness and equal opportunities may further negatively impact employment and skills matching. According to a 2017 Eurobarometer survey on fairness, inequality, and intergenerational mobility, less than 40 percent of Romanians believe they have equal opportunities to advance in life, nearly 20 percent lower than in the EU (EC 2018). Recent studies have also demonstrated that perception of corruption may discourage citizens from attempting to integrate the labor force and, conversely, may motivate emigration (Ariu and Squicciarini 2013; Cooray and Schneider 2014).

Finally, limited levels of digital inclusion, computer use, and internet access in some regions is another potential factor contributing to skills mismatches. In 2017, about 27 percent of Romanians claimed to have never used a computer, nearly double the EU average of 14 percent. Similarly, about 81 percent of Romanian households had internet access in 2018 compared to 89 percent across the EU. There are also significant regional variations of the level of digital inclusion in the country.

SOCIOCULTURAL INFLUENCES

While more women have achieved tertiary qualifications, employment of women and their share of managerial positions is low. Half of the Romanian population ages 15–64 who have completed at least a preprimary education level are women. However, in 2017, only 43 percent of employed people were female. Women are also underrepresented in managerial positions, despite representing more than half (53 percent) of the employed population with a tertiary education, a level of education primarily required for managerial positions. Indeed, only about 30 percent of managerial positions are held by women.

Traditional perceptions regarding the role of women in the household may explain that bias. Over two-thirds of Romanians believe that the most important role of a woman is to take care of her home and family, while less than that share approves of the idea of a man taking parental leave from work (EC 2017). These types of gender biases, combined with the extensive maternity leave to which Romanian women are entitled (one to two years), may have a negative impact on the career progression of highly skilled women and contribute to vertical skills mismatches for managerial positions, with more men who possess lower education levels than required.

Social exclusion of the ethnic Roma population may also prevent skills matching for a significant share of the working-age population. In addition to inequality of opportunities that Roma face due to their restricted access to vital public services, their chances of finding employment that matches their skills level is deterred by the prevalence of ethnic discrimination in the country. Official national figures estimate the share of the Roma population is 3.5 percent of the total Romanian population, while the European Commission estimate is nearly four times as much (World Bank

2014a).[8] According to the Second Survey on Minorities and Discrimination in the EU (EU FRA 2017), one in three Roma persons felt discriminated against when they looked for work in the past five years, and one in five stated they felt discriminated against in the workplace in the same period. Although it is challenging to accurately measure the impact of discrimination on labor market access, the relatively low employment rates of Roma people compared to non-Roma, for all levels of education, suggest that the former might face additional barriers to employment that are not necessarily skills related (World Bank 2014a).

Ongoing efforts to combat discrimination against Roma people in the labor market have yet to achieve significant results. The government has introduced multiple programs and legislation to combat Roma discrimination in the labor market. Yet, like the impact of the diminished capacity of the National Employment Agency on combating information asymmetries in the Romanian labor market, institutional capacity constraints have a negative impact on the government's capacity to address discrimination meaningfully (World Bank 2014b). In 2016, the share of Roma people who stated that they are aware of organizations that offer support or advice to victims of discrimination remained low in absolute terms, in comparison to other EU member states[9] and relative to the share in 2011.

RESPONDING TO SKILLS MISMATCHES WITH WORK-BASED TRAINING

Most enterprises do not provide continued vocational training (CVT), one way in which companies might respond to skills mismatches. The main reasons include a view that (i) existing qualifications, skills, and competencies correspond with the current needs of enterprises (84 percent); (ii) employers are recruiting people with the right skills needed for the job (78 percent); (iii) the high cost of CVT (34 percent), with the average cost of CVT per participant being lei 1,705 in 2015 (NIS 2017); and (iv) considerations for the high workload and limited time available for staff to participate in CVT (26 percent). The number of Romanian enterprises providing CVT declined significantly between 2005 and 2010 but increased slightly between 2010 and 2015. By comparison, most other EU-28 countries show a progressive increase in providers over the same periods.

However, more people, and more highly skilled people, are taking part in CVT in Romania. In 2010, around 18 percent of Romanian employees took part in CVT courses, increasing to 21 percent in 2015 (NIS 2017). The likelihood of participation in education and training is related to levels of educational achievement, so people with a tertiary level education are more likely to participate in work-based training (66 percent for the EU-28 and 16 percent for Romania), while those having completed at most upper secondary or postsecondary levels are second most likely (41 percent for the EU-28 and 6 percent for Romania), and those with at most lower secondary education least likely (24 percent for the EU-28 and only 1 percent for Romania) (Eurostat 2018). Only 4 percent of Romanians indicated that they participated in on-the-job training to improve skills relating to the use of computers, software, or applications in 2018, while an additional 3 percent indicated that their employers either paid for or provided such training. By comparison, 12 percent of Romanians reportedly engaged in free online or self-study to improve their ICT skills (Eurostat 2019). When looking at the rates of participation by industry, 67 percent of the financial and insurance field participates in CVT, followed by 49 percent, respectively, for the fields of electricity, gas, steam and air conditioning supply, and

ICT. The lowest participation rates are in the construction (27 percent) and other service fields (29 percent) (NIS 2017).

Employers provide close to half of all work-based training, most likely through nonformal education sources. In Romania, employers make up 46 percent of training providers. Training activities are most likely to take place through non-formal education (29 percent), followed by commercial institutions where education and training is not the main activity (9 percent), formal education institutions (5 percent), and individual or other training providers (4 percent each). CVT provided by Romanian enterprises primarily takes the form of courses (79 percent). Most companies (71 percent) use external providers, while 60 percent use internal providers. Beyond nonformal courses, 59 percent of companies also use guided on-the-job training, 53 percent use self-directed learning/e-learning, and 19 percent use learning or quality circles (NIS 2017).

WORKPLACE TRAINING PRACTICES: CASE STUDY EVIDENCE

A sample of seven firms was interviewed for this report to solicit a richer, qualitative understanding of workplace training practices.[10] In these seven firms, a wide range of types of training is provided to staff. Most companies have a strong onboarding process, comprising direct training from the human resources department as well as peer-to-peer learning. After the initial onboarding, most companies provide additional training that lasts between three to six months and is usually linked to a probationary review period. In some cases, direct managers and employees work together to develop individualized training plans for the year beyond the initial training. These training plans are then reviewed annually. Some companies do this more comprehensively than others, while most that have individualized training plans (irrespective of how they are developed) also review them annually.

The interviewed firms provide most training internally. For firms that are heavily involved in manual manufacturing of products, the facilities or factories themselves are the training sites, as employees need to be trained on the equipment itself. The exception to this was an information technology (IT) company, but this was largely because most of their employees receive highly technical training that is internationally certified and required for their various IT services.

Specific training in soft skills is most likely to be outsourced to external parties. This is particularly relevant to managerial training, where the goal of the training is to develop leadership and management skills, as opposed to technical skills. Most firms had established partnerships with training providers.

The seven firms also differentiated the type of training offered through classification of employees according to the nature of their work. Training for blue-collar workers tended to be more intensive and structured than for white-collar workers and often lasted longer. For the smaller percentage of white-collar workers at these firms, there was a more flexible training program that predominantly involved general professional development skills. This is outsourced to external providers. There are also differences across companies regarding the number of hours each type of worker receives training.

Most firms bear the entire cost of training and have allocated budgets to do so. Although firms did not disclose the budget, all stated that they pay for all work-related training for employees and ensure that it is conducted during work hours. Exceptions to this are online training opportunities in which some employees engage and that they can access at any time. A few firms stated that literacy and comprehension levels affect how much they invest in online training programs. Depending on the nature of the industry, most training is done face-to-face.

With one exception, all companies stated that training forms a significant part of an employee's annual review and promotion but is regarded as only one factor in a holistic approach to employee performance, and therefore not directly linked to promotions.

Most of the companies reported that they are not participating in structured, formalized relationships with the government or government ministry bodies. Most have relationships with state universities and TVET schools, ensuring that internships and scholarships are available to students at the high school or university level. There is a strong focus on ensuring that they can create an opportunity for investment in the population at an earlier stage, as this directly affects their talent pipeline. There are formal, signed memoranda of understanding between both parties to invite students for internships, share information on industry best practices, invite representatives from the company or the university to give a talk at either location, and sometimes even advertise and directly recruit employees from universities. The firms appear to highly value relationships with state universities.

Most companies were aware of a retraining program introduced by the National Employment Agency, but few participate in it. Largely, these firms do not engage the government with their workplace training programs. Most noted that they engage with government when they are mandated by law to follow certain health and safety, data protection, or industry standard regulations. Firms ensure that all staff are trained in accordance with national or international law standards but are not actively partnering with government agencies to achieve this.

IDENTIFYING OPPORTUNITIES TO RESPOND TO THE CHALLENGES

There are significant opportunities for Romania to develop new models of skills development that will position it well to benefit from the possibilities of the fourth industrial revolution. This will require a strong determination to introduce new models and approaches, as it is clear that business as usual will not move Romania in the direction it wishes to head. From this perspective, the so-called precision training framework provides a strong conceptual model for introducing suitable new approaches.

"Precision training" hinges on the concept of demand-driven training, offered to individuals where they already are and typically through their employers. Public-private partnerships can help to compensate for market failures and a lack of inclusivity by sharing responsibility between firms and government. The precision training framework starts with good governance, a dynamic business environment, strong connectivity infrastructure, and a well-trained workforce. Although all are important, workforce skills are the focus of this chapter. With increased uncertainty and accelerated rates of change arriving in the workplace, Romania should consider such new forms of skills-development arrangements that can better support workers moves through quicker skills-depreciation cycles and adjust through different segments of the age profile. New forms can more readily prepare them for reskilling throughout their lives. Precision training is a promising model that promotes such continuous skills development.

A key aspect of precision training is the notion of a "lifelong learning ladder." This represents the fluctuation of the relevance of an individual's skills throughout her working life. At some points, those skills may be in demand and highly relevant; at others, they may become outdated and be of low relevance. In a precision training environment, she can reenter training exactly when, where, and in the manner required to update her skills. Given the extent of skills mismatches evident in Romania, such an approach will be essential to enable the country to align its labor supply with changing economic demands.

There are three key innovations worth considering in Romania: individualized learning opportunities offered through technology, workplace-based training provided by employers, and public-private partnerships to incentivize training and make it accessible to all. Harnessing all three can create an agile, demand-driven skills environment in which individuals can receive skills training and retraining through various means as and when they need it throughout their lives.

The most efficient way to make training accessible to individuals is to serve them where many already are: at work. Like their global counterparts, Romanian employers are uniquely positioned to offer relevant, in-demand skills training to large numbers of individuals. Compared to traditional education and training institutions, they may be more aware of and adaptive to market trends, better at profiling workers and their skills needs, and better positioned to integrate learning opportunities into real-world contexts (ManpowerGroup 2018). They may also be better equipped to offer real-time evaluation and support (box 6.1). In general, successful training of this kind involves hands-on learning, accountability, and individualized learning plans.

Market failures can limit the availability and relevance of training. Not all employers offer training to their employees, and not all individuals are employed in the workforce. In many cases, the labor market fails to deliver preemployment or workplace training to workers at various skill levels. Imperfect credit markets mean that firms and individuals may be unwilling to pay most of the out-of-pocket cost of training up front (Almeida and Aterido 2010). Lack of coordination between training providers and employers can lead to individuals whose skills are not well matched to their jobs (Almeida, Behrman, and Robalino 2012), a trend evident in Romania. Firms often fear poaching—why invest in an employee's skills when she can then take those skills to a competitor? Access to training at work may also be more limited for members of marginalized groups and for employees of small and medium enterprises (SMEs), which may lack training resources.

Public-private partnerships offer one way to address these market failures. Public-private partnerships represent a spectrum of programs characterized by cooperation between government and the private sector, as well as shared risks

BOX 6.1

Taking training to the workplace in Romania

An automotive parts manufacturing company based in Sibiu has approximately 1,100 employees who are all trained from the start of their careers on-site. The company has personalized training plans for each employee, and all employees on average receive 80–100 hours of training per year. The factory has a well-developed training facility on-site, which has infrastructure to deliver all necessary training, from introductions to health and safety standards required at work to specific information about the manufacturing line on which employees work. The training facility also supports employees who require retraining, while one-on-one personal training is delivered by a member of the training team. This approach is important because there are few opportunities to learn the practical skills required before employment.

and rewards. Public-private partnerships present a valuable solution not only for addressing market failures in training provision but also in bridging gaps between the demand for workforce skills and knowledge learned in schools. The Technical Education and Skills Development Authority (TESDA), for example, coordinates training activities in the Philippines. TESDA provides incentives to industry to generate support and commitment for "training, expanding, and purposively directing scholarships and other assistance to fund the development of critical and hard-to-find skill [and] higher technologies and to incentivize the Technical Vocational Institutions" (OECD 2016a). Furthermore, unemployed or less-educated individuals, members of marginalized groups, and employees of SMEs may not have the same access to training as workers at larger firms. Public-private partnerships offer mechanisms to tackle these challenges.

CONCRETE STEPS TO OVERHAUL ROMANIA'S SKILLS-DEVELOPMENT SYSTEM

A series of interrelated policy actions can help Romania to overhaul its skills-development system and move its economy closer to the global frontier. While some actions, particularly those associated with educational reform at the secondary school level and technical and university education, may take longer to implement, others can be implemented relatively quickly and deliver rapid changes to the country's economy.

Implement appropriate reforms in primary and secondary schooling to ensure that learners and workers entering the skills-development ecosystem in Romania have acquired the required literacy, numeracy, socioemotional skills, and other core foundational competencies necessary to prepare them for further studies and integration into a rapidly modernizing economy. At the heart of problems with skills mismatches and gaps in Romania are problems at the primary and secondary levels of schooling, and they are at the center of challenges that employers encounter with their workforce, particularly for lower-skilled positions. Chapter 5 provided possible policy actions for tackling these challenges in the education sector. For working-age adults who are already in the labor force, considering remedial programs to address foundational skills gaps might be required before moving forward with more job-specific or specialized training.

Undertake ongoing review, rationalization, and streamlining of all vocational programs and qualifications to ensure that formal skills-development programs in both TVET schools and universities are relevant, up to date, and sufficiently flexible to allow for reskilling at different points in individuals' labor market trajectories. This should include decommissioning of outdated curricula and programs that are either preparing students for jobs that no longer exist or that train students in skills that are no longer required in the workplace, underpinned by ongoing, structured interaction with the industry to determine what skills are most in demand in the labor market. As part of this process, it will be worth considering delaying the stage at which students are tracked into vocational programs at school level, to ensure that students entering those programs have already acquired the necessary foundational skills to succeed in the workplace and to be well prepared to engage in a series of ongoing lifelong learning engagements before they begin to specialize. Linked to this, it will also be important to *reskill those trainers and educators responsible for program delivery,* given that they will be central to successful implementation and may resist curriculum transformation efforts if they feel that they lack the skills to move into new program areas.

Stimulate and support new skills-development arrangements that can better support workers through quicker skills-depreciation cycles and more readily prepare them for reskilling throughout their lives. The precision training framework outlined in this report offers strategies that can be adopted to develop a comprehensive skills-development ecosystem for Romania that would be significantly more responsive to changing labor market demands than the current system, thereby reducing skills mismatches and positioning Romania more effectively to move to the economic frontier. Of specific relevance would be the following:

- *Policy and financing incentive mechanisms to implement public-private partnerships, combined with clear guidelines for participation.* These would constitute a specific strategy to share the cost, risk, and reward between government and the private sector in skills areas where vacancies are highest and skills supply is not readily available in the labor market. This could also facilitate the growth of new kinds of skills in economic growth areas where training providers are not yet in a position to run formal programs that meet changing labor market demands. This process should include consultation with the private sector to identify the most suitable public-private partnership models for implementation in Romania, considering its specific political economy. Part of this process should focus explicitly on how public-private partnerships could be implemented to stimulate regionally specific skills-development initiatives in lagging regions within Romania.

- *Provision of guidance to employers on how best to engage in and offer workplace-based training.* This should focus on providing hard evidence on the return on investment of workplace-based training to industry leaders, as well as information about successful workplace-based training initiatives within Romania and from around the world. This could helpfully include a focus on suitable strategies specifically for deployment in SMEs, given the likely key role they will play in driving growth in frontier economic sectors.

- *Development and adoption of suitable occupational competence standards for priority professions and jobs in key economic sectors to facilitate the creation of new skills-development programs and services by both public and private training providers, with emphasis on being able to provide workplace-based training services to employers.* Adoption of such standards could help to develop trust in, and facilitate growth of, the skills-development industry in Romania to support workplace-based training, as well as facilitating new forms of delivery of skills-development programs that harness blended learning methods.

- *Overhaul recognition-of-prior-learning (RPL) processes to enable more flexible completion of skills-development programs, accumulation of credits, portability of credentials, and flexible entry into programs depending on skills, knowledge, and competencies acquired through self-study and/or workplace practices.* The success registered by high- and low-skilled Romanian expatriates integrating into labor markets across Europe provides clear evidence that many Romanians are developing strong, relevant skills through a variety of informal mechanisms. Effective RPL enables easier individualized accumulation of skills, while allowing opportunities for formal recognition of those skills once they have been acquired. This can help skilled employees secure better wages while also serving to reduce the extent of reported skills mismatches in national, subnational, regional, and global statistics.

- *Establish structured mechanisms to enable effective coordination of efforts between all the key players in Romania on whom a skills-development ecosystem for the country will depend.* While Romania has excellent policies and strategies on skills development in different areas, current initiatives appear to be implemented in isolation, and there is very limited evidence of sustained coordination between different branches of government (particularly the Ministries of Trade and Industry, Labor, and Education), employers, and public and private training providers. If Romania wishes to move its economy to the global frontier, then this coordination will be essential to ensure both that there is sustained focus on agreed areas of key national need and that investments in skills development are effectively aligned to achieve maximum impact. This process of coordination should focus on identifying and prioritizing investment in those economic sectors that show greatest potential for simultaneously driving economic growth and employment generation.

- *Invest in active labor market policies and improve efficiency of ALMP expenditures to remove information asymmetries.* This will help current and future workers reduce search times to find jobs that fit their skills profile and to find suitable skills programs to prepare them best for future employment and career growth. There should be a focus on women, youth, and those in rural areas. As part of this, it may be worth engaging with employment centers to ensure they offer modern profiling, job search support, and information services to help individuals find jobs and skills-development opportunities, especially individuals from vulnerable groups (for example, ethnic minorities, the long-term unemployed, and economically inactive citizens) and that they advertise these services effectively. Strong emphasis should be placed on targeting lagging regions through this investment to ensure that ALMPs help to accelerate growth in those regions.

- *Introduce regular monitoring, evaluation, and research strategies to assess the effectiveness and impact of national strategies to stimulate the skills-development ecosystem.* Although there have been various efforts to research skills-development systems in Romania, these have tended to take the form of once-off initiatives that are seldom sustained; there have also been limited efforts to assess the impact of projects being implemented. The types of research and evaluation to consider might include regular labor market gap analyses, disaggregated by region, to measure gaps between supply and demand; longitudinal impact evaluations of new forms of skills development to inform government investment strategies; and tracer studies to assess the effectiveness of formal training programs. Table 6.1 explores some policy recommendations.

TABLE 6.1 Policy options to overhaul Romania's skills-development system

SHORT TERM	MEDIUM TERM
System level	
Implement appropriate reforms in primary and secondary schooling to ensure that learners and workers entering the skills-development ecosystem in Romania have acquired the required literacy, numeracy, and socioemotional skills and other core foundational competencies necessary to prepare them for further studies and integration into a rapidly modernizing economy.	Establish a feedback mechanism that brings together policy and decision makers in general education, training providers, and tertiary education institutions to communicate strengths in, weaknesses in, and areas to improve the quality of foundational skills sets of young people. Make available remedial education curricula targeting young and working-age adults whose core foundational competencies and skills need to be upgraded before entering further education and training.
Undertake ongoing review, rationalization, and streamlining of all vocational programs and qualifications to ensure that formal skills-development programs in both TVET schools and universities are relevant, up to date, and sufficiently flexible to allow for reskilling at different points in individuals' labor market trajectories.	Reorganize the education system to delay streaming into vocational areas to a later stage in the educational trajectory. Enhance the quality of secondary education to include communication and socioemotional skills that will be needed for further education, training, or employment.

continued

TABLE 6.1, *continued*

SHORT TERM	MEDIUM TERM
Service delivery	
Introduce new skills-development arrangements that can better support workers through quicker skills depreciation cycles and more readily prepare them for reskilling throughout their lives. This can begin on a pilot basis, and, based on evidence, it can be scaled up.	• Introduce policy and financing incentive mechanisms to implement public-private partnerships, combined with clear guidelines for participation, as a specific strategy to share the cost, risk, and reward between government and the private sector in skills areas where vacancies are highest and skills are not readily available in the labor market and to facilitate growth of new kinds of skills in economic growth areas where training providers are not yet positioned to run formal programs that meet changing labor market demands. • Provide systematic guidance to employers on how best to engage in and offer workplace-based training. This should focus on providing hard evidence on the return on investment of workplace-based training to industry leaders, as well as information about successful workplace-based training initiatives within Romania and from around the world. Adopt suitable (and flexible) occupational competence standards for priority professions and jobs in key economic sectors to facilitate the creation of new skills-development programs and services by both public and private training providers, with emphasis on being able to provide workplace-based training services to employers.
Information	
Design recognition-of-prior-learning (RPL) processes to enable more flexible completion of skills-development programs, accumulation of credits, portability of credentials, and flexible entry into programs depending on skills, knowledge, and competencies acquired through self-study and/or workplace practices.	Implement an RPL system to underpin the development of a precision training framework to ensure workers can access training when they need it, where they need it, and how they need it. This may require the use of technologies and online training platforms.
Establish structured mechanisms to enable effective coordination of efforts between all the key players in Romania on whom a skills-development ecosystem for the country will depend.	Ensure the sustainability of the effective coordination with a combination of legislation, funding, and well-publicized strategic leadership from the government and industry.
Invest in active labor market policies and improve efficiency of ALMP expenditures to remove information asymmetries, thereby helping current and future workers reduce search times to find jobs that fit their skills profile and to find suitable skills programs to prepare them best for future employment and career growth, with a focus on women, youth, and those in rural areas.	Establish an evaluation system to gauge the effectiveness and impacts of different types of ALMPs and expand program coverage based on accumulated evidence. Make information on programs available to employment centers, providers, employers, and prospective users.
Introduce regular monitoring, evaluation, and research strategies to assess the effectiveness and impact of national strategies to stimulate the skills-development ecosystem.	Make information available online and through different social media to ensure that students, workers, trainers, and employers understand the system, how to make effective use of the program offerings, and how to establish new programs, including through public-private partnerships.

Note: ALMP = active labor market policies; RPL = recognition of prior learning; TVET = technical and vocation education and training.

NOTES

1. This chapter is authored by Neil Butcher, Vincent Belinga, Sonja Loots, Myra Murad Kahn, Ioana Ciucanu, Michal Tulwin, Alina Sava, Zohar Ianovici, Mohamed Mukhtar Qamar, and Alexandria Valerio.
2. See the background paper on skills for a comprehensive description of the education and training system in Romania (World Bank 2019b).
3. For more information, there is a background paper that was prepared for this chapter (World Bank 2019b).
4. Peers include Bulgaria, Hungary, and Poland.
5. ALMPs include six categories: training, employment incentives, supported employment rehabilitation, direct job creation, and start-up incentives.
6. This percentage is below what would be predicted for Romania's level of ALMP expenditures, signaling a certain degree of inefficiency.

7. According to official figures of the Ministry of Finance, the central and local administration account for 1.23 million employees, or 14 percent of the labor force, and SOEs account for nearly 200,000 employees, or 3 percent of the labor force.
8. Difficulties in finding an accurate estimate of the size of Roma people signal the barriers they face to successful integration in Romanian society.
9. The selection of countries was based on the availability of data.
10. The research methodology and detailed case studies are presented in a background paper to this report (World Bank 2019b).

REFERENCES

Almeida, R., and R. Aterido. 2010. "Investment in Job Training: Why Are SMEs Lagging So Much Behind?" Policy Research Working Paper 5358, World Bank, Washington, DC.

Almeida, R., J. Behrman, and D. Robalino, eds. 2012. *The Right Skills for the Job? Rethinking Training Policies for Workers.* Washington, DC: World Bank.

Ariu, A., and M. P. Squicciarini. 2013. "The Balance of Brains—Corruption and Migration." *EMBO Reports* 14 (6): 502–4.

Cooray, A., and F. Schneider. 2014. "Does Corruption Promote Emigration? An Empirical Examination." IZA Discussion Paper 8094, Institute for the Study of Labor (IZA), Bonn.

EC (European Commission). 2017. *Eurobarometer 465: Gender Equality.* Brussels: Directorate-General for Communication. https://data.europa.eu/euodp/data/dataset/S2154_87_4_465 _ENG.

———. 2018. *Eurobarometer 471: Fairness, Inequality and Intergenerational Mobility.* Brussels: Directorate-General for Communication. http://data.europa.eu/euodp/en/data /dataset/S2166_88_4_471_ENG.

EC (European Commission) and Eurydice. 2019. "National Life Long Learning Strategy 2015–2020." Brussels. https://eacea.ec.europa.eu/national-policies/eurydice/content/lifelong-learning -strategy-64_en.

EU (European Union). 2018. *Eurostat Regional Yearbook. 2018 Edition.* Luxembourg: Publications Office of the European Union. https://ec.europa.eu/eurostat/documents/3217494/9210140 /KS-HA-18-001-EN-N.pdf/655a00cc-6789-4b0c-9d6d-eda24d412188.

EU FRA (European Union Agency for Fundamental Rights). 2017. *Second European Union Minorities and Discrimination Survey: Main Results.* Luxembourg: Publications Office of the European Union. https://fra.europa.eu/sites/default/files/fra_uploads/fra-2017-eu-midis-ii-main-results _en.pdf.

Eurostat. 2018. Eurostat (database), European Commission, Brussels, "Adult Learning Statistics." https://ec.europa.eu/eurostat/statistics-explained/index.php/Adult_learning_statistics.

———. 2019. Eurostat (database), European Commission, Brussels, "Way of Obtaining ICT Skills." http://data.europa.eu/euodp/data/dataset/V0NU6krlZdcI11ZUl5FtA.

Hardy, W., R. Keister, and P. Lewandowski. 2016. "Technology or Upskilling? Trends in the Task Composition of Jobs in Central and Eastern Europe." IBS Working Paper 2016–40, Institute of Structural Research, Warsaw.

Manpower Group. 2018. *Employment Outlook Survey Romania: Q3 2018.* Bucharest: Manpower-Group Romania.

Marrez, H. 2015. "The Role of State-Owned Enterprises in Romania." *ECFIN Country Focus* 12 (1): 1–8.

NACS (National Agency of Civil Servants). 2015. *Analiză cu privire la sistemele actuale de recrutare și evaluare a personalului, din perspectiva punerii în aplicare a normelor în vigoare* (Analysis Regarding the Current Systems for Recruiting and Evaluating the Personnel, from the Perspective of Applying the Norms in Force). Bucharest: NACS.

NIS (National Institute of Statistics). 2017. "Labour Market Press Release." No. 269, October, Bucharest.

OECD (Organisation for Economic Co-operation and Development). 2016a. *OECD Competition Assessment Reviews: Romania.* Paris: OECD Publishing.

———. 2016b. *PISA 2015 Results (Volume I): Excellence and Equity in Education.* Paris: PISA, OECD Publishing. http://dx.doi.org/10.1787/9789264266490-en.

UN-DESA (United Nations Department of Economic and Social Affairs) and OECD (Organisation for Economic Co-operation and Development). 2013. "World Migration in Figures." A joint contribution by UN-DESA and the OECD to the United Nations High-Level Dialogue on Migration and Development, 3–4 October 2013, New York and Paris. https://www.oecd.org/els/mig /World-Migration-in-Figures.pdf.

World Bank. 2014b. "Achieving Roma Inclusion in Romania: What Does It Take?" World Bank, Washington, DC. https://openknowledge.worldbank.org/handle/10986/18663.

———. 2014b. "Diagnostics and Policy Advice for Supporting Roma Inclusion in Romania." World Bank, Washington, DC. https://openknowledge.worldbank.org/handle/10986/17796.

———. 2018. *From Uneven Growth to Inclusive Development: Romania's Path to Shared Prosperity.* Washington, DC: World Bank.

———. 2019a. *World Development Report 2019: The Changing Nature of Work.* Washington, DC: World Bank.

———. 2019b. "Precision Training for Workforce Romania. Romania's Skills Challenge: Ending Mismatches with Training-Ready Workers. Preparing Current and Future Workers to Thrive in a Changing Labor Market." World Bank, Washington, DC.

World Bank and NACS (National Agency of Civil Servants). 2017. "Regulatory Impact Assessment Report: Better Employment System within Romania's Central Public Administration." World Bank, Washington, DC. https://sgg.gov.ro/new /wp-content/uploads/2016/04 /RIA-Report-NACS_EN.pdf.

7 Policy Recommendations

As noted throughout this report, Romania has experienced impressive economic growth over the past two decades. The economy has opened to foreign trade and investment. Meanwhile, the country's income per capita rose from 26 percent of the EU-28 average in 2000 to 63 percent in 2017.

The good news, however, sits atop a stressed foundation. This report addresses two essential and inextricably bound structural components of that foundation in depth: markets and people. If Romania is to continue to grow—indeed, if it is to avoid slipping backward—it must address market flaws that frustrate growth and barriers that prevent people from enhancing their human capital, their ability to participate in and benefit from economic growth.

The recommendations in chapter 7 address these two components. They are detailed in two extensive tables. Table 7.1 focuses on competition in markets.

MARKET COMPETITION

State control of the economy and barriers to entry and competition in markets, especially in services, are roadblocks on the path to sustainable economic growth in Romania. Table 7.1 outlines measures that could streamline administrative procedures to market entry for businesses, remove unneeded entry requirements for professional services, and reassess (with an eye toward eliminating or at least minimizing) the application of minimum and maximum prices and of recommended price guidelines for various professions.

The government also hinders growth through its use of state-owned enterprises (SOEs). These can be beneficial entities where markets for essential goods or services do not exist and are unlikely to be created by the private sector. However, in too many instances, SOEs can crowd out private enterprise in Romania, because they do not face the same competitive pressures as private companies. Detailed recommendations focus on leveling the playing field by moving SOEs out of markets when feasible and by making them answerable to increased accountability and transparency where they operate.

These recommendations must also include process improvements. Often, those responsible for coordinating and managing entrance requirements are entities that

TABLE 7.1 **Boosting market competition**

	A. PRODUCT MARKET REGULATION			
	EXPECTED IMPACT LOW = LEAST TRANSFORMATIONAL HIGH = MOST TRANSFORMATIONAL	TIME HORIZON SHORT TERM = < 1 YEAR MEDIUM TERM = 1–3 YEARS	FISCAL IMPLICATIONS	COMMENTS
ECONOMYWIDE				
Streamline burdensome administrative procedures for businesses to facilitate easy market entry. In particular, consider reducing unnecessary requirements applied to entrepreneurs in the preregistration stage of the start-up process.	High	Short term	Yes (potential cost savings)	Reduction of administrative burden and simplification of rules are favorable to competition, as they reduce transaction costs for businesses. This will be an essential complement to systematic application of procompetitive policies and antitrust enforcement.
Facilitate access to information on notifications and licenses as well as access to issuance or acceptance notifications and licenses by setting up (at the local level, if possible) single contact points and making the information available via the internet.	Medium	Medium term	Yes (potential cost savings)	An environment that encourages market entry and ensures competition and transparency in the granting of licenses is key to limiting administrative burden for potential market entrants.
SECTOR-SPECIFIC				
Transport				
Consider extending cabotage to foreign firms in the road freight market.	Medium	Short term	No	The impact on competition may be limited if entry barriers for potential entrants are high. Further liberalizing entry in the road freight market can improve the quality of service, at competitive prices.
Limit interventions by the trade associations in the entry decision in road freight services.	High	Short term	No	By limiting the opportunity of incumbents to veto entry in the sector, the risk of collusive agreements is also reduced. The impact on competition can also be enhanced if burdensome administrative entry procedures are minimized.
Ensure that entry decisions in the road freight sector regulations follow public safety guidelines as well as transparent, neutral, and adequate technical and financial fitness criteria.	Medium	Medium term	No	
Consider removing unnecessary entry requirements for road freight services that may be excessive: for example, the requirement to notify the government or regulatory agency and wait for approval before road freight businesses can start operation.	High	Medium term	Yes (potential cost savings)	Reduction of administrative burden and simplification of rules reduce transaction costs and can increase contestability. This will be an essential complement to a systematic application of procompetitive policies and antitrust enforcement.
Energy				
Reassess recent legislative changes regarding price controls in the gas and electricity sectors for end-user prices and the wholesale market for gas.	Medium	Short term	No	Unnecessary price controls may reduce incentives for additional investments and chill competition in these markets. Further sectoral liberalization may be beneficial for consumers.
Promote regulatory changes that require ownership separation between the production and distribution segments (in electricity and gas).	Low	Medium term	No	

continued

TABLE 7.1, *continued*

A. PRODUCT MARKET REGULATION

	EXPECTED IMPACT LOW = LEAST TRANSFORMATIONAL HIGH = MOST TRANSFORMATIONAL	TIME HORIZON SHORT TERM = < 1 YEAR MEDIUM TERM = 1–3 YEARS	FISCAL IMPLICATIONS	COMMENTS
Retail trade				
Minimize limitations to promotions and discounts that do not qualify as predatory pricing practices in retail distribution.	Low	Short term	No	Limiting regulatory intervention in business decisions can boost sector dynamics.
Promote fierce competition in the retail distribution by lifting restrictions on the timing of sales and promotions.	Low	Short term	No	
Professional services				
Consider removing excessive and unnecessary entry requirements for professional services; for example, unnecessary membership requirements in professional associations, or double licensing from public and professional bodies to lawyers and engineers.	High	Short term	Yes (potential cost savings)	Tackling entry restrictions helps reduce transaction costs and increase contestability, but the impact on competition will be limited if the number of exclusive tasks remains high or price regulation persists.
Review the rationale for shared exclusive rights in all four professional services: legal, accounting, architecture, and engineering.	Medium	Medium term	No	Incentives to compete need to be put in place to avoid collusive behavior and anticompetitive outcomes.
Review the limitations on the corporate forms for the provision of legal and engineering services.	Low	Medium term	No	
Reassess the application of the minimum and maximum price for lawyers and the recommended price guidelines for engineers and architects.	High	Medium term	No	
Support the elimination of advertising and marketing restrictions for legal professional services. Likewise, improve the ability of these professionals to associate and cooperate with other professionals.	Low	Medium term	No	Advertising and marketing reduce information incompleteness and asymmetry. However, competition may be harmed if other complementary measures are not implemented addressing the large number of exclusive tasks that limits the synergies from such associations or price regulation.
Adopt internationally harmonized standards and certification procedures for the legal, engineering, and architecture professions to foster competition and secure a minimally acceptable level of quality of service.	Low	Medium term	No	Competition and benefits for consumers can be fostered when greater standard harmonization allows for the free movement of service providers and market entry.

continued

TABLE 7.1, *continued*

B. STATE-OWNED ENTERPRISES (SOES)

	EXPECTED IMPACT LOW = LEAST TRANSFORMATIONAL HIGH = MOST TRANSFORMATIONAL	TIME HORIZON SHORT TERM = < 1 YEAR MEDIUM TERM = 1–3 YEARS	FISCAL IMPLICATIONS	COMMENTS
ECONOMYWIDE				
Undertake competition assessments in selected markets with significant SOE presence to understand their effects on market outcomes.	Low	Medium term	No	SOE presence should derive from a clear economic rationale; the participation of the government in the economy should not crowd out the private sector.
Restrict publicly controlled firms to markets where the presence of the state is needed as a last resort, and in those sectors where private and public firms coexist, ensure competitive neutrality.	High	Medium term	Yes (potential cost savings)	
Pursue reforms on streamlining SOE management and ensure avoidance of conflicts of interest: including separation between regulatory and operational functions.	Medium	Short term	Yes (potential cost savings)	SOE performance can be improved in the presence of checks and balances to limit undue public influence on strategic decisions.
Require that SOEs must achieve a rate of commercial return and show positive net present value.	High	Short term	Yes (potential cost savings)	The market investor principle will help ensure effective SOE management and limit unnecessary losses and potential associated state aid, while enhancing the efficiency of public spending.
Ensure transparency with respect to (i) state aid granted to SOEs vs. non-SOEs, (ii) the beneficiaries of state aid measures, and (iii) the size of illegal state aid to be recovered and the beneficiaries of such aid, including SOEs and the private sector.	Medium	Short term	No	Increased transparency of state aid to SOEs will minimize competition distortions and foster more efficient public spending.
Ensure that government interventions in markets follow the principle of the subsidiarity role of the state in the economy, with a clear economic rationale.	High	Medium term	No	Identifying a clear economic rationale for SOEs can facilitate investment, better service delivery, and increased value added, and limit crowding out of the private sector.
Minimize the government intervention (at any level) in strategic choices of publicly controlled firms.	Medium	Medium term	Yes (potential cost savings)	To foster a level playing field, SOEs' decisions should be based on efficiency considerations, limiting interference from public bodies in corporate decisions of SOEs.

continued

TABLE 7.1, *continued*

	B. STATE-OWNED ENTERPRISES (SOEs)			
	EXPECTED IMPACT LOW = LEAST TRANSFORMATIONAL HIGH = MOST TRANSFORMATIONAL	TIME HORIZON SHORT TERM = < 1 YEAR MEDIUM TERM = 1–3 YEARS	FISCAL IMPLICATIONS	COMMENTS
Require that state equity holdings in publicly controlled firms be managed by an independent body entity instead of any ministry connected to the SOE.	Medium	Medium term	Yes (potential cost savings)	SOE performance can be improved in the presence of checks and balances to limit undue public influence on strategic decisions. However, limited impact on market dynamics can be expected if this is not implemented as a part of broader competitively neutral policies.
Ensure systematic application of the EU state aid rules to SOEs, including control of illegal state aid.	Medium	Medium term	No	The effectiveness of applying remedies under the EU state aid law may be limited, and systematic monitoring of SOE performance is needed.
SECTOR-SPECIFIC				
Transport				
In the airline sector, reassess the economic rationale of SOE participation, and ensure competitive neutrality.	Medium	Medium term	Yes (potential cost savings)	SOE performance should guide the decisions on maintaining SOE presence in the market and minimize unnecessary public spending associated with SOE operations, while minimizing competition distortions.
Consider removing any legal or constitutional constraints on the sale of the stakes held by the government in the railway infrastructure segment.	Low	Medium term	Yes (potential cost savings)	Limiting command-and-control regulation can complement procompetition policies in the sector.
Energy				
Ensure competitive neutrality between existing SOEs and private firms.	Medium	Medium term	No	A comprehensive policy to foster competition in the sector, including access to essential facilities and incentives for operators to enter segments open to competition, can strengthen market dynamics.
Promote regulatory changes that require ownership separation between the production and distribution segments (particularly in electricity and gas).	Medium	Medium term	No	
Retail trade				
Ensure competitive neutrality between private firms and any public firm and ensure that publicly controlled firms are restricted to markets where the presence of the state is needed as last resort (for example, the pharmaceutical sector).	Low	Medium term	No	The impact on competition may be enhanced when SOEs are subject to market discipline and provide goods that the private sector cannot provide by itself in an efficient manner.

Note: EU = European Union; SOE = state-owned enterprise.

stand to gain from their continued existence, and the state entities that oversee SOEs likewise have a stake in their continuation. Table 7.1 presents specific recommendations to improve these processes, outlining their costs and benefits as well.

HUMAN CAPITAL

The foundation of any economy—not to mention society and culture—is people. They harness their skills, knowledge, and labor to create economic enterprises whose purpose, in the end, is to generate wealth, products, and services to improve the lives of those people in a virtuous cycle.

Table 7.2 presents detailed recommendations in two fundamental generators of human capital: the educational system and both public and private efforts to ensure that the supply of skills matches the economy's demand, in both quantity and quality.

As noted earlier in the report, a child born in Romania is expected to reach only 60 percent of his or her productive potential as an adult. If he or she received the full benefit of a high-quality education and health available in other European Union countries, the expectation would be 100 percent.

This gap is associated directly with a lack of quality in education. Table 7.2 presents recommendations to achieve effective reform by using evidence to hold systems and stakeholders accountable for student learning; implementing more flexible approaches to teacher development and appraisal, one that rewards success rather than straightjackets pedagogy; upgrading the teaching profession by using innovative teacher recruitment, motivation, and development practices; providing schools with the ability to plan school-level improvements tailored to their needs; and offering systematic support to schools so administrators and teachers can learn methodologies that engage students meaningfully.

A good part of the educational endeavor must prepare students to be lifelong learners, as their jobs, careers, and even professions may change several times in modern, fast-changing marketplaces. This will entail teaching sociobehavioral skills as well as subject-oriented skills: often, tasks are taught on the job, but the ability to work as a team and at a comfortable level in adapting to change have become essential prerequisites for modern workers. To enhance educational practices that address these factors, the government, the private sector, the educational system, and other stakeholders must tend to the macro issues of supply and demand in marketable skills.

Recommendations in table 7.2 call for public-private partnerships to address the provision of training and retraining needs, a public review and rationalization of vocational programs and qualifications, and ongoing evaluations of supply-and-demand mismatches in terms of skills and capabilities. The Romanian economy suffers from too many people in positions they are not adequately prepared for and too many in positions for which they are overqualified, because mismatches are (i) not detected and (ii) not addressed when identified. Human capital well matched to employers' needs—whether in self-employment as an entrepreneur or a staff member in a large corporation—is oil that lubricates the economy. The recommendations in table 7.2 can help ensure that such a lubricant is available and of high quality.

TABLE 7.2 **Building human capital**

A. EDUCATION

	EXPECTED IMPACT LOW = LEAST TRANSFORMATIONAL HIGH = MOST TRANSFORMATIONAL	TIME HORIZON SHORT TERM = < 1 YEAR MEDIUM TERM = 1–3 YEARS LONG TERM = > 3 YEARS	FISCAL IMPLICATIONS	COMMENTS
System level: Funding				
Review current school funding mechanisms to ensure that finances are directed to those schools and students that need them most.	Medium Financial support is important for transformation, but if there is no buy-in and commitment from school governing bodies and other stakeholders, or if there is a lack of optimal or responsible use of financial support, the impact will not be as expected.	Short term	Increased funding for schools that need it most implies either allocating additional funds to the system or redirecting current funding streams. The latter might need some consultation with current recipients of funding.	The assumption is that better financially resourced schools would be able to provide better educational resources (including physical and human resources). However, helping schools to manage increased funding well is a critical component that will play a key role in maximizing the impact of increased funding.
Introduce dynamic changes in the school funding formula to incentivize learning and close educational gaps across regions. This will require improvements in the system's monitoring and evaluation system to track results, make decisions, and hold stakeholders accountable to achieving learning outcomes.	Medium There is possibility of high impact if monitoring and evaluation results in accountability and continuous improvement. However, there is still uncertainty about the impact of incentivized learning.	Medium term	Financial implications will depend on the nature of incentives. Monitoring and evaluation planning and implementation will require some resources if implemented at scale.	Before such changes are implemented to incentivize learning, research studies are needed to determine the impact of different possibilities. This is because of the lack of or uncertainty about the impact regarding teacher and other resource incentives.
System level: Institutional development				
Incorporate stakeholder consultations into educational reform efforts to build consensus, ensure buy-in during implementation, and enable more rapid scale-up and long-term sustainability.	Medium	Short term	Low costs involved.	Consultations need to establish credibility, and processes need to ensure that stakeholders' feedback is used meaningfully.
Use evidence, including international and national student assessment information, to hold the system and stakeholders accountable for achieving student learning.	High	Medium term	Monitoring and evaluation will initially require some investment. However, costs might decline with standardized or automated ways of using data.	There are administrative data that could be used more effectively, as a starting point.
Track progress of program interventions through systematic efforts to measure program impacts.	High	Medium term	Monitoring and evaluation will initially require some investment. However, costs might decline with standardized or automated ways of using data.	Having robust evidence can help programs survive short political cycles.
School level: Teachers				
Design and implement a more flexible approach to teacher development and appraisal that focuses on improving teaching performance and the students' learning experience.	High	Long term	Low cost (consultation/research; conceptual change to teaching development). Cost of implementation may be higher depending on approach taken.	This needs to be implemented in consultation with teachers. A research study on teachers' development needs might be necessary before making such changes.

continued

TABLE 7.2, *continued*

A. EDUCATION

	EXPECTED IMPACT LOW = LEAST TRANSFORMATIONAL HIGH = MOST TRANSFORMATIONAL	TIME HORIZON SHORT TERM = < 1 YEAR MEDIUM TERM = 1–3 YEARS LONG TERM = > 3 YEARS	FISCAL IMPLICATIONS	COMMENTS
Upgrade the teacher profession using innovative teacher recruitment, motivation, and development practices that recognize teachers as valued professionals.	High	Medium term	Costs might be related to study bursaries, evaluating and adapting teacher-training programs, and investing in a marketing and development campaign.	Specific attention needs to be given to make the prospect of teaching in a rural or disadvantaged school attractive. Typically, good teachers tend to go to better schools, thereby not breaking the cycle of disadvantage in poorer schools. This will require significant investment of time and resources to change perceptions.
Introduce a system that links professional development to student performance and offer coaching to teachers who are at the beginning of their careers or who need to upgrade their practices to be in line with changes in curricula and modern teaching methods that engage students meaningfully in their learning journey.	Medium	Medium term	Low cost for the initial research and development of such a rubric. There might be larger financial implications for sustained relationships and use of training providers.	In practice, this will imply a generic assessment (maybe in the form of a rubric) of teachers' development needs, which must be related to students' performance. It would also require buy-in from schools, teachers, and training providers. A research study to determine the parameters of such a rubric might be needed beforehand.
School level: Students				
Consider introducing student mentoring programs to reduce early school leaving and develop socioemotional skills.	Medium	Short term	At scale, this might have considerable costs.	This might have indirect impact on academic achievement or retention. Tracking and impact studies will be needed to determine feasibility.
Introduce a system that provides schools with the ability to plan school-level improvements that are tailored to the teaching force and diverse needs of the student populations they serve.	High This impact depends on initiatives being managed well and given appropriate support.	Medium term	Providing adequate support to schools might have some financial implications.	The majority of schools might need considerable guidance to identify and implement tailor-made interventions and programs to help their student populations. There are ongoing efforts in country that could be proven effective (for example, the Romania Secondary Education Project).
Offer systematic support to school leaders and teachers to ensure there is relevant training and there are guides available to prepare school staff on methodologies that can engage students meaningfully, especially students from vulnerable groups and disadvantaged homes who endure multiple constraints. Recognize schools and groups of teachers who make substantive progress in improving student outcomes and student learning.	High	Medium term	Investment in providing such support might be substantial.	Empowering schools and stakeholders is key.

B. SKILLS

	EXPECTED IMPACT LOW = LEAST TRANSFORMATIONAL HIGH = MOST TRANSFORMATIONAL	TIME HORIZON SHORT TERM = < 1 YEAR MEDIUM TERM = 1–3 YEARS LONG TERM = > 3 YEARS	FISCAL IMPLICATIONS	COMMENTS
System level				
Implement appropriate reforms in primary and secondary schooling to ensure that learners and workers entering the skills development ecosystem in Romania have acquired the required literacy, numeracy, and socioemotional skills and other core foundational competencies necessary to prepare them for further studies and integration into a rapidly modernizing economy.	High	Long term	Depending what the "appropriate reforms" are, improving literacy, numeracy, and socioemotional skills will require changes in curricula, teaching and learning, and monitoring and evaluation. At scale, this will require considerable effort, coordination, and cost.	
Establish a feedback mechanism that brings together policy and decision makers in general education, training providers and tertiary education institutions to communicate strengths, weaknesses, and areas to improve the quality of foundational skills set of young people.	Medium A feedback mechanism might not lead to tangible changes in practice.	Medium term	Low cost	Key ideas here are collaboration and coordination among different role players and making data driven decisions to monitor interventions and progress. Some effort will be required to put such mechanisms in place, but the continuous review of progress toward improving foundational skills will be crucial to keep up with changing skills needs.
Make available remedial education curricula targeting young and working age adults whose core foundational competencies and skills need to be upgraded before entering further education and training.	Medium	Medium term	Costs should subside with increased quality of basic education (which would imply less need for such remedial programs).	It is very important to raise an individual's literacy level to ensure they can participate meaningfully in training.
Undertake ongoing review, rationalization, and streamlining of all vocational programs and qualifications to ensure that formal skills development programs in both technical and vocational education and training (TVET) schools and universities are relevant, up to date, and sufficiently flexible to allow for reskilling at different points in individuals' labor market trajectories.	High	Short term	Funding is already in place, but additional funding might be needed.	Taking a hard look at the system and rationalizing institutions or programs as needed is important to ensure that students who go into the TVET stream move into training programs that are of high quality and that provide skills needed today and develop students' ability to learn new technical skills in the future.

continued

	EXPECTED IMPACT LOW = LEAST TRANSFORMATIONAL HIGH = MOST TRANSFORMATIONAL	TIME HORIZON SHORT TERM = < 1 YEAR MEDIUM TERM = 1–3 YEARS LONG TERM = > 3 YEARS	FISCAL IMPLICATIONS	COMMENTS
B. SKILLS				
Reorganize the education system to delay streaming into vocational areas until a later stage in the educational trajectory.	Medium	Medium term	There is a low cost to organize such changes, but they may entail high costs of implementation depending on the institutional adjustments required.	
Enhance the quality of secondary education to include communication and socioemotional skills that will be needed for further education, training, or employment.	Medium	Medium term	This should not have considerable cost implications if such graduate attributes or generic skills are worked into existing curricula (although additional teacher training may be needed).	Adding these skills to curricula will necessitate assessments to ascertain the extent to which students develop the skills, and some coordination is required to determine the logistics and extent of adding such skills into curricula.
Service delivery				
Introduce new skills development arrangements that can better support workers by helping them move through increasingly quick skills depreciation cycles and more readily prepare them for reskilling throughout their lives. This can begin on a pilot basis, and, based on evidence, it can be scaled up.	Medium There is a possibility of High impact later when the effort is scaled up and reaching more people.	Short to medium term	Costs need not be too high if arrangements are beneficial for all parties.	Companies might need help mediating between training providers and educational institutions.
Introduce policy and financing incentive mechanisms to implement public private partnerships, combined with clear guidelines for participation, as a specific strategy to share the cost, risk, and reward between government and the private sector in skills areas where vacancies are highest and skills are not readily available in the labor market, and to facilitate growth of new kinds of skills in economic growth areas where training providers are not yet positioned to run formal programs that meet changing labor market demands.	High	Medium term	Costs need not be too high if arrangements are beneficial for all parties.	Public-private partnerships are vital for early identification of and response to emerging skills needs.
Provide systematic guidance to employers on how best to engage in and offer workplace based training. This should focus on providing hard evidence on the return on investment of workplace based training to industry leaders, as well as information about successful workplace based training initiatives within Romania and from around the world.	Low	Short term	Low costs would be associated with research, distribution of information, and advocacy.	This should be done in consultation and collaboration with training and education providers as a facilitative process forming relationships between workplaces and training providers.

continued

B. SKILLS

	EXPECTED IMPACT LOW = LEAST TRANSFORMATIONAL HIGH = MOST TRANSFORMATIONAL	TIME HORIZON SHORT TERM = < 1 YEAR MEDIUM TERM = 1–3 YEARS LONG TERM = > 3 YEARS	FISCAL IMPLICATIONS	COMMENTS
Adopt suitable (and flexible) occupational competence standards for priority professions and jobs in key economic sectors to facilitate the creation of new skills development programs and services by both public and private training providers, with emphasis on being able to provide workplace based training services to employers.	Medium	Medium term	Low cost would be entailed for developing standards. Higher costs would be related to implementation, monitoring, and evaluation.	As with any other policy goals and guidelines, occupational standards are only as good as their measure of implementation.
Information				
Design recognition of prior learning (RPL) processes to enable more flexible completion of skills development programs, accumulation of credits, portability of credentials, and flexible entry into programs depending on skills, knowledge, and competencies acquired through self study and/or workplace practices.	High	Short term	Low costs would be entailed to design the process. There might be a higher cost to implement it, depending on the approach designed.	
Implement an RPL system to underpin the development of a precision training framework to ensure workers can access training when they need it, where they need it, and how they need it. This may require the use of technologies and online training platforms.	High	Medium term	Low cost is entailed in the development of an RPL system and precision training framework. The development of online training programs specific to companies' needs will require initial funding.	
Establish structured mechanisms to enable effective coordination of efforts among all the key players in Romania on whom a skills development ecosystem for the country will depend.	High	Short term	Low to no cost	
Ensure the sustainability of the effective coordination with a combination of legislation, funding, and well publicized strategic leadership from the government and industry.	High	Short term	Low to no cost	High impact is possible if implementation is monitored and evaluated.

continued

B. SKILLS

	EXPECTED IMPACT LOW = LEAST TRANSFORMATIONAL HIGH = MOST TRANSFORMATIONAL	TIME HORIZON SHORT TERM = < 1 YEAR MEDIUM TERM = 1–3 YEARS LONG TERM = > 3 YEARS	FISCAL IMPLICATIONS	COMMENTS
Invest in active labor market policies and improve efficiency of active labor market policy (ALMP) expenditures to remove information asymmetries, thereby helping current and future workers to reduce search times to find jobs that fit their skills profile and to find suitable skills programs to best prepare them for future employment and career growth, with a focus on women, youth, and those in rural areas.	Medium The impact could, however, be transformational for rectifying skills alignment.	Short term	Potentially low, especially if some dedicated funding is redirected toward more effective programs.	High impact is possible if implementation is monitored and evaluated.
Establish an evaluation system to gauge the effectiveness and impacts of different types of ALMPs and expand program coverage based on accumulated evidence. Make information on programs available to employment centers, providers, employers, and prospective users.	Medium	Medium term	High initial costs to develop the evaluation system. Once a system is in place, there would be fewer financial requirements when data and information gathering and reporting is done in cycles.	
Introduce regular monitoring, evaluation, and research strategies to assess the effectiveness and impact of national strategies to stimulate the skills development ecosystem.	Medium	Short term	Initial costs to develop a monitoring and evaluation system might be high, then there would be fewer financial requirements when data and information gathering and reporting is done in cycles. There would be costs for ongoing research.	
Make information available online and through different social media to ensure students, workers, trainers, and employers understand the system, how to make effective use of the program offerings, and how to establish new programs, including through public-private partnerships.	Medium	Medium term	Continuous limited costs.	It is important to make sure that relevant information reaches relevant people, and that all (particularly people from rural areas) are included as recipients of relevant information.

Note: ALMP = active labor market policies; TVET = technical and vocation education and training.

APPENDIX

Selected Indicators

Basic indicators

	AVERAGE				
	2000–08	2009–15	2016	2017	2018
Real economy					
GDP (nominal, billion lei)	264.7	604.1	765.1	856.7	944.2
Real GDP growth					
Romania	*6.1*	*0.8*	*4.8*	*7.0*	*4.1*
Czech Republic	4.3	0.9	2.5	4.4	2.9
Hungary	3.4	0.6	2.3	4.1	4.9
Poland	4.2	3.1	3.1	4.8	5.1
Slovak Republic	5.7	1.8	3.1	3.2	4.1
EU-15	2.1	0.4	1.9	2.3	1.8
Euro area	2.0	0.2	2.0	2.4	1.9
EU-28	2.2	0.5	2.0	2.4	2.0
GNI per capita, Atlas method (US$)	3,854	9,083	9,530	9,990	11,290
Fiscal accounts (percent of GDP)					
Revenues	33.2	33.4	31.8	30.9	32.0
Expenditures	35.8	37.6	34.5	33.6	35.0
General government balance (ESA 2010)					
Romania	*-2.6*	*-4.2*	*-2.7*	*-2.7*	*-3.0*
Czech Republic	-3.6	-2.9	0.7	1.6	0.9
Hungary	-6.1	-3.4	-1.6	-2.2	-2.2
Poland	-4.1	-4.8	-2.2	-1.5	-0.4
Slovak Republic	-4.7	-4.6	-2.2	-0.8	-0.7
EU-15	-1.9	-4.4	-1.7	-1.0	-0.6
Euro area	-2.0	-4.0	-1.6	-1.0	-0.5
EU-28	-2.2	-4.3	-1.7	-1.0	-0.6
Public and publicly guaranteed debt (ESA 2010)	18.5	33.9	37.3	35.2	35.0
Selected monetary accounts					
Interest (key policy rate, in percent)	19.5	4.9	1.8	1.8	2.5
Inflation (Consumer Price Index, average)	17.5	3.6	-1.5	1.3	4.6
Balance of payments (percent of GDP)					
Current account balance					
Romania	*-8.0*	*-3.2*	*-2.1*	*-3.2*	*-4.5*
Czech Republic	-3.9	-1.4	1.6	1.1	0.8

continued

TABLE A.1, *continued*

	AVERAGE				
	2000–08	2009–15	2016	2017	2018
Hungary	-7.2	1.4	6.1	3.2	0.4
Poland	-5.0	-3.2	-0.5	0.2	-0.7
Slovak Republic	-7.0	-1.6	-2.2	-2.0	-2.5
EU-15	-0.4	1.0	2.1	2.8	2.3
Euro area	-0.2	1.3	3.2	3.2	3.0
EU-28	-1.1	0.3	1.3	1.3	1.2
Foreign direct investment	5.2	2.0	2.7	2.6	2.4

Sources: Data compiled from Eurostat (database), European Commission, Brussels, https://ec.europa.eu/eurostat/data/database; National Bank of Romania, https://www.bnro.ro/Home.aspx; National Institute of Statistics, http://www.insse.ro/cms/en; and World Development Indicators, World Bank, Washington, DC, https://datacatalog.worldbank.org/dataset/world-development-indicators.
Note: ESA 2010 = European System of Accounts 2010; EU-15 = for list of countries see Note 4 on page 20; EU-28 = for list of countries see Note 3 on page 20; GDP = gross domestic product; GNI = gross national income.

TABLE A.2 Investment

	AVERAGE				
	2000–08	2009–15	2016	2017	2018
Total investment (by institutional sectors, percent of GDP)					
Private					
Romania	*21.4*	*20.7*	*19.3*	*19.9*	...
Czech Republic	24.0	21.5	21.7	21.4	...
Hungary	19.9	16.7	16.5	17.7	...
Poland	17.1	15.2	14.8	...	...
Slovak Republic	23.6	18.1	18.1	18.2	...
EU-15	18.4	16.6	17.3	17.5	...
Euro area	19.5	17.5	18.1	18.2	18.6
EU-28	18.9	17.0	17.7	17.9	18.1
Public					
Romania	*4.1*	*5.1*	*3.6*	*2.6*	...
Czech Republic	5.1	4.7	3.3	3.4	...
Hungary	4.1	4.3	3.1	4.5	...
Poland	3.3	4.9	3.3	...	...
Slovak Republic	3.5	4.0	3.2	3.2	...
EU-15	3.0	3.1	2.7	2.7	...
Euro area	3.2	3.1	2.6	2.6	2.68
EU-28	3.1	3.2	2.7	2.8	2.89
Investment (by structural elements, percent of total)					
New construction	39.2	44.2	40.3	37.5	...
Installations	54.4	49.1	52.9	52.9	...
Geological works	1.4	2.2	2.1	2.0	...
Other	5.0	4.4	4.7	7.6	...
Investment (by economic activity, percent of total)					
Agriculture, forestry, and fishing	5.2	4.4	4.5	6.5	...
Industry	37.2	38.7	34.7	30.7	...
Construction	10.0	11.4	10.3	11.0	...
Wholesale and retail trade	13.4	9.8	10.4	11.9	...

Sources: Eurostat (database), European Commission, Brussels, https://ec.europa.eu/eurostat/data/database; National Institute of Statistics, http://www.insse.ro/cms/en.
Note: EU-15 = for list of countries see Note 4 on page 20; EU-28 = for list of countries see Note 3 on page 20; GDP = gross domestic product; ... = not available.

TABLE A.3 **Labor**

	AVERAGE				
	2000–08	2009–15	2016	2017	2018
Population, total (million)	21.6	20.1	19.8	19.6	19.5
Population, working age (percent)	68.4	68.0	67.1	66.6	66.2
Net migration (thousand)	-621	-300	...	-150	...
Age dependency ratio (percent of working-age population)	46.0	46.6	48.7	49.5	...
Unemployment rate (percent)					
Total (ages 15–64)					
Romania	*7.3*	*6.9*	*5.9*	*4.9*	*4.2*
Czech Republic	7.2	6.6	4.0	2.9	2.2
Hungary	6.6	9.7	5.1	4.2	3.7
Poland	15.8	9.2	6.2	4.9	3.9
Slovak Republic	16.0	13.3	9.7	8.1	6.5
EU-15	7.7	10.0	9.0	8.2	7.5
Euro area	8.5	10.8	10.0	9.1	8.2
EU-28	8.5	9.9	8.6	7.6	6.8
Ages 15–24					
Romania	*18.7*	*22.6*	*20.6*	*18.3*	*16.2*
Czech Republic	16.1	17.1	10.5	7.9	6.7
Hungary	15.5	24.5	12.9	10.7	10.2
Poland	33.8	24.1	17.7	14.8	11.7
Slovak Republic	31.1	31.3	22.2	18.9	14.9
EU-15	16.4	21.4	18.9	17.2	15.6
Euro area	17.7	22.5	20.9	18.8	16.9
EU-28	18.2	21.9	18.7	16.8	15.2
Employment rate (percent)					
Total (ages 15–64)					
Romania	*64.0*	*64.8*	*65.6*	*67.3*	*67.8*
Czech Republic	70.4	71.8	75.0	75.9	76.6
Hungary	60.7	64.2	70.1	71.2	71.9
Poland	64.3	66.5	68.8	69.6	70.1
Slovak Republic	69.4	69.5	71.9	72.1	72.4
EU-15	70.6	72.9	73.9	74.1	74.4
Euro area	69.4	71.9	72.9	73.1	73.5
EU-28	69.5	71.6	73.0	73.4	73.7
Ages 15–24					
Romania	*34.5*	*30.6*	*28.0*	*30.0*	*29.5*
Czech Republic	36.3	31.4	32.0	31.7	30.4
Hungary	29.9	26.8	32.3	32.4	32.3
Poland	36.0	33.6	34.5	34.8	35.1
Slovak Republic	39.4	30.9	32.4	33.2	32.3
EU-15	48.0	45.4	44.0	43.8	43.9
Euro area	44.3	41.4	39.7	39.9	40.1
EU-28	44.6	42.4	41.7	41.7	41.7

continued

TABLE A.3, *continued*

	AVERAGE				
	2000–08	2009–15	2016	2017	2018
Employment rate (percent)					
Less than primary, primary, and lower secondary education (ages 15–64)					
Romania	*43.0*	*42.6*	*41.0*	*42.5*	*42.6*
Czech Republic	24.9	22.1	23.7	26.1	26.5
Hungary	28.0	27.8	36.6	38.5	39.4
Poland	24.9	23.3	23.0	23.3	23.6
Slovak Republic	15.4	15.8	19.8	21.4	21.1
EU-15	51.2	47.0	46.9	47.7	48.6
Euro area	49.4	45.6	44.9	45.7	46.5
EU-28	47.8	44.5	44.6	45.6	46.4
Upper secondary and postsecondary education (ages 15–64)					
Romania	*64.7*	*63.9*	*65.2*	*67.5*	*68.6*
Czech Republic	72.3	72.3	77.4	78.9	80.1
Hungary	65.6	63.3	71.5	73.1	73.7
Poland	58.9	62.4	65.6	67.0	68.1
Slovak Republic	66.8	66.4	70.9	72.5	74.0
EU-15	71.4	69.9	70.8	71.3	71.9
Euro area	70.0	68.9	69.7	70.4	71.1
EU-28	69.4	68.4	70.0	70.9	71.7
Tertiary education (ages 15–64)					
Romania	*83.8*	*83.4*	*86.2*	*87.9*	*88.4*
Czech Republic	85.0	81.8	83.4	84.2	85.6
Hungary	81.5	79.2	84.4	84.3	85.1
Poland	82.0	83.1	85.8	86.8	87.6
Slovak Republic	84.2	76.7	77.3	78.5	79.3
EU-15	83.2	82.1	83.1	83.6	84.1
Euro area	82.3	81.5	82.4	83.1	83.6
EU-28	83.3	82.2	83.4	84.0	84.5

Sources: Eurostat (database), European Commission, Brussels, https://ec.europa.eu/eurostat/data/database; National Institute of Statistics, http://www.insse.ro/cms/en; World Development Indicators, World Bank, Washington, DC, https://datacatalog.worldbank.org/dataset /world-development-indicators.
Note: EU-15 = for list of countries see Note 4 on page 20; EU-28 = for list of countries see Note 3 on page 20; . . . = not available.

TABLE A.4 **Human capital**

	AVERAGE				
	2000–08	2009–15	2016	2017	2018
PISA Scores*					
Math					
Romania	*420.2*	*438.7*	. . .	. . .	. . .
Czech Republic	510.2	495.4	. . .	. . .	. . .
Hungary	490.1	481.9	. . .	. . .	. . .
Poland	486.7	506.1	. . .	. . .	. . .
Slovak Republic	495.3	485.3	. . .	. . .	. . .
EU-15	500.7	497.9	. . .	. . .	. . .
Euro area	494.6	490.4	. . .	. . .	. . .
EU-28	495.2	490.4	. . .	. . .	. . .
Reading					
Romania	*412.0*	*432.1*	. . .	. . .	. . .
Czech Republic	490.6	487.1	. . .	. . .	. . .
Hungary	481.8	484.5	. . .	. . .	. . .
Poland	495.8	508.7	. . .	. . .	. . .
Slovak Republic	468.0	465.0	. . .	. . .	. . .
EU-15	498.2	498.8	. . .	. . .	. . .
Euro area	490.1	488.6	. . .	. . .	. . .
EU-28	491.1	488.9	. . .	. . .	. . .
Science					
Romania	*429.8*	*434.2*	. . .	. . .	. . .
Czech Republic	517.9	501.2	. . .	. . .	. . .
Hungary	501.5	491.9	. . .	. . .	. . .
Poland	493.9	512.5	. . .	. . .	. . .
Slovak Republic	491.9	475.0	. . .	. . .	. . .
EU-15	500.8	502.8	. . .	. . .	. . .
Euro area	497.1	496.2	. . .	. . .	. . .
EU-28	497.6	496.1	. . .	. . .	. . .
Early leavers from education and training (ages 18-24, percent of total age group)					
Romania	*20.4*	*18.0*	*18.5*	*18.1*	*16.4*
Czech Republic	5.8	5.4	6.6	6.7	6.2
Hungary	12.4	11.5	12.4	12.5	12.5
Poland	5.9	5.5	5.2	5.0	4.8
Slovak Republic	6.3	5.7	7.4	9.3	8.6
EU-15	17.9	13.6	11.1	10.9	11.0
Euro area	17.9	13.7	11.1	11.0	11.0
EU-28	15.7	12.6	10.7	10.6	10.6
Tertiary education attainment (ages 30–34)					
Romania	*11.1*	*21.5*	*25.6*	*26.3*	*24.6*
Czech Republic	13.3	24.6	32.8	34.2	33.7
Hungary	17.7	29.8	33.0	32.1	33.7

continued

TABLE A.4, *continued*

	AVERAGE				
	2000–08	2009–15	2016	2017	2018
Poland	20.2	38.5	44.6	45.7	45.7
Slovak Republic	12.8	24.1	31.5	34.3	37.7
EU-15	29.1	37.2	39.7	40.4	41.4
Euro area	27.6	35.1	37.6	38.4	39.6
EU-28	27.6	35.8	39.2	39.9	40.7

	2017				
Human Capital Index	HCI	U-5 SR	ASR	EYS	HTS
Romania	*0.60*	*0.992*	*0.87*	*12.2*	*452*
Czech Republic	0.78	0.997	0.92	13.9	522
Hungary	0.70	0.996	0.87	13.0	516
Poland	0.75	0.995	0.89	13.2	537
Slovak Republic	0.69	0.994	0.89	13.0	500
EU-15	0.77	0.996	0.94	13.6	519
Euro area	0.75	0.996	0.92	13.4	517
EU-28	0.75	0.996	0.92	13.4	515

Sources: Eurostat (database), European Commission, Brussels, https://ec.europa.eu/eurostat/data/database; Organisation for Economic Co-operation and Development (OECD) PISA, https://www.oecd.org/pisa/; Human Capital Project, World Bank, Washington, DC, https://www .worldbank.org/en/publication/human-capital.
Note: ASR = adult survival rate; EU-15 = for list of countries see Note 4 on page 20; EU-28 = for list of countries see Note 3 on page 20; EYS = expected years of school; HCI = Human Capital Index; HTS = harmonized test scores; PISA = Program for International Student Assessment; U-5 SR = under-5 survival rate; . . . = not available.
* The PISA is conducted once every three years. The averages are calculated based on the assessments in 2000, 2003, 2006, 2009, 2012, and 2015.

TABLE A.5 **Business environment**

	PRODUCT MARKET REGULATION*		
	2003	2008	2013
Overall score			
Romania	...	...	*1.69*
Czech Republic	1.89	1.51	1.41
Hungary	2.11	1.54	1.33
Poland	2.42	2.04	1.65
Slovak Republic	2.18	1.62	1.29
EU-15	1.69	1.47	1.34
Euro area	1.80	1.52	1.41
EU-28	1.80	1.73	1.63
State control			
Romania	...	...	*2.78*
Czech Republic	2.61	2.14	1.98
Hungary	2.47	2.03	2.05
Poland	3.57	3.32	3.06
Slovak Republic	3.07	2.36	2.17
EU-15	2.48	2.22	2.07
Euro area	2.72	2.28	2.10
EU-28	2.46	2.41	2.35
Barriers to entry and rivalry			
Romania	...	...	*2.06*
Czech Republic	2.19	1.90	1.82
Hungary	2.30	2.20	1.69
Poland	3.11	2.49	1.64
Slovak Republic	2.15	1.74	1.15
EU-15	2.08	1.79	1.59
Euro area	2.10	1.81	1.68
EU-28	2.13	2.02	1.86
Barriers to trade and investment			
Romania	...	...	*0.22*
Czech Republic	0.85	0.48	0.42
Hungary	1.57	0.38	0.24
Poland	0.59	0.33	0.24
Slovak Republic	1.30	0.77	0.55
EU-15	0.50	0.41	0.35
Euro area	0.57	0.46	0.46
EU-28	0.79	0.74	0.68

continued

TABLE A.5, *continued*

	DOING BUSINESS**				
	AVERAGE				
	2000–08	2009–15	2016	2017	2018
Overall					
Romania	...	*66.0*	*72.7*	*72.8*	*72.3*
Czech Republic	...	70.6	76.0	72.8	72.3
Hungary	...	67.7	71.2	71.9	72.3
Poland	...	70.1	77.1	77.3	77.0
Slovak Republic	...	70.7	74.8	74.9	75.2
EU-15	...	75.4	76.8	76.9	77.1
Euro area	...	72.7	75.3	75.4	75.6
EU-28	...	72.9	75.6	75.7	75.9
Starting a business					
Romania	*87.7*	*89.8*	*89.5*	*89.7*	*83.9*
Czech Republic	71.9	79.3	83.0	83.6	83.6
Hungary	76.0	89.5	87.3	87.6	87.9
Poland	56.6	80.4	82.8	82.8	82.9
Slovak Republic	71.3	80.7	81.9	82.0	82.0
EU-15	82.3	88.2	90.9	91.0	91.1
Euro area	81.9	87.5	90.1	90.5	90.4
EU-28	79.3	87.3	89.4	89.7	89.5
Dealing with construction permits					
Romania	*62.7*	*56.8*	*58.1*	*58.1*	*58.2*
Czech Republic	54.3	56.9	56.2	56.2	56.2
Hungary	67.0	67.9	66.2	66.2	66.7
Poland	50.3	65.2	75.2	75.2	75.2
Slovak Republic	61.2	60.8	59.3	59.3	59.3
EU-15	70.8	74.6	76.2	76.2	76.4
Euro area	64.1	70.1	73.9	74.3	74.5
EU-28	66.1	69.5	72.3	72.6	72.8
Getting electricity					
Romania	...	*40.5*	*53.2*	*53.3*	*53.5*
Czech Republic	...	86.1	95.4	95.4	95.4
Hungary	...	62.0	63.3	63.3	63.3
Poland	...	68.4	81.4	81.4	81.4
Slovak Republic	...	78.5	83.2	83.2	83.2
EU-15	...	80.3	85.6	85.9	86.6
Euro area	...	77.3	83.3	83.7	84.0
EU-28	...	76.6	81.9	82.1	82.4
Registering property					
Romania	*70.3*	*79.7*	*73.9*	*74.8*	*75.0*
Czech Republic	62.6	77.3	79.7	79.7	79.7
Hungary	57.4	76.4	80.1	80.1	80.1
Poland	52.3	70.3	76.5	76.5	76.1
Slovak Republic	89.2	91.6	90.2	90.2	90.2

continued

TABLE A.5, *continued*

	DOING BUSINESS**				
	AVERAGE				
	2000–08	2009–15	2016	2017	2018
EU-15	65.8	70.8	73.1	73.1	72.6
Euro area	61.6	70.8	73.2	73.2	72.8
EU-28	66.9	72.9	74.6	74.7	74.4
Getting credit					
Romania	*67.5*	*84.3*	*80.0*	*80.0*	*80.0*
Czech Republic	72.5	67.9	70.0	70.0	70.0
Hungary	62.5	68.9	70.0	75.0	75.0
Poland	78.8	85.7	75.0	75.0	75.0
Slovak Republic	67.5	71.4	70.0	70.0	70.0
EU-15	64.4	60.8	54.0	54.3	55.7
Euro area	55.4	56.7	53.9	54.7	56.1
EU-28	65.4	63.7	58.8	59.5	60.4
Protecting minority investors					
Romania	*55.8*	*58.1*	*60.0*	*60.0*	*60.0*
Czech Republic	50.0	54.0	58.3	58.3	58.3
Hungary	43.3	46.2	50.0	50.0	50.0
Poland	59.2	60.7	61.7	61.7	61.7
Slovak Republic	46.7	49.5	53.3	53.3	53.3
EU-15	56.2	60.2	63.4	63.8	63.8
Euro area	41.1	57.3	61.7	62.0	62.1
EU-28	55.5	58.9	62.4	62.7	62.9
Paying taxes					
Romania	*48.0*	*61.9*	*80.4*	*80.3*	*80.3*
Czech Republic	49.0	74.4	81.8	81.2	81.4
Hungary	65.4	70.1	71.6	71.6	73.8
Poland	51.4	68.4	79.1	79.5	76.5
Slovak Republic	59.1	68.3	80.5	80.5	80.6
EU-15	75.2	81.3	83.4	83.9	83.8
Euro area	69.1	78.5	82.9	83.4	83.4
EU-28	71.7	78.6	82.1	82.2	82.3
Trading across borders					
Romania	*67.8*	*83.3*	*100*	*100*	*100*
Czech Republic	79.5	84.2	100	100	100
Hungary	74.4	82.6	100	100	100
Poland	80.4	86.2	100	100	100
Slovak Republic	74.7	82.6	100	100	100
EU-15	85.9	89.9	97.1	97.1	97.1
Euro area	83.6	88.4	96.7	96.7	96.7
EU-28	82.0	87.7	97.4	97.4	97.4
Enforcing contracts					
Romania	*68.0*	*67.0*	*72.3*	*72.3*	*72.3*
Czech Republic	64.2	64.5	56.4	56.4	56.4

continued

TABLE A.5, *continued*

	DOING BUSINESS**				
	AVERAGE				
	2000–08	2009–15	2016	2017	2018
Hungary	69.3	67.6	69.1	71.0	71.0
Poland	53.9	61.2	63.4	63.4	64.4
Slovak Republic	65.1	62.2	58.7	64.3	66.1
EU-15	66.5	68.9	66.0	65.9	66.3
Euro area	63.3	67.2	66.1	66.3	66.5
EU-28	67.9	66.9	65.8	66.0	66.4
Resolving insolvency					
Romania	*19.7*	*41.8*	*59.2*	*59.8*	*59.9*
Czech Republic	19.9	63.0	79.6	79.8	80.1
Hungary	41.1	46.4	54.4	54.8	55.0
Poland	35.4	53.8	76.4	77.7	76.5
Slovak Republic	46.1	62.1	70.5	66.1	66.9
EU-15	78.2	78.0	78.4	77.3	77.6
Euro area	67.0	68.4	72.2	70.9	71.2
EU-28	61.1	66.0	71.4	70.6	70.8

Sources: Indicators of Product Market Regulation, OECD, Paris, https://www.oecd.org/economy/reform/indicators-of-product-market-regulation/; Doing Business (database), World Bank, Washington, DC, https://datacatalog.worldbank.org/dataset/doing-business.
Note: EU-15 = for list of countries see Note 4 on page 20; EU-28 = for list of countries see Note 3 on page 20; . . . = not available.
 * The OECD indicators of product market regulation (PMR) measure regulatory barriers to firm entry and competition on a scale of 0–6 from least to most restrictive.
** Doing business (DB) reflects the performance from the previous calendar year. This was considered in the table (for example, data for 2018 is based on World Bank 2019). The average for 2000–08 reflects the period 2004–08. The DB scores capture the gap of each economy from the best regulatory performance observed on each of the indicators across all economies in the sample. An economy's score is reflected on a scale from 0 to 100, where 0 represents the lowest and 100 represents the best performance.

REFERENCE

World Bank. 2019. *Doing Business 2019: Training for Reform*. Washington, DC: World Bank. https://openknowledge.worldbank.org/handle/10986/30438.